The Imaginary Sea

This catalog is published
in conjunction with the
exhibition ***The Imaginary Sea***,
presented at the Villa Carmignac
in Porquerolles from May 20th
to October 17th 2021.
Exhibition Curator: Chris Sharp.

Cover: Jochen Lempert
Untitled (Seadragon), 2016
Untitled (Plastic Bag III), 2017
Courtesy BQ, Berlin
and ProjecteSD, Barcelona
ADAGP, Paris, 2021

ISBN 978-2-36568-046-2

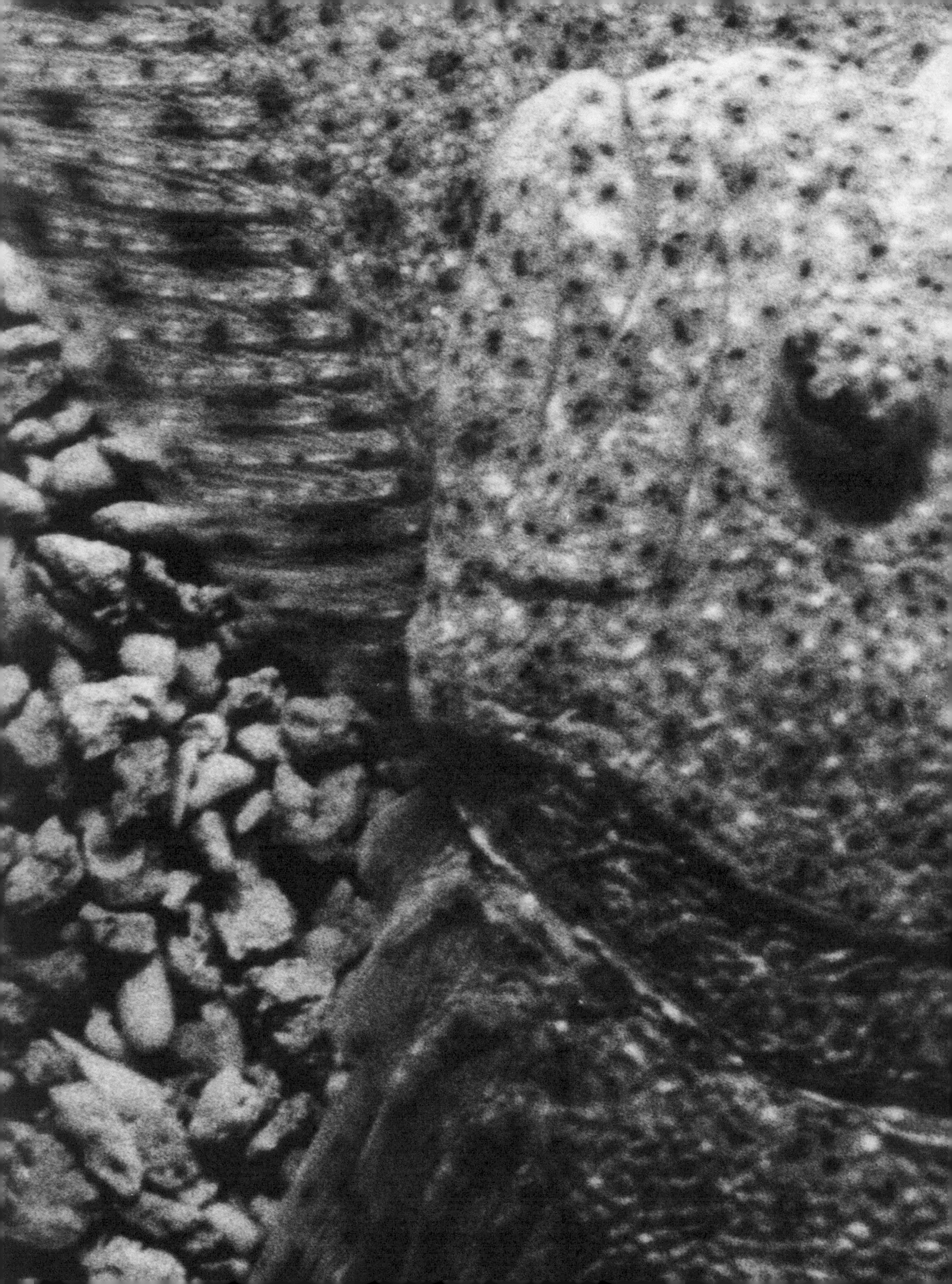

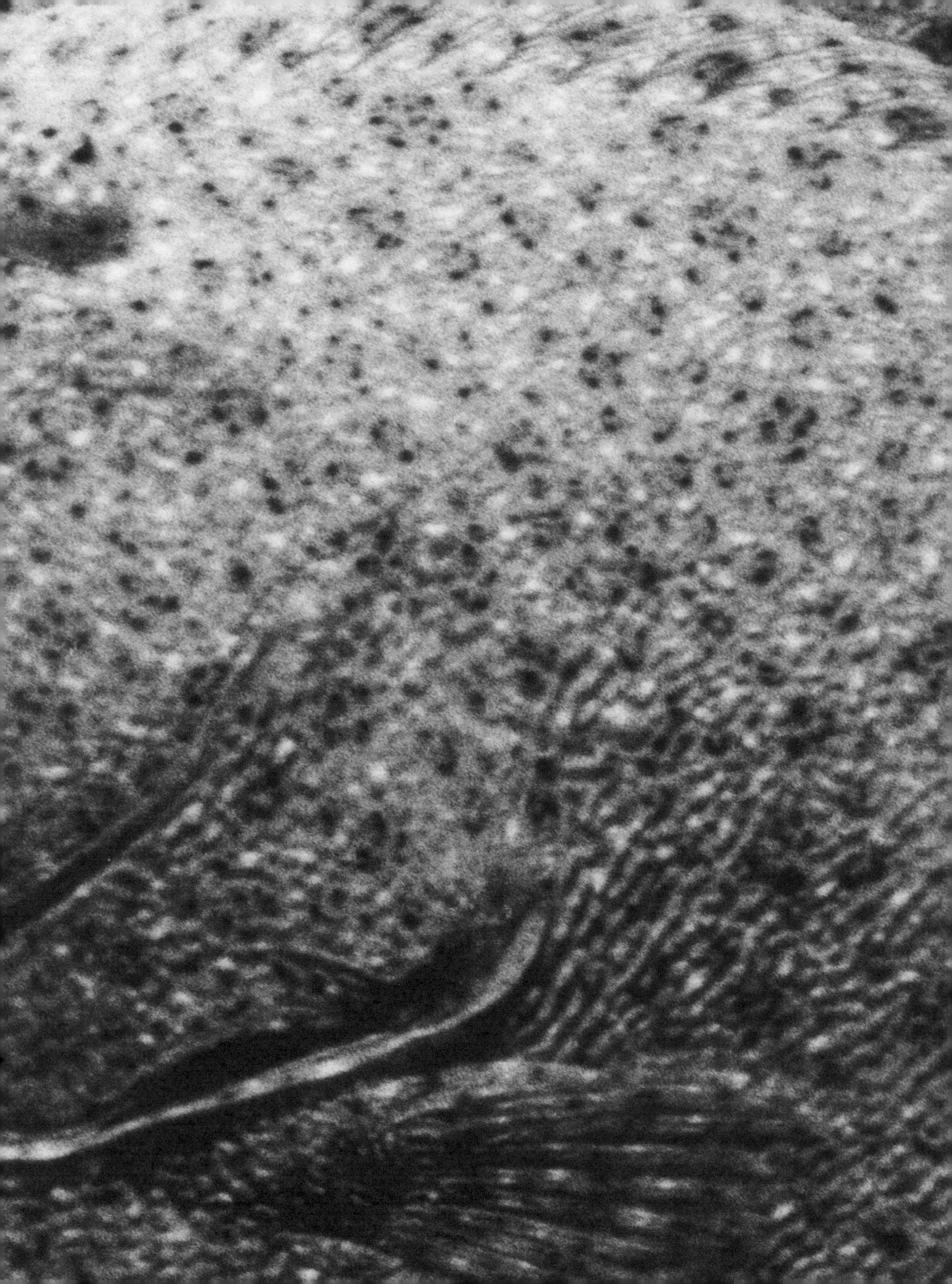

Foreword — **Charles Carmignac**

Can we experience nostalgia for things that have not yet disappeared?

Perhaps it is strange to anticipate the experience of absence, and yet a new sense of anxiety about the loss or degradation of the familiar environment — that we know and love — does exist. Australian philosopher Glenn Albrecht identifies and describes this feeling as "solastalgia". Thus, feeling "homesick" is conceivable without having to be far from home. The mere idea that our natural habitat is being damaged, lost, dying, is enough to evoke it. Looking out at the sea, this enchanted and mysterious territory which becomes devastated before our eyes is this feeling of solastalgia that compellingly emerges.

The Imaginary Sea exhibition confronts us with this future, immediately and without pursuing the stages of agony predicted for the coming years. For the artists, it is at once like unrestrained phantasmagoria born from this environment, but also the sea remaining in the imagination, like a happy memory after its disappearance. The exhibition thus displays the abyss in which these fantastic creatures created by the artists, phantoms of majestic species that are sometimes unknown, or that have disappeared before humans could even know what they are.

As the saying goes, we don't realize the value of something until after we lose it. The ambition of *The Imaginary Sea* is to have us experience this tragic sense of loss today, through a temporal shift, a play on time, of which the writer and curator Chris Sharp is accustomed. When I first met him, he was sitting under a sonorous palm tree which enumerated elements that have disappeared: models of cars, plant and animal species... In this installation that artist Dane Mitchell designed for the New Zealand pavilion at the Venice Biennale* in 2019, the visitor learns of the existence of a thing and simultaneously its loss. This mechanism gives way to a feeling that is at once luminous and melancholy, confirming for the Fondation Carmignac the relevance of inviting Chris Sharp to curate the upcoming exhibition in Porquerolles.

*58th Venice Biennale, May 2019. New Zealand Pavilion, "Post hoc," Dane Mitchell. Exhibition curators: Zara Stanhope and Chris Sharp.

On-site in our spaces, Chris Sharp immediately envisioned an underwater natural history museum from a distant future, made up of works imagined by artists. A proposal that enticed us with its poetry and its skillful detour through fiction, to speak to us about ecology and the human-animal connection.

Beyond the exhibition, in this catalog, Portuguese writer Filipa Ramos and French art historian Vincent Normand have analyzed this human-animal link with power and subtlety. These essays are responded to by the text-capsules of Christina Catherine Martinez and Andrew Berardini, which shed light on the vision of the works in this exhibition.

All of these contributions were impelled by Chris Sharp, whom I would like to warmly thank here for the intelligence, pertinence and musicality he has shown in the conception of this magical exhibition that graces this place.

Finally, I would like to express my gratitude to all the members of the Fondation and of the Villa Carmignac, who have actively participated in this exhibition, as well as to all of our partners and core service provider.

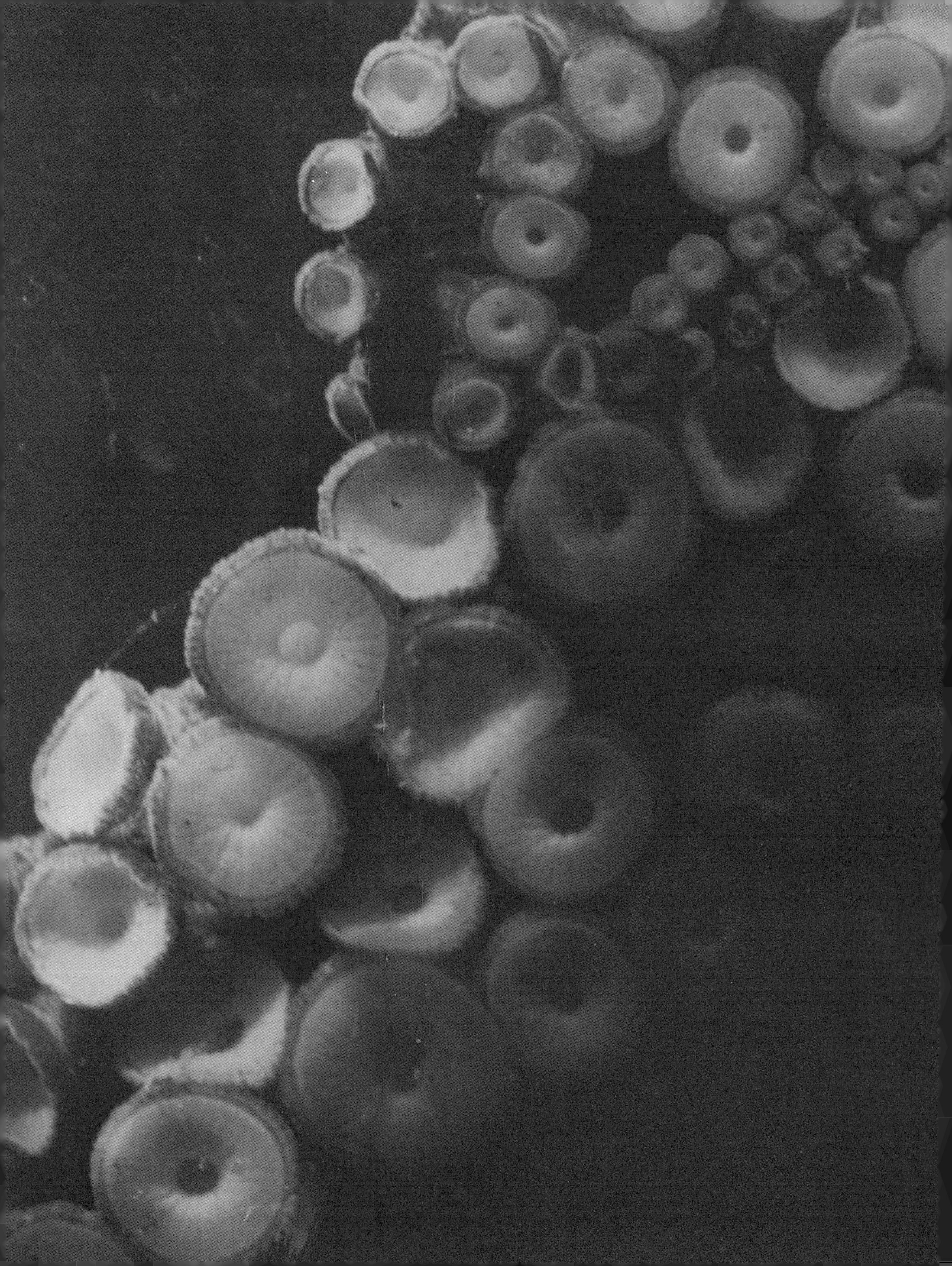

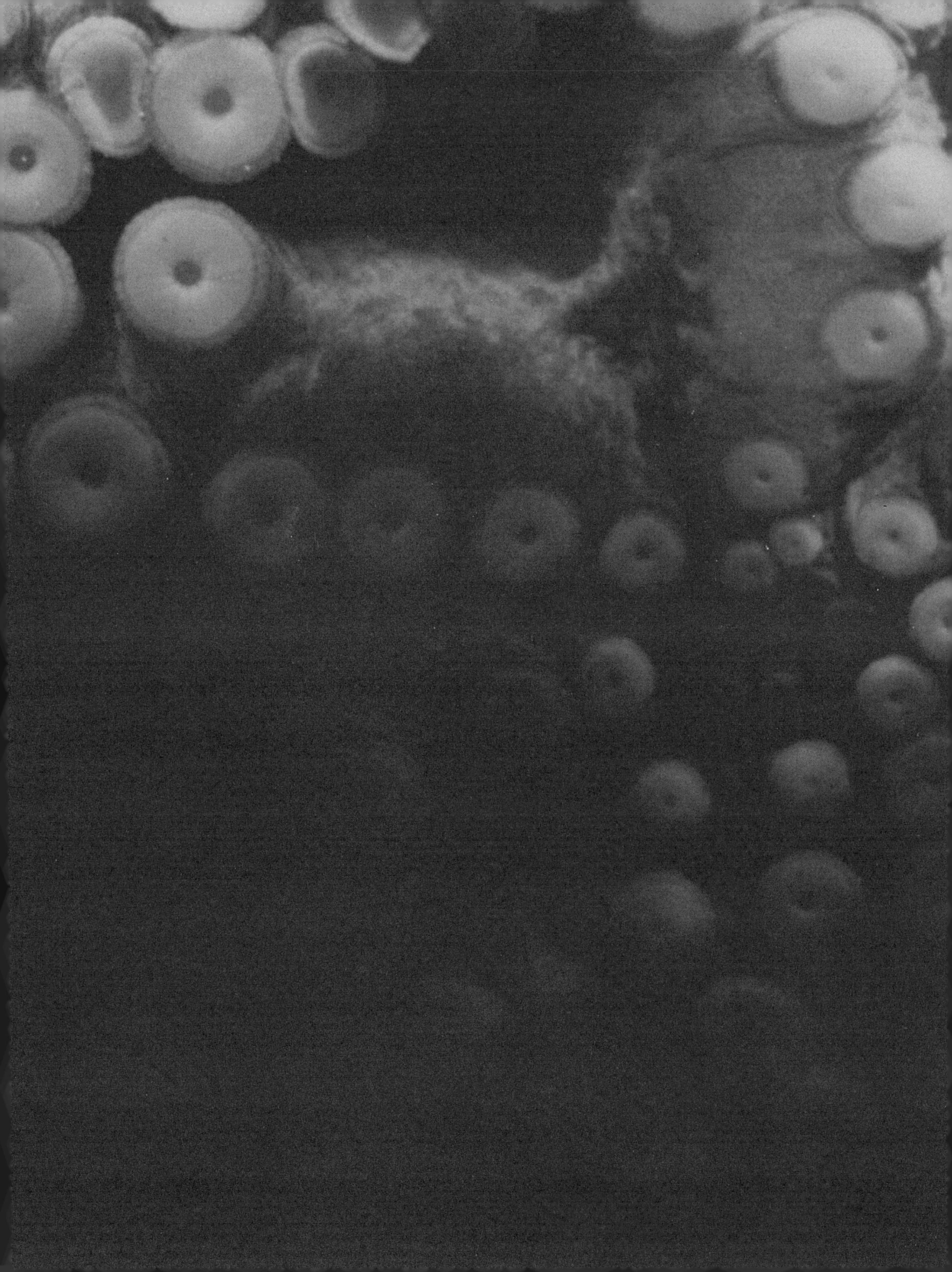

The Imaginary Sea — **Chris Sharp**

The origins of *The Imaginary Sea* can be traced all the way back to a novel by Vladimir Nabokov, *Bend Sinister* (1947) which I read in my early twenties in the late 90s. I remember being struck by and particularly puzzled by the protagonist's — who is a philosopher — apparent disdain for "People who are amused by trained animals." Why? What, exactly, was wrong with being amused by trained animals? Where was the misdemeanor? The error of thought? The human foible? I am not sure that I was able to answer the question at the time, but it opened a proverbial rabbit hole that would accompany all my subsequent intellectual development and which would gradually proceed along increasingly anti-Cartesian lines[1]. The quandary was, if not solved, then productively complicated later when I encountered Franz Kafka's short story, *A Report to an Academy* (1917) which tells the story of an ape recounting to an academy how, captured in Africa, he trained himself to behave and speak like a human being in order to avoid the further captivity of being held in a zoo. This story daily becomes more relevant with the advent of the Internet and ubiquity of social media; the frequency with which I encounter videos or stories of animals allegedly behaving like "human beings" is bewildering. It is as if nothing has changed in the intervening 100 years since Kafka penned his prescient tale. Animals, as John Berger rightly points out[2], can only be tolerated among us if they obediently imitate or reflect us[3].

These issues functioned as points of suspicion for many years until I encountered the work of the German photographer Jochen Lempert, and not much later, that of the American sculptor Michael E. Smith. Lempert, a trained biologist who did his field work on dragonflies and possesses an encyclopedic knowledge of natural history, took — still takes — black-and-white photos which addressed these very issues, focusing largely on the animal kingdom in urban environments. His recourse to anthropomorphism in many photos is so nuanced, conspicuous and over the top that it assumes a critically self-reflexive and comically absurd quality. And in the work of Michael E. Smith, the fatal and fatalistic extremes to which animals are subject touches upon a particularly

1
That same anti-Cartesianism can also be traced back to Nabokov, who writes, precisely one sentence later in *Bend Sinister*, "All those who are because they do *not* think…"

2
See John Berger's "Why Look at Animals" (Penguin, New York, 2008).

3
One imagines a piece of dystopian science fiction which consists of a kind of animal conspiracy in which one animal convinces a whole host of other animals that they can only survive *as a nonhuman species* if they learn how to behave like human beings. Forsaking their animal nature, they eventually learn, like Kafka's ape, to walk, talk and eat like their human counterparts. To the threat of literal extinction from the world, they cannily, if tragically, respond with their own symbolic extinction. And the true tragedy of this science fiction is that it, like most instances of the genre, is not science fiction…

stark and telling truth about our relationship to the animal kingdom. Little more than the tangential recipients of an incidental violence, animals, in Smith's work, always seem to be at the wrong place at the wrong time; innocent bystanders in our — the human species — intractable and psychopathic will to self-destruct. As such, the work of both artists directly and indirectly meditates on the nature/culture divide at the core of Cartesian thought in novel and refreshing ways, ultimately helping me realize the gravity of these issues.

This experience of urgency was compounded by the emergence of a post-Kantian philosophical development known as Speculative Realism or Object-oriented Ontology[4]. The main thrust of this largely foredoomed movement was an attempt to try and think the world from a non-anthropocentric point of view. Patently impossible, it was nevertheless important, and indicative of turning away from the self-centered humanism that had dominated western thought since the Renaissance. This movement was succeeded by the popularization of the contested geological paradigm shift known as the "Anthropocene." First brought to my attention by Jochen Lempert in 2013, this shift describes a new geological epoch characterized by being permanently impacted by human activity. The earth's surface, according to the theorizers of the Anthropocene, had been forever and irrevocably modified by humankind's sojourn upon it, and not necessarily for the better. This lent an even greater sense of urgency to the impetus behind Lempert and Smith's work, as well as similarly motivated practices, which could be said to include many others such as Pierre Huyghe, Lin May Saeed, Henrik Håkansson, Cosima von Bonin, Daniel Steegmann Mangrané, to name but a few.

4 See work by Quentin Meillassoux, Graham Harman, Ray Brassier, to name but a few of the core Speculative Realists.

For if, at first glance, it seemed that these developments helped frame and provide context to what these artists were doing, it was because these artists were already ahead of the curve in trying to think and reevaluate a post-Cartesian relationship to the animal kingdom or so-called nature. They were, as per usual, a few steps ahead of us. It was not a matter of them catching up with the humanities, it was, rather, a matter of the humanities catching up with them. While I had already worked with the likes of Jochen Lempert and Michael E. Smith on different projects, it wasn't until I was on a research trip in Brazil, and I encountered a work by Renata Lucas[5], that it occurred to me to organize a show around this specific theme. Tentatively titled, "A Museum of Natural History", the exhibition project gradually took shape over the next few years in my head and on paper but never really found a home. But from the moment I visited the Villa Carmignac in 2019, with its semi-submerged architecture, in situ fountain of floating bronze fish by Bruce Nauman, panoramic painting of sea life by Miquel Barceló, and perhaps, most importantly, its glass ceiling cum shallow pool, I knew the exhibition had not only found a home, but also one that would transform it into its most ideal manifestation, that of a large, wholly improbable and fantastical approximation of an aquarium. Plunging it underwater, so to speak, added an entire quotient of both the unknown and the unknowable proportionate to the unknowability of the sea and ocean, and the ways in which precisely this quotient has, over the ages, and continues to fire the imagination of artists. Thus, the context of the Villa, aided by the fact that it is situated on an island and predominately frequented by vacationing families, helped unearth a whole new range of positive and negative complexity with regard to the original idea. Hence, *The Imaginary Sea*, whose double entendre — a sea that is at once imagined and an imaginary in itself, with the all implications these states of evocation carry— is wholly and entirely intended.

5
Barulho de fundo, 2005, a collaboration with Daniel Steegmann Mangrané and Dionís Escorsa, in which the artists released a black panther in Oscar Niemeyer's Ibirapuera park building and record its appearance on the security equipment. This work is somewhat reminiscent of Francis Alÿs, *The Nightwatch*, 2004, a video which follows the same principle, but releases a fox in London's National Portait Gallery in the middle of the night. In both works, instances of "nature" are loosed in edifices of "culture."

Far from a wholesale critical condemnation of anthropocentrism, the exhibition seeks to present a balanced, multifaceted perspective of our evolving relationship with the natural world. It operates if not in different temporalities, then, let's say, different imaginaries. Akin to the emotional range of a Shakespearian comedy — or tragedy —, it intends to evoke joy, mystery, wonder, and, inevitably, melancholy as well as loss. Because, it goes virtually without saying, our relationship to the natural world, especially the sea and its enigmatic and unfathomable contents, is quite complex and fraught. It cannot be necessarily reduced to black-and-white evaluations of right or wrong. As such, the work of the pioneer underwater filmmaker, and celluloid poet Jean Painlevé is very much the spiritual father of this exhibition. Driven as much by an idiosyncratic form of scientific inquiry as he was by a love of the natural world as well as cinema, a version of which he established and called, "scientific-poetic cinema," Painlevé made over two hundred films in his lifetime, took photos, and was, though he didn't officially align himself with their movement, championed by the surrealists. His complete absorption in, poetic depiction and ultimate interpretation of his preferred subject matter, the life of the sea, is what renders him such a spiritually influential figure here. Painlevé continually reminds us how difficult it is to disavow the sea as such a fertile source of the imagination.

The elegant, entrancing, and all but dream-like quality of his photos helps set the mood of the show, which resonates with the work of a variety of artists, ranging from Dora Maar to more contemporary practitioners like Leidy Churchman, Jean-Marie Appriou and Bianca Bondi and her massive, crystalized whale, among many others brought together here. Here is an aquarium populated by a multitude of oneiric, subaquatic scenarios, positions and fantastical fauna, as potentially perceived in the fathomless depths of sleep. The mixing of metaphor ripples out throughout the entirety of the exhibition, touching upon joy as much as it does upon nightmare, sometimes in one and the same work. The sense of unmitigated joy in Jeff Koons' inverted lobster or Henri Matisse's conflation of the sea and sky cannot be denied, nor can the droll humor of Allison Katz' gloriously anatomically incorrect depiction of a whale or Cosima von Bonin's unwieldy, but pedagogically pliable, stuffed killer whale. There is as much here to guffaw as there is to marvel at, what with Shimabuku's magnificent floating leafy seadragon, not to mention Micha Laury's motley forest of multicolored jellyfish. And yet the exhibition is liable to careen from joy and wonder to sadness and perplexity in an instant. Consider the juxtaposition of Jochen Lempert's black-and-white photo of a father and baby gazing at school of fish in an aquarium hung next to a painting by the late Gilles Aillaud depicting a group of neglected fish bleakly gazing out at the viewer in a half-filled aquarium. This particular pairing, which is seen almost at the beginning of the show, assumes a special significance because the viewer both sees themselves observing (Lempert) and observed (Aillaud). My hope and intention with this juxtaposition is that the strange, contradictory quality of this encounter will create a heightened, even self-critical awareness, in which any emotion the viewer might experience will be tempered by a self-interrogation and perhaps even an interrogation of the whole exhibition apparatus as a framing device and methodology of oppression. Meanwhile the numerous works of Michael E. Smith, ranging from his totem of blowfish to his dismembered starfish reconfigured to resemble a geometric cube, are dark and twisted reminders of our propensity to abuse and bend nature to culture's will. Meanwhile Yuji Agematsu's frayed and tattered amalgamations of trash resemble jellyfish, as if organically engendered by some effluence of urban refuse. They are oddly capable of registering as ersatz surrogates for the beings they poorly, if evocatively represent. Indeed, considered generally, the sundry and assorted agglomeration of objects and images gathered here could be read as some kind of dystopian interpretation of a museum of natural history. Retrospectively perched from a remote future, *The Imaginary Sea* becomes an attempt to represent an extinct sea life world from the perspective of a humanity so far removed from any knowledge of nature that these inspired recreations are the best that can be done with the little information available. As such, they become the speculative and symbolic populace of a truly imaginary sea, and consequently an involuted, cautionary tale of loss.

Behold these fleeting, subaquatic riches, this exhibition states — the riches of the sea and the human imagination. Indissociable from a certain impending natural and human poverty, they are nevertheless marked by affirmation. For no matter what happens, I chose to see these works, and art in general, as ultimately affirmative of the best of humanity, the best of what we as a species have to offer, the present, the future and the past.

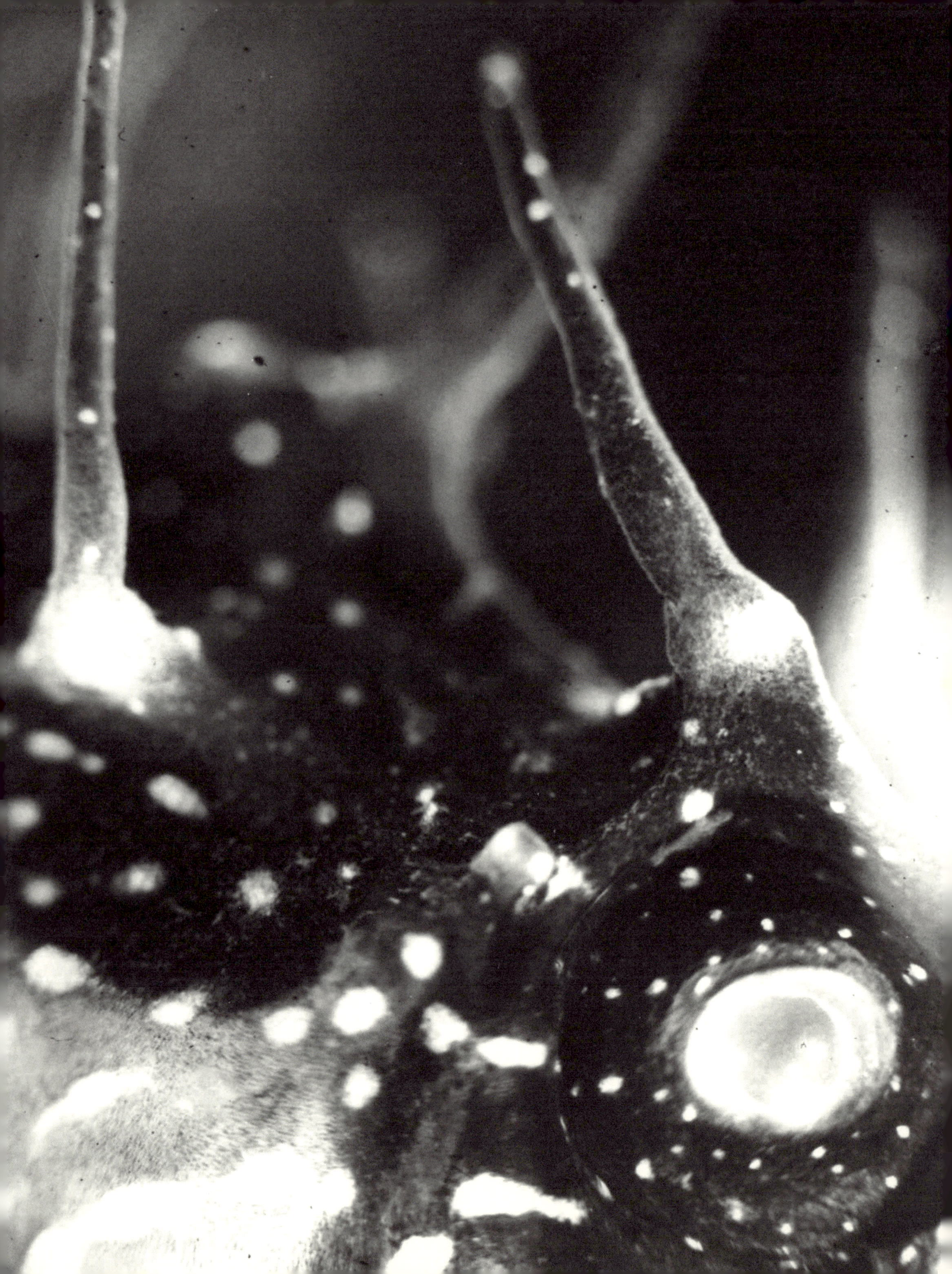

Exhibition

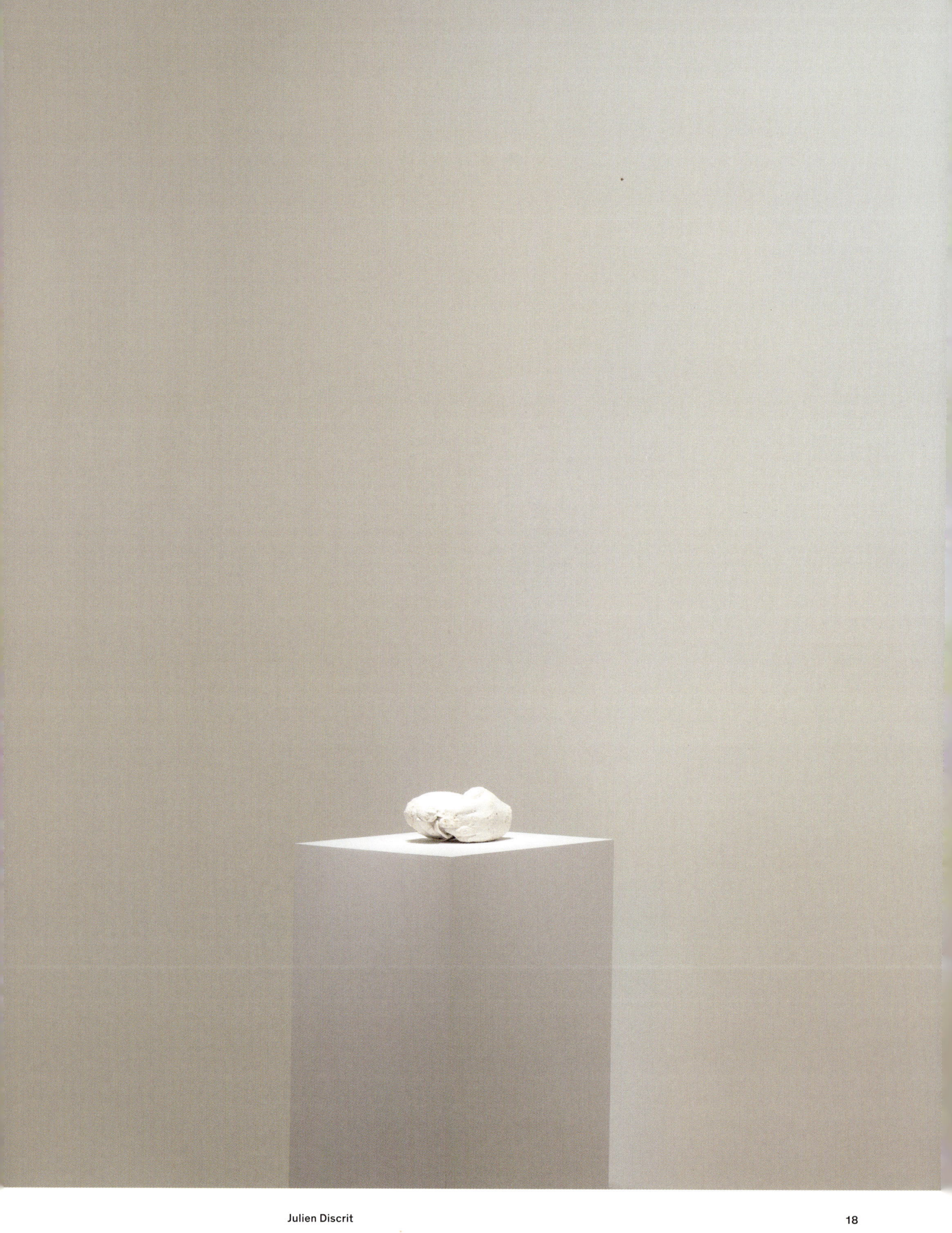

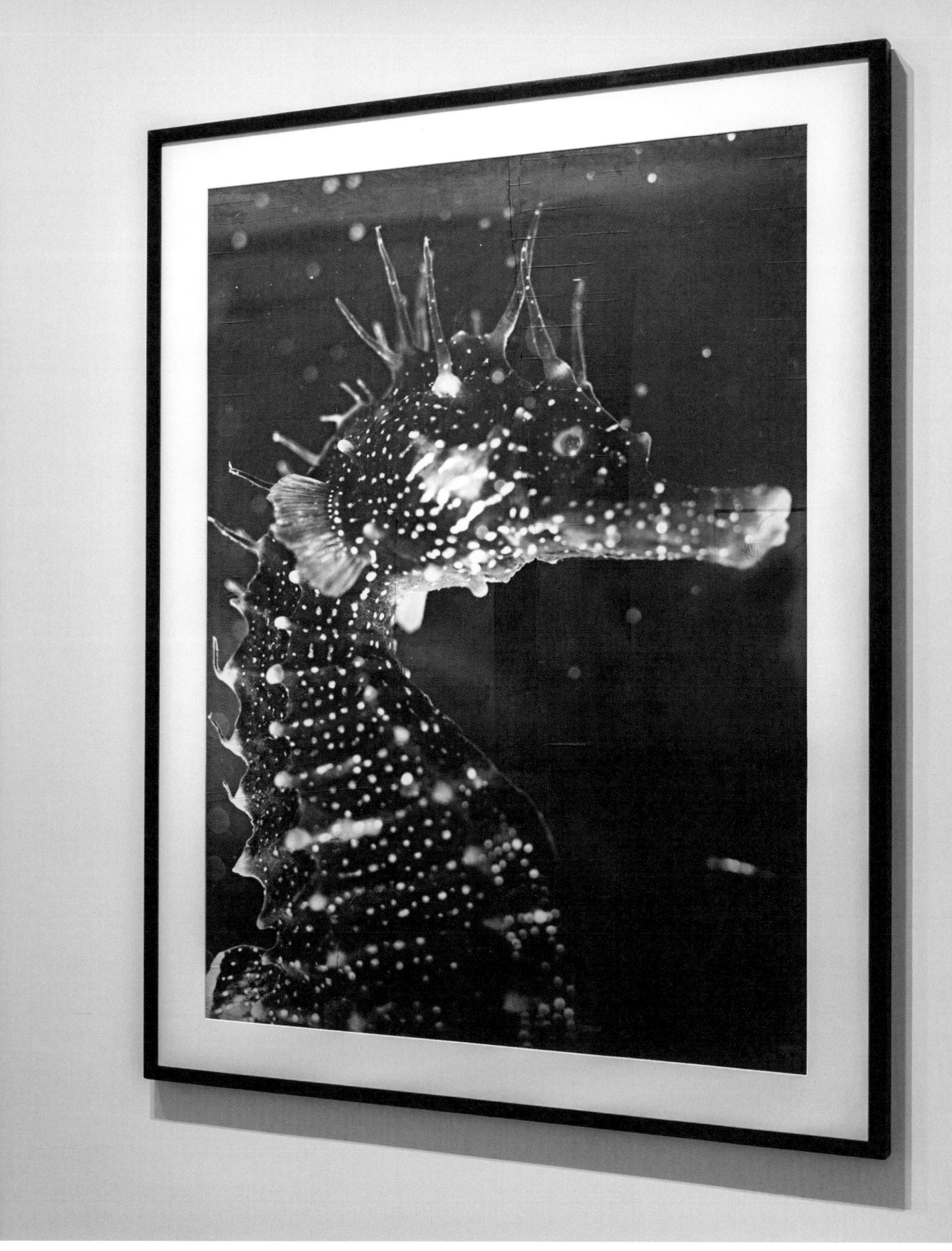

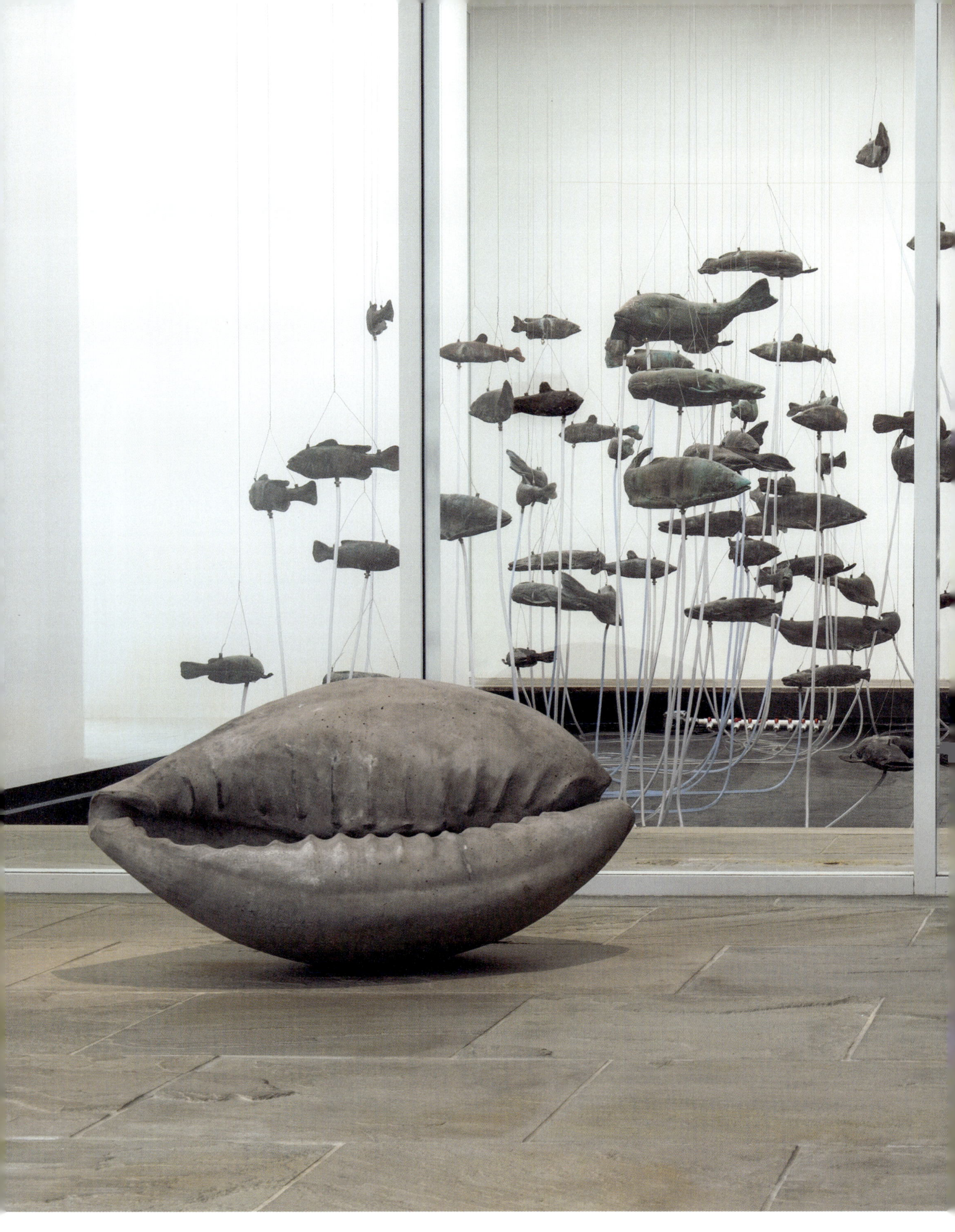

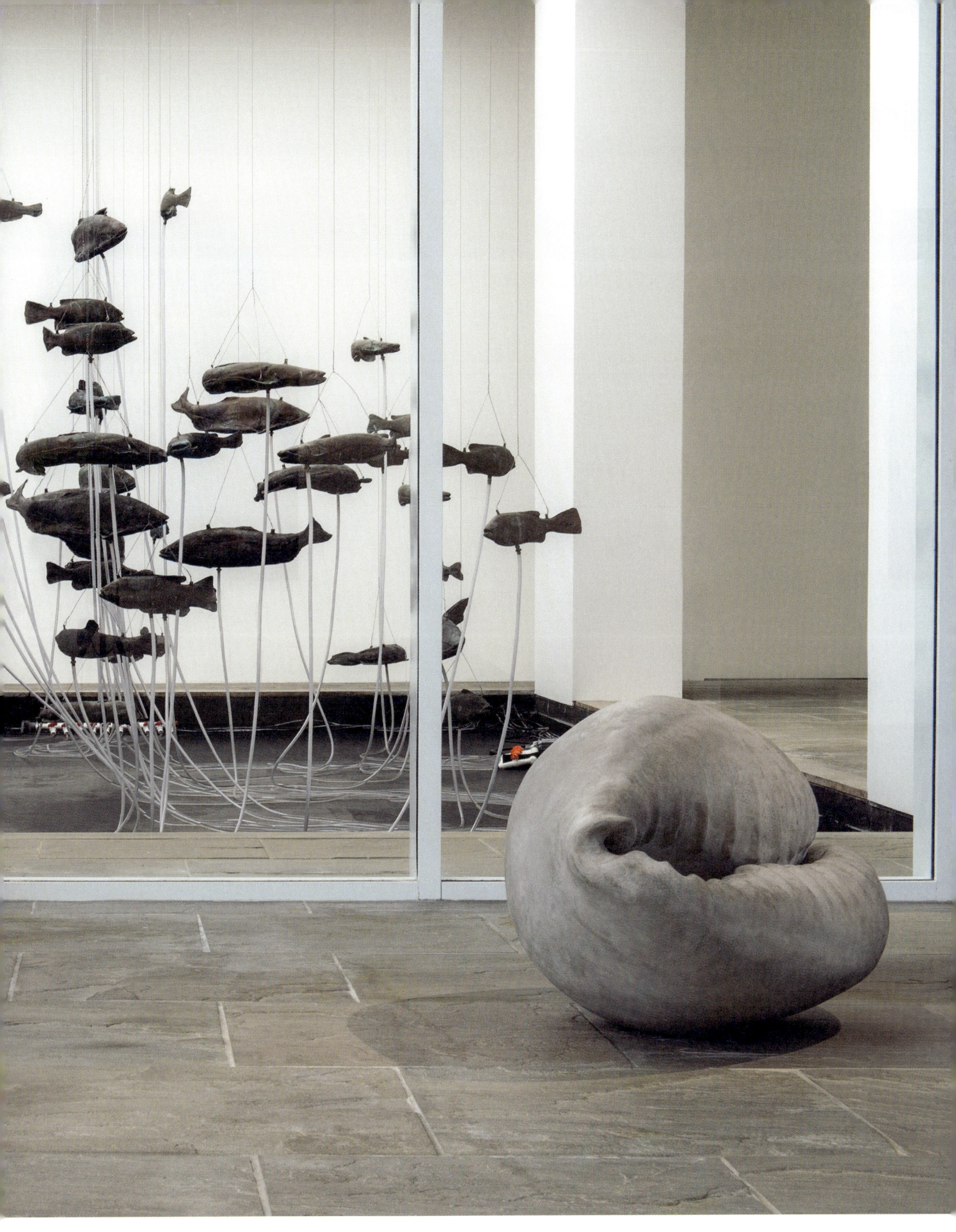

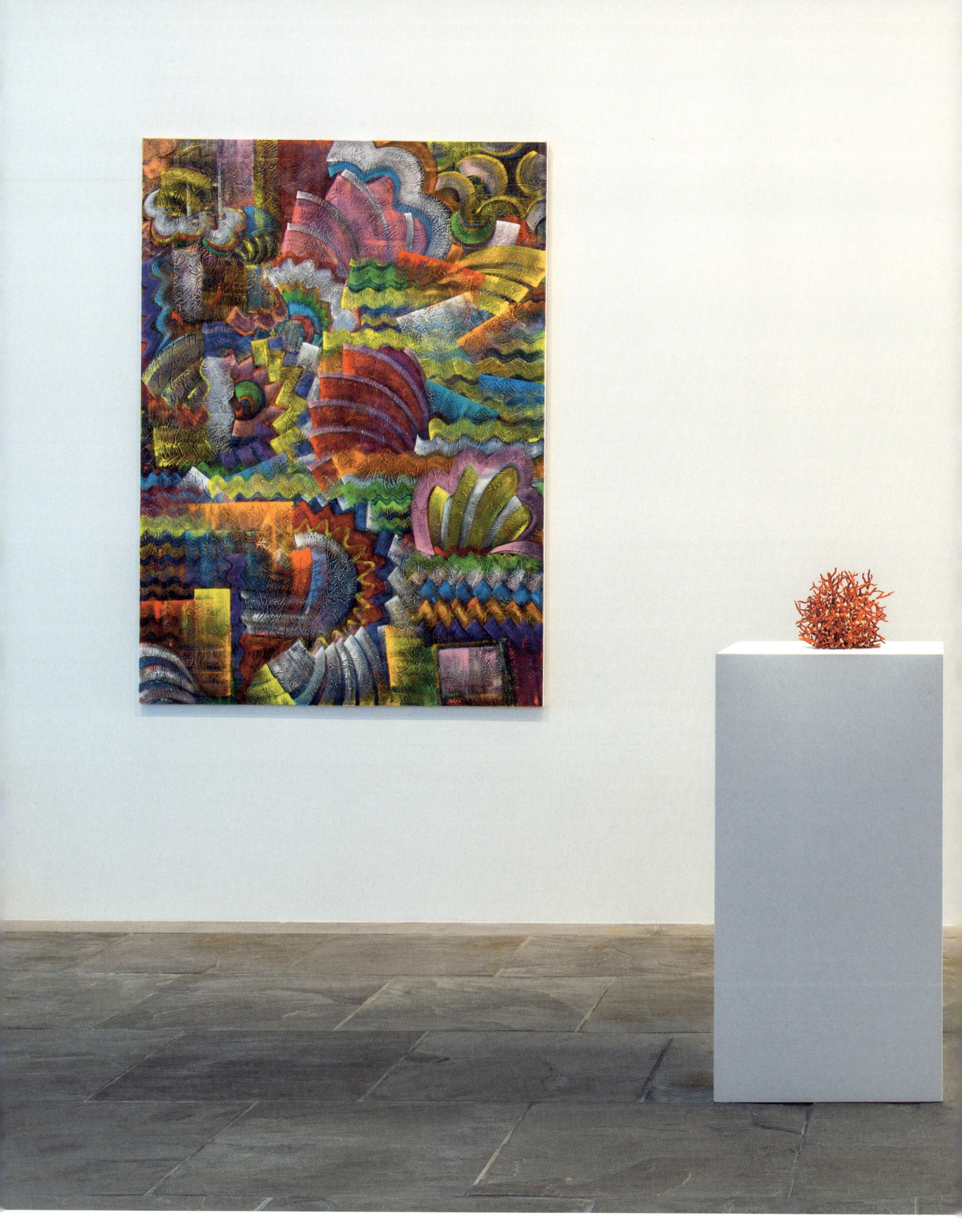

Alex Olson

Hubert Duprat

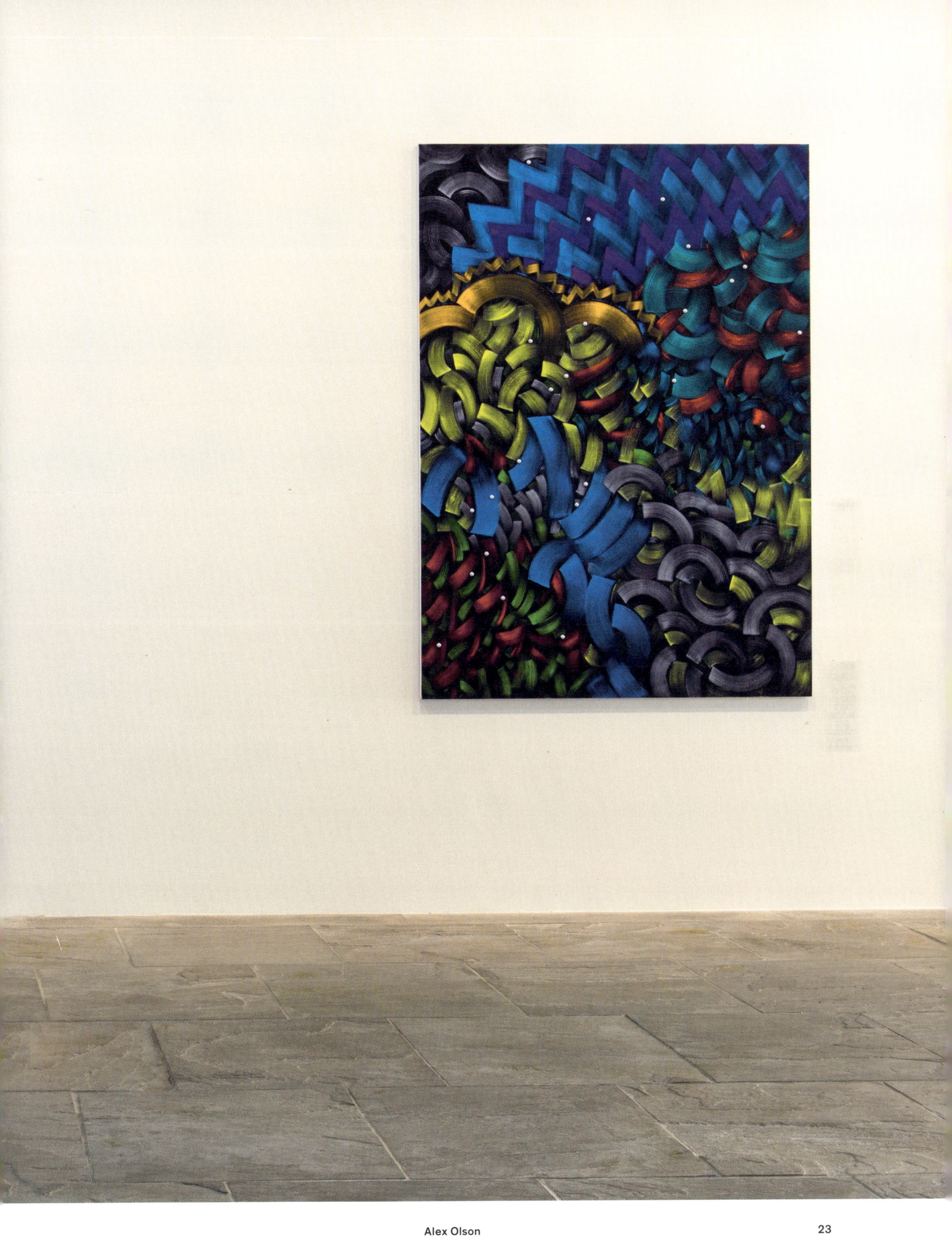

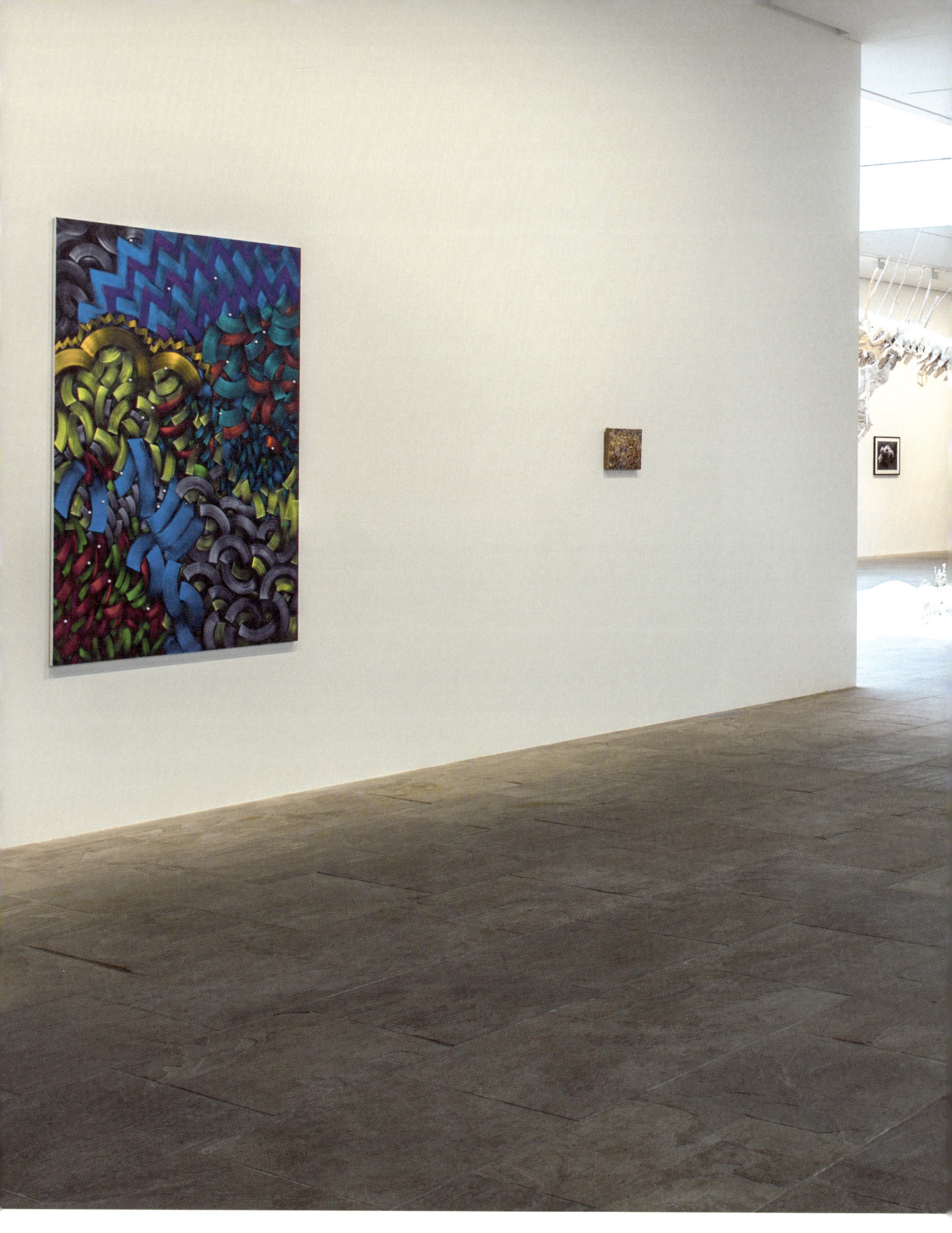

Alex Olson

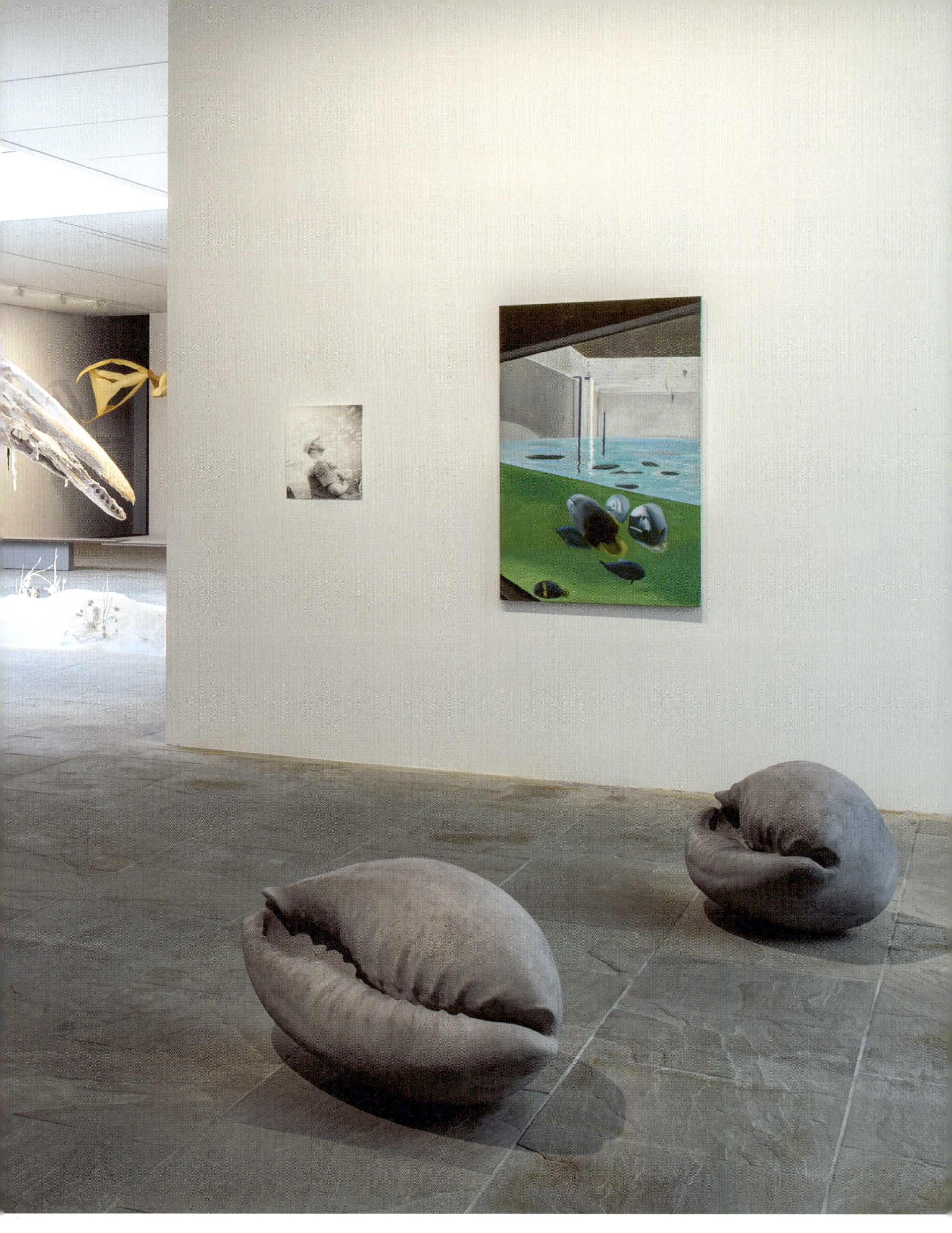

Jochen Lempert Gilles Aillaud Melik Ohanian

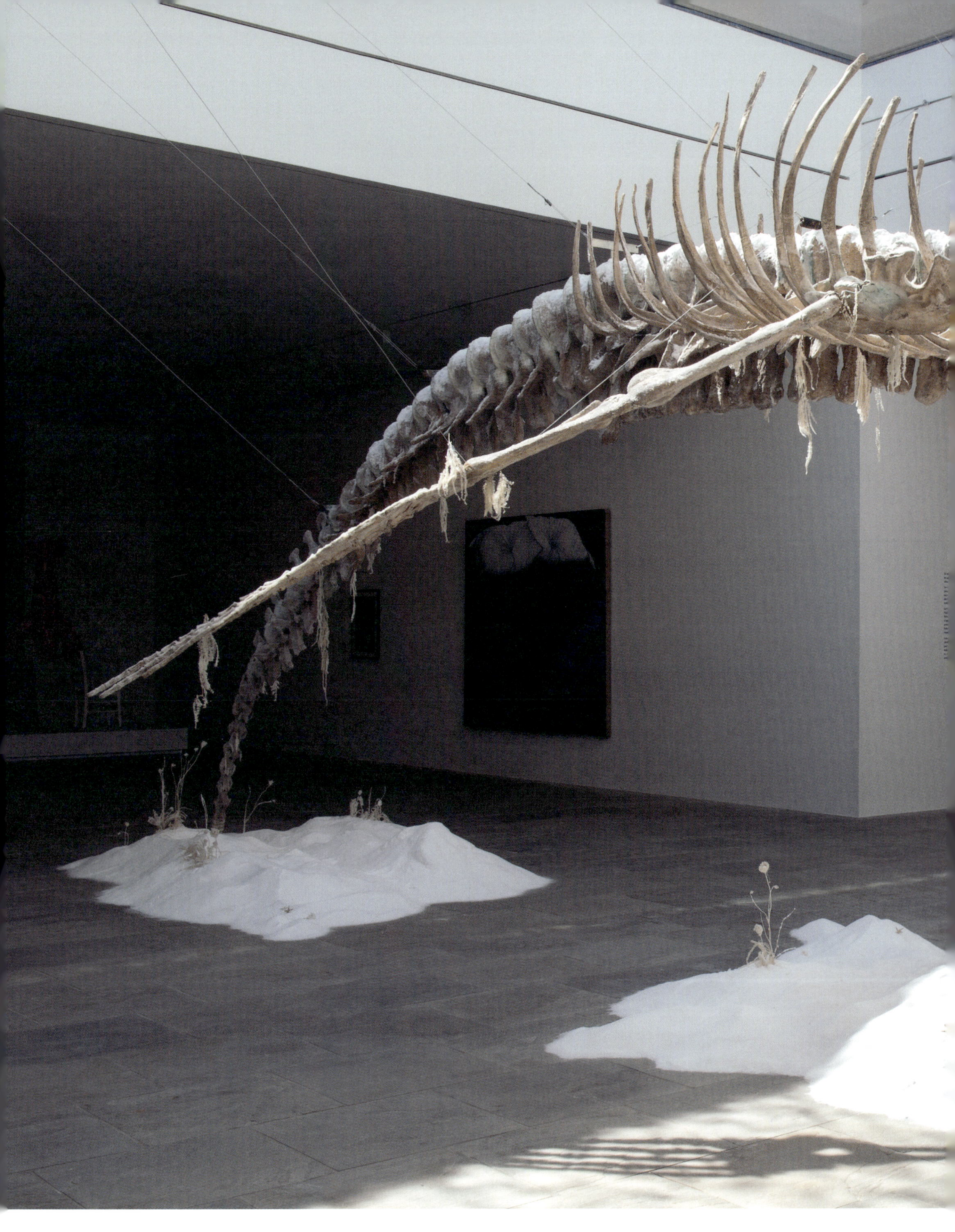

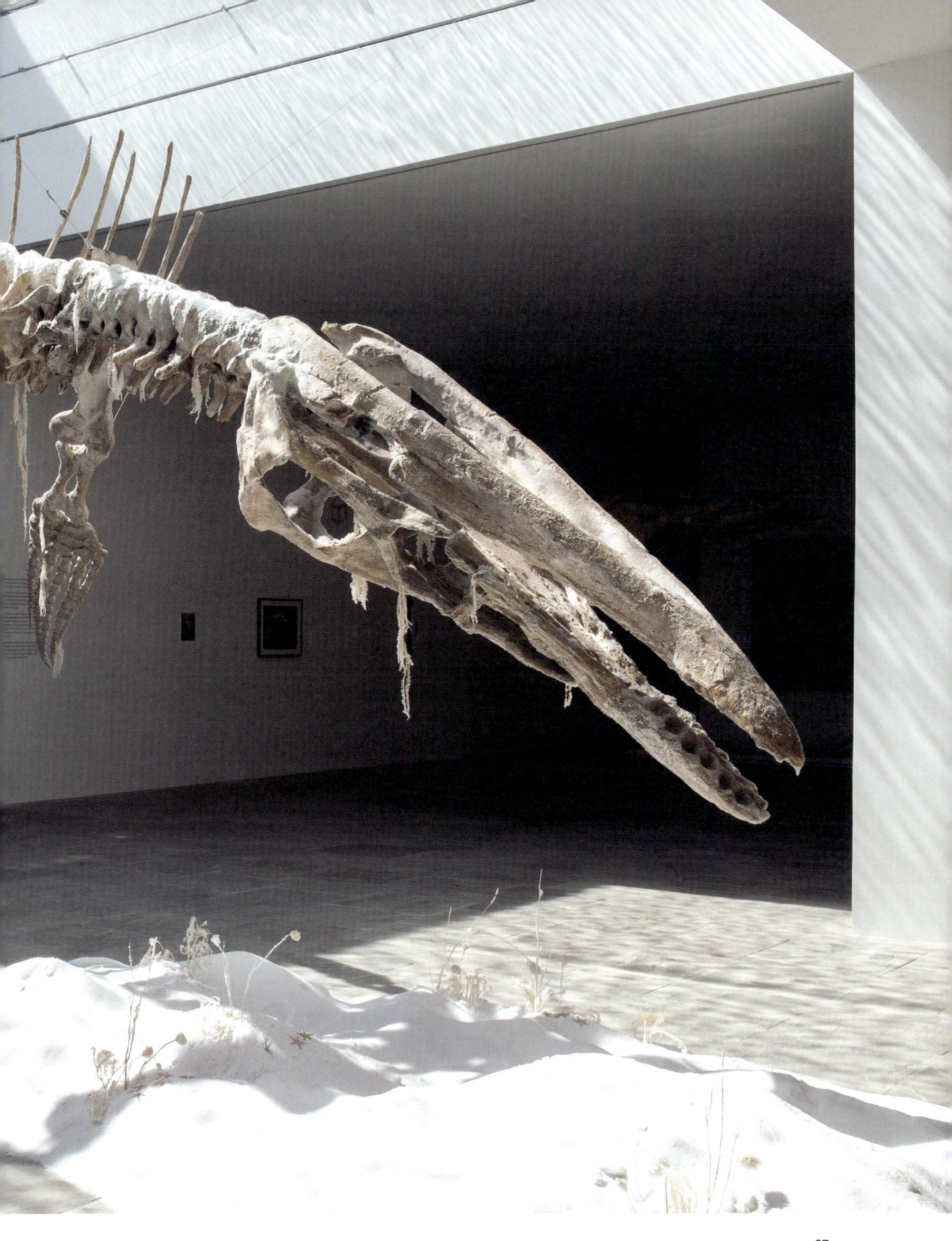

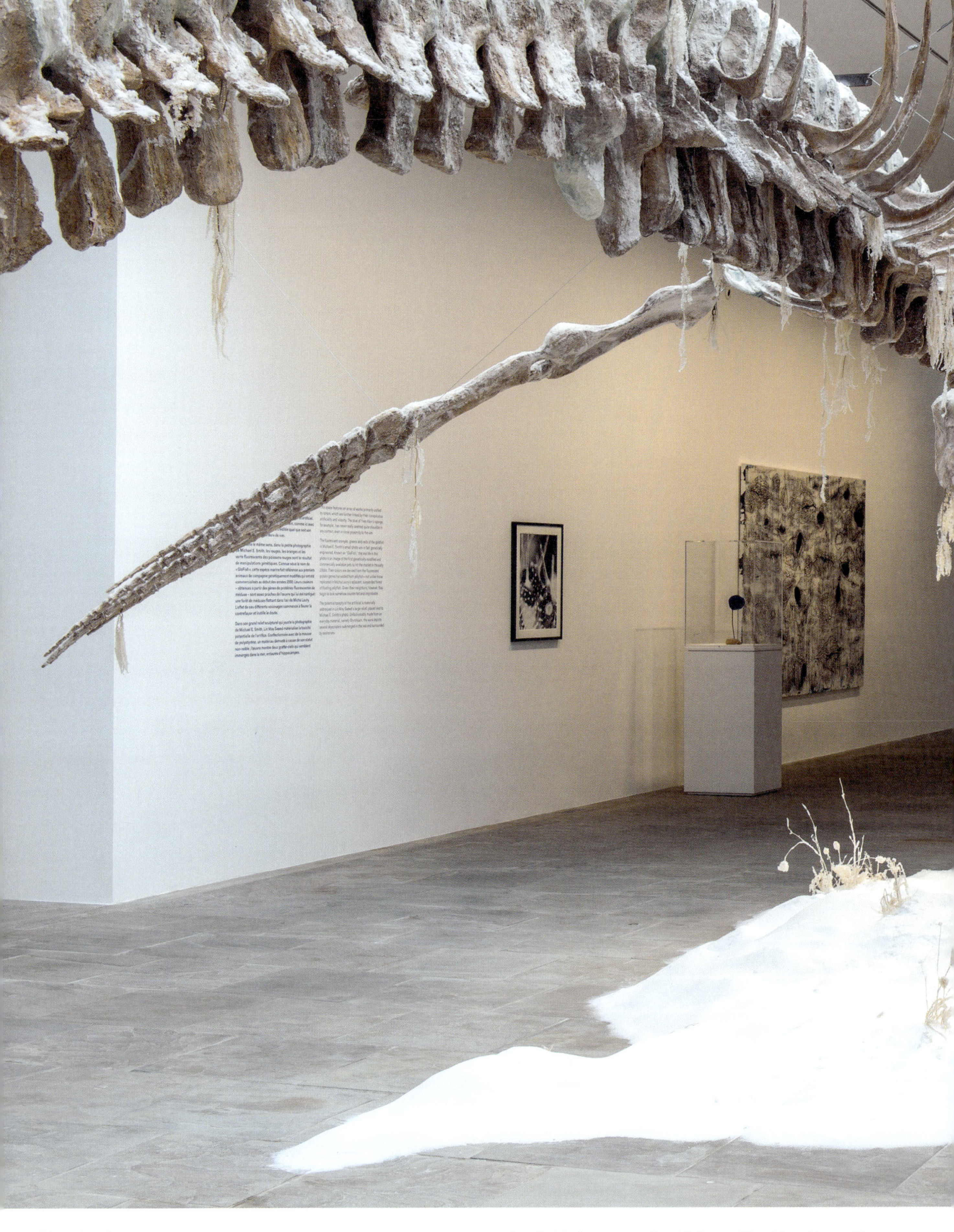

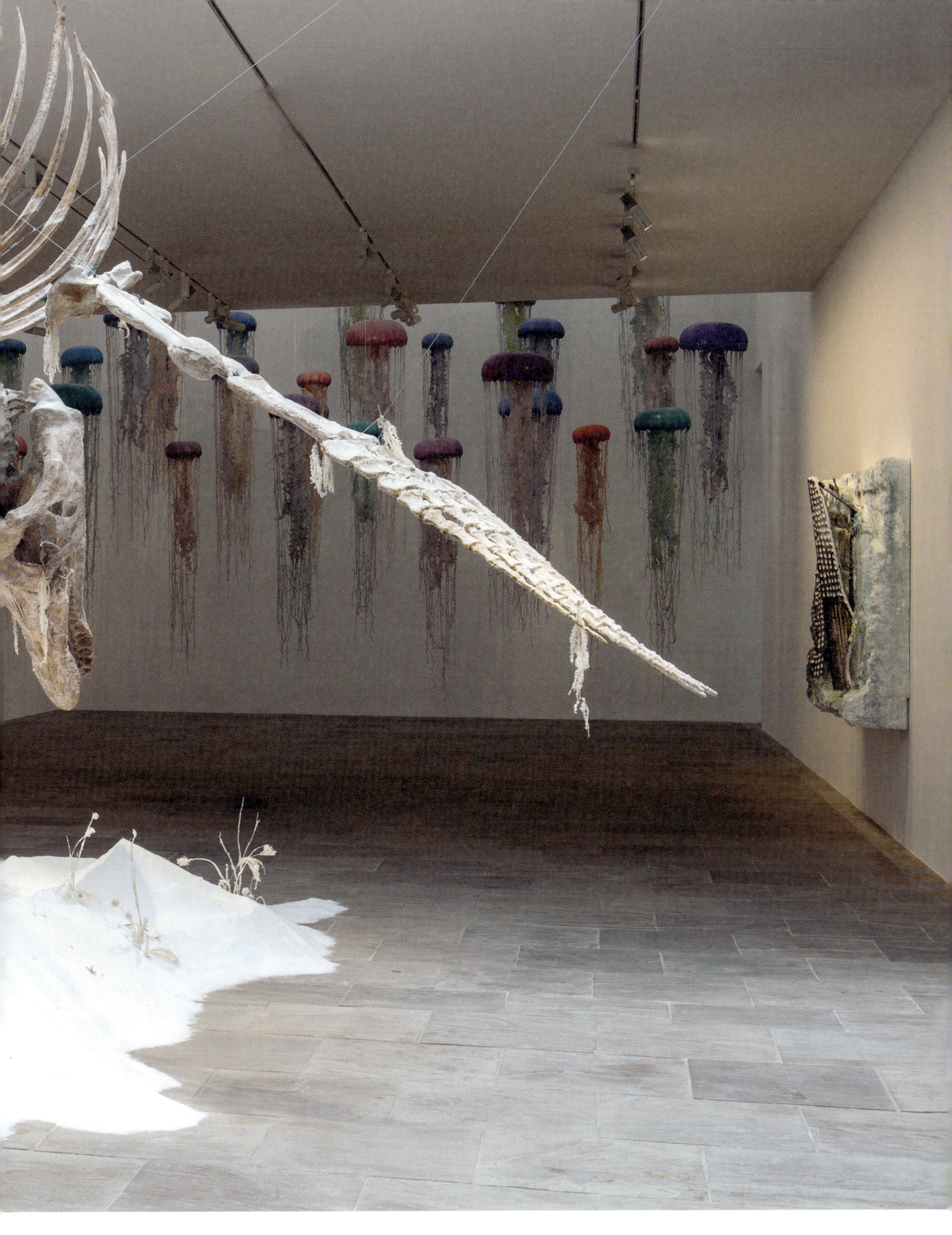

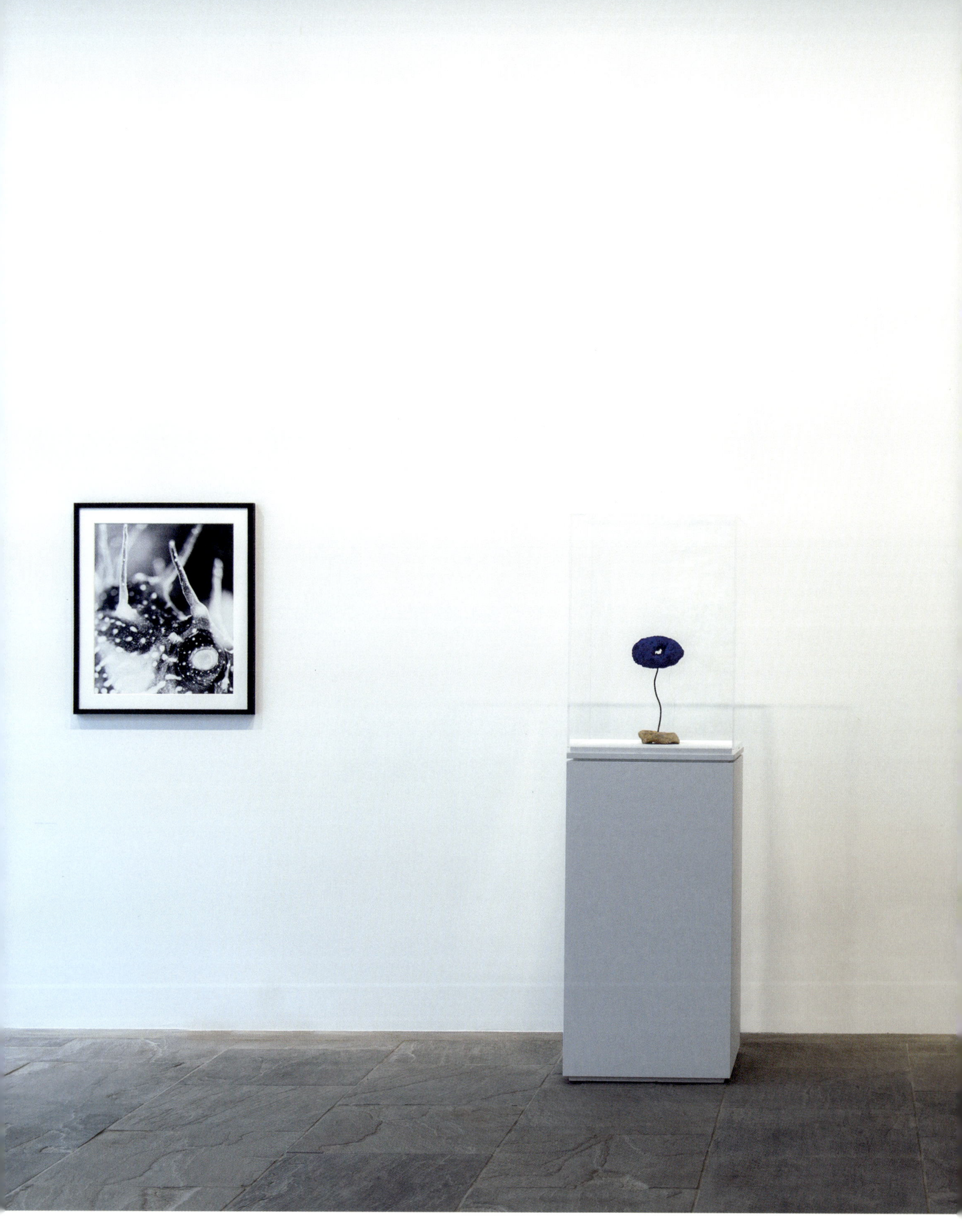

Jean Painlevé

Yves Klein

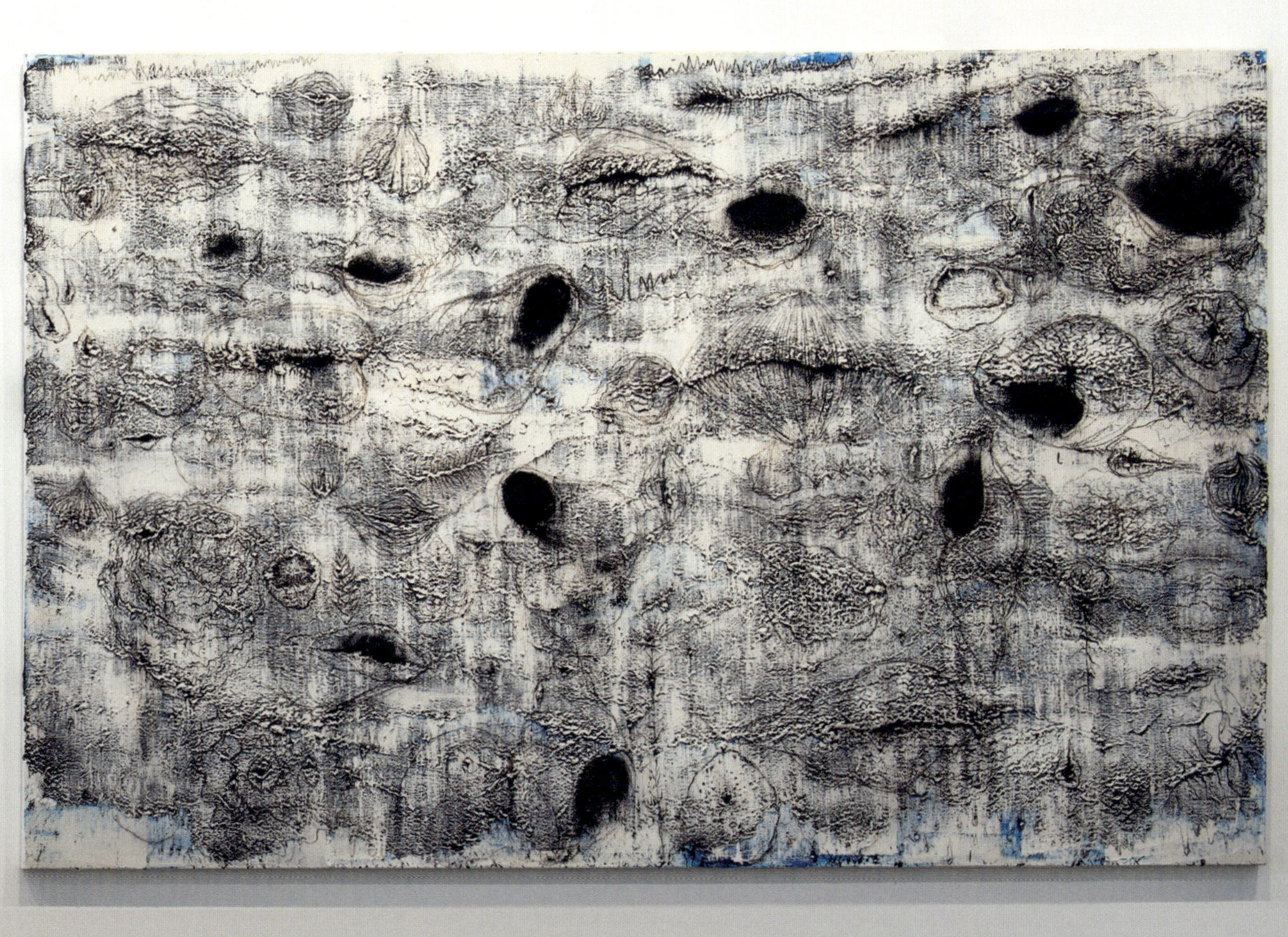

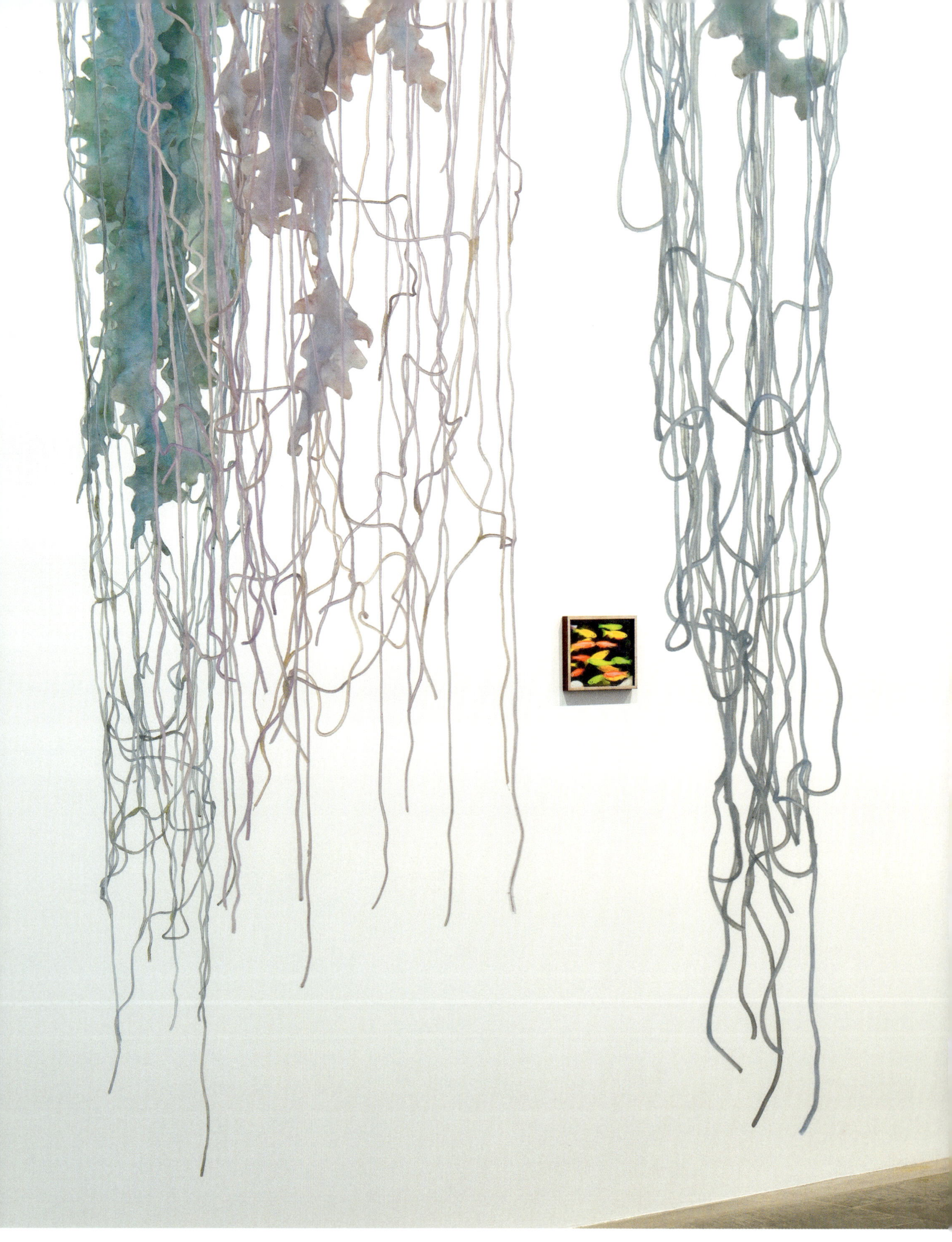

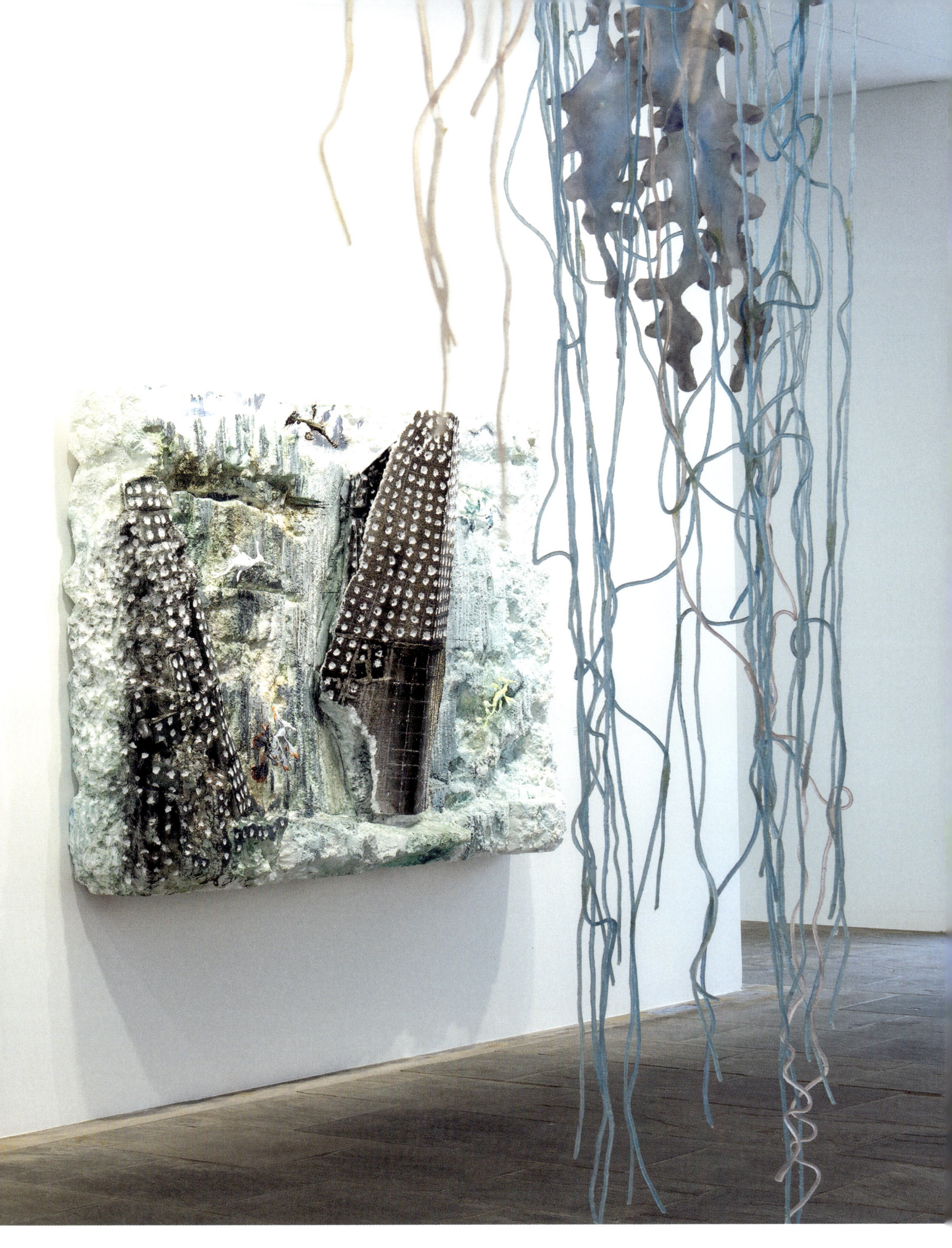

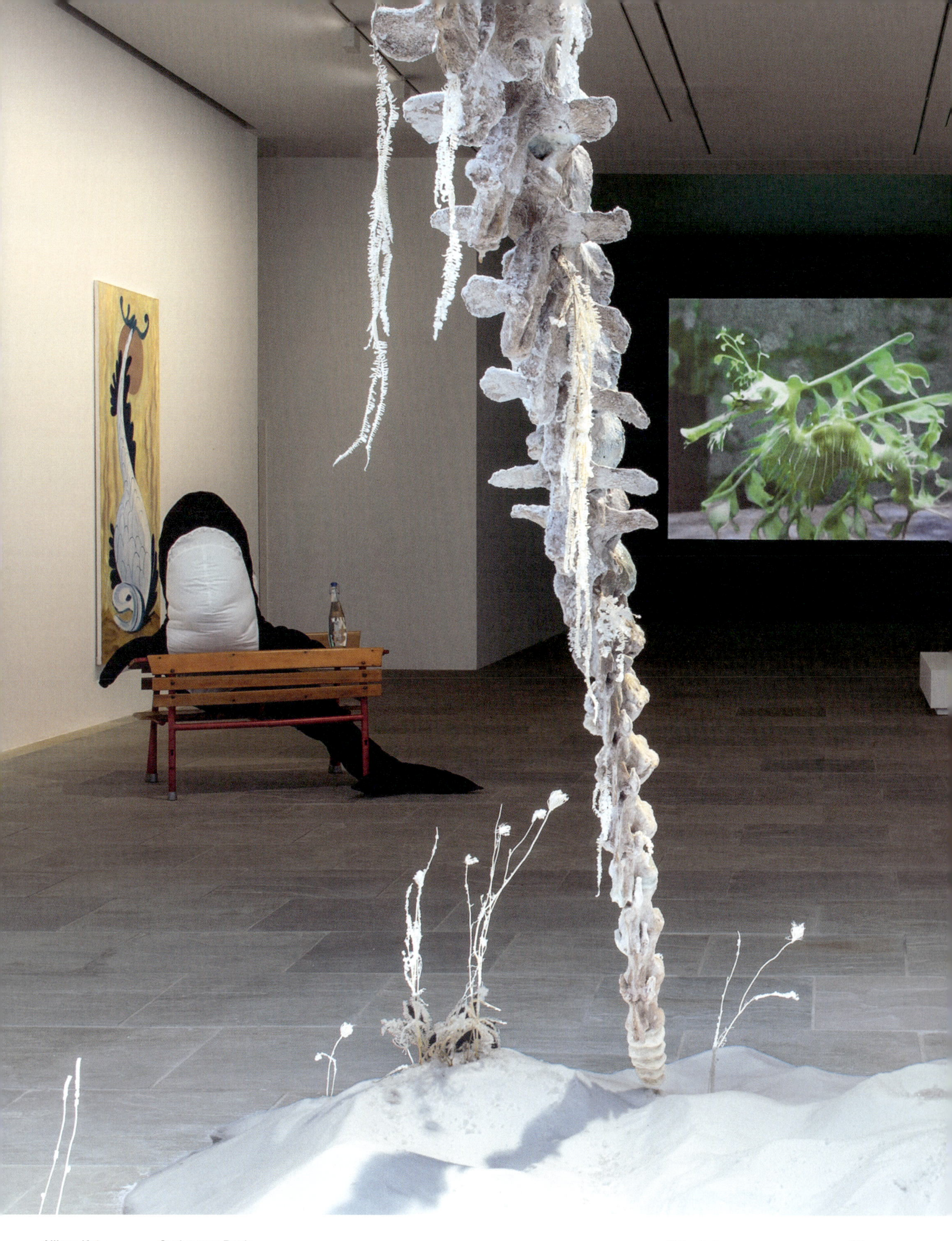

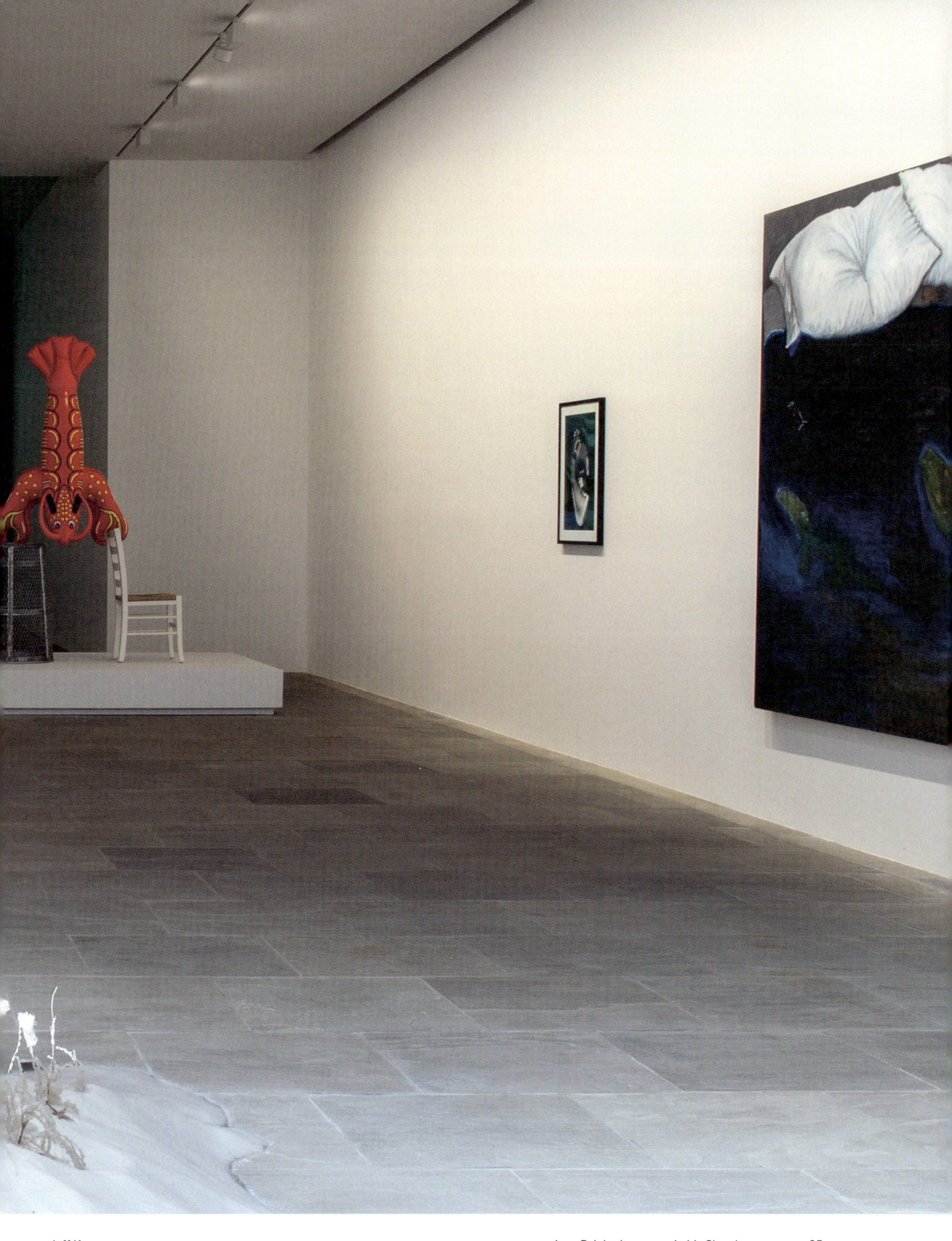

Jeff Koons Jean Painlevé Leidy Churchman

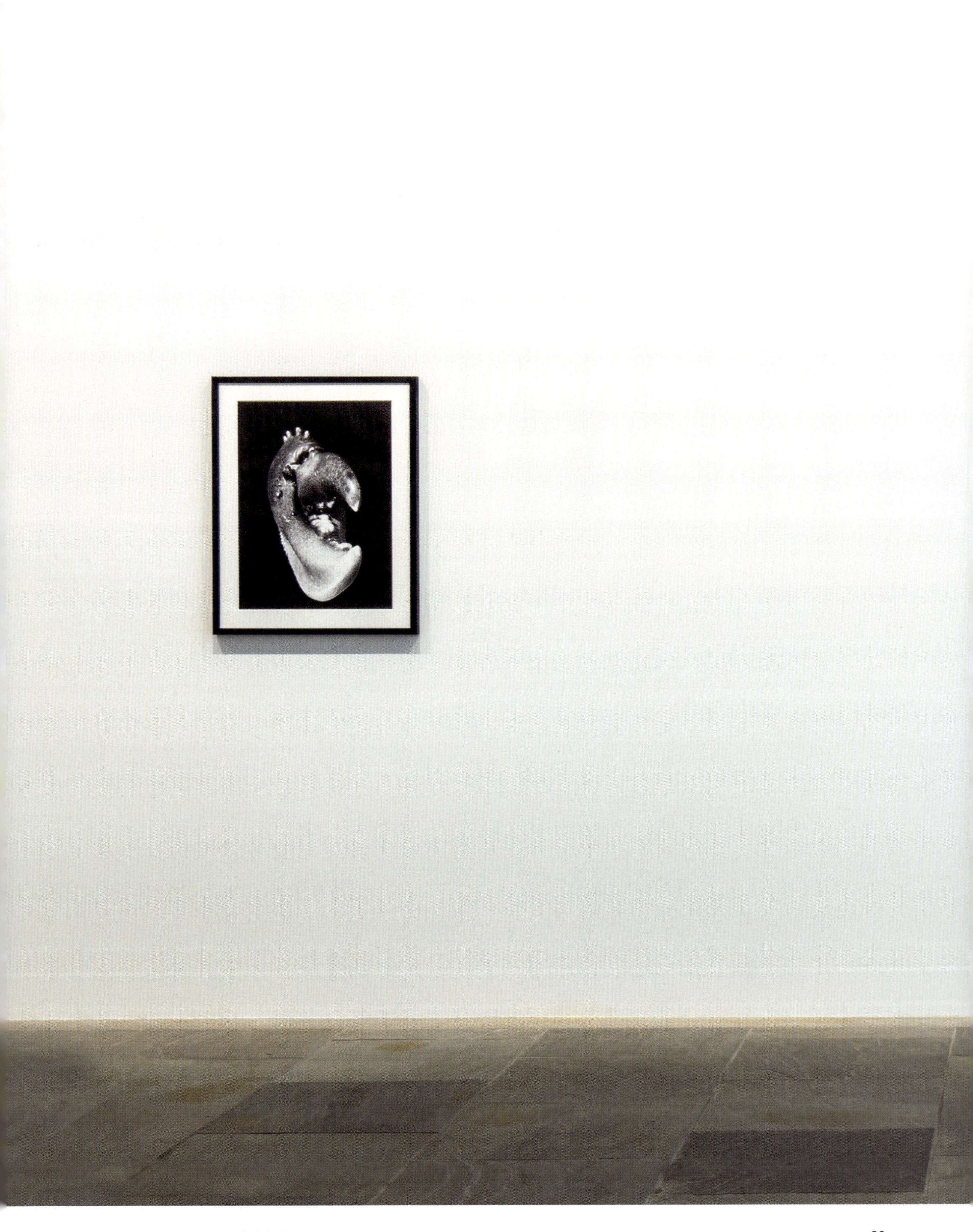

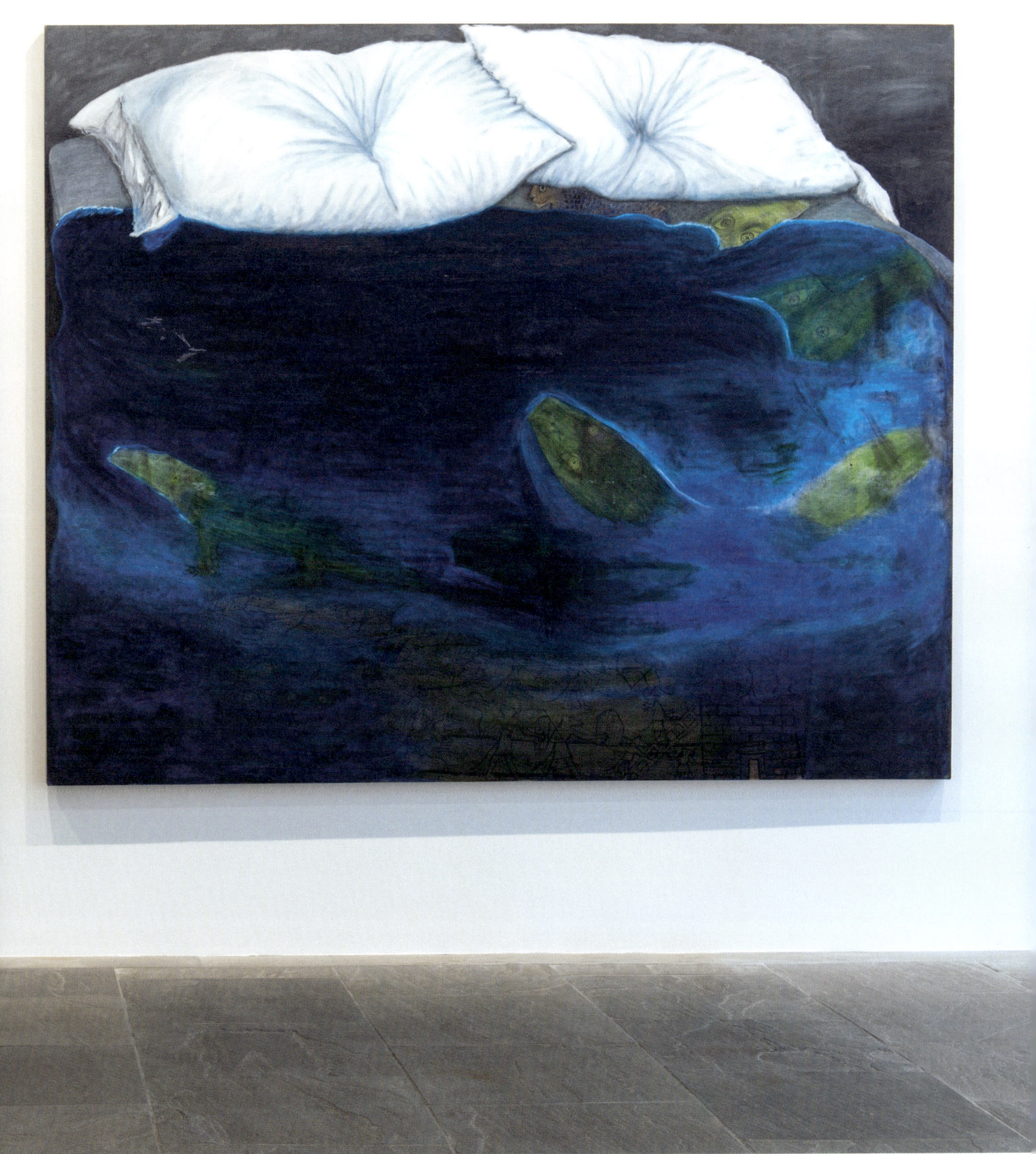

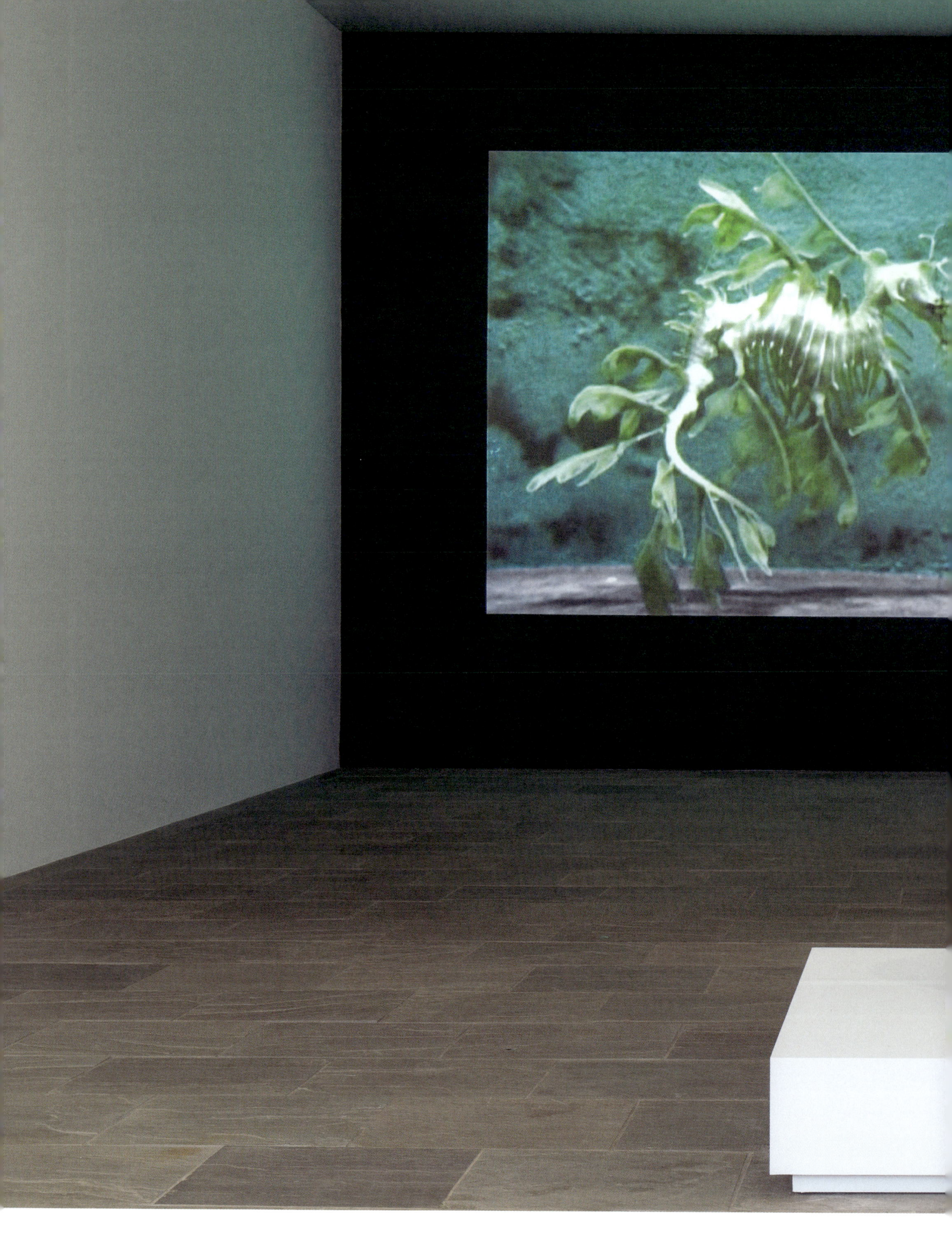

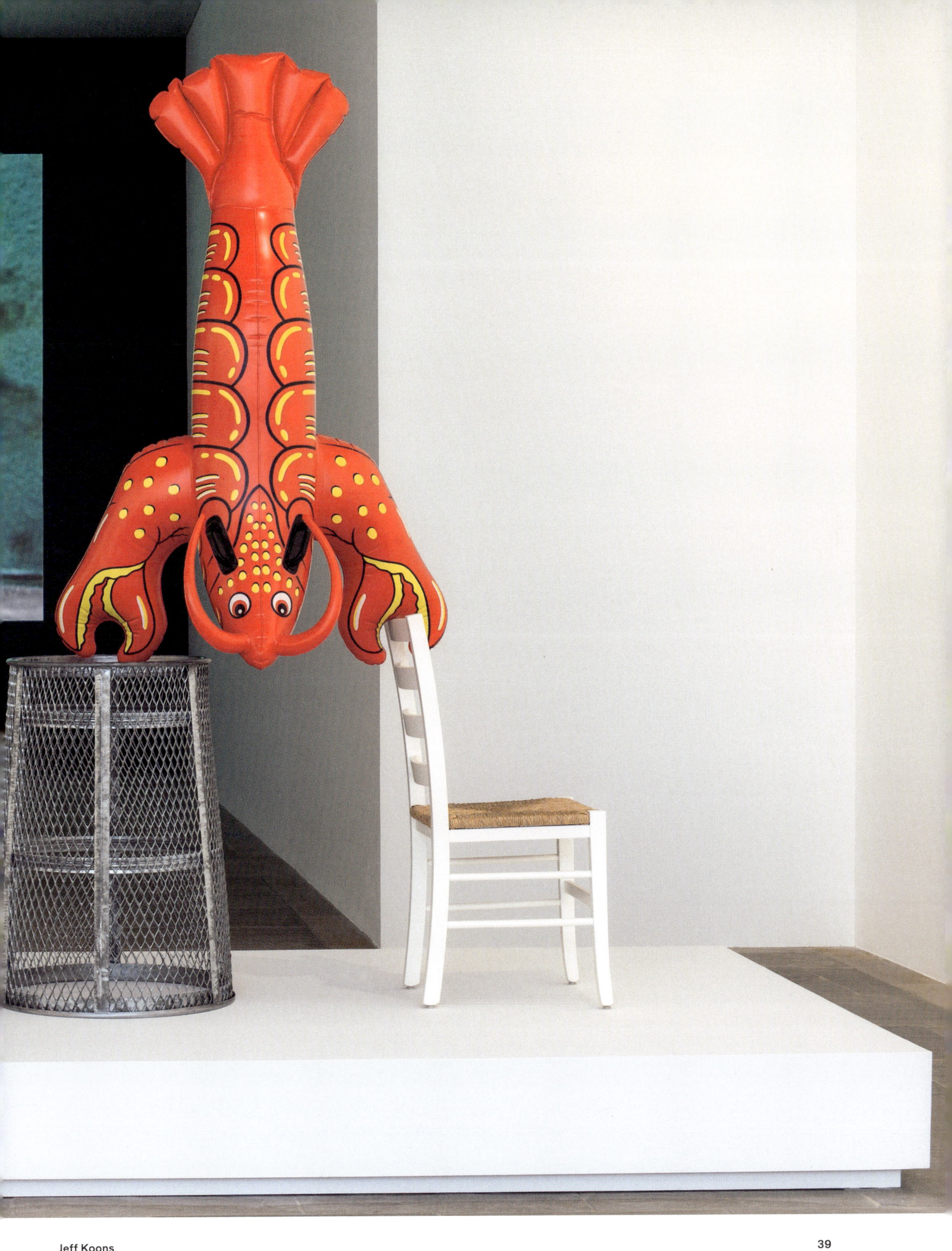

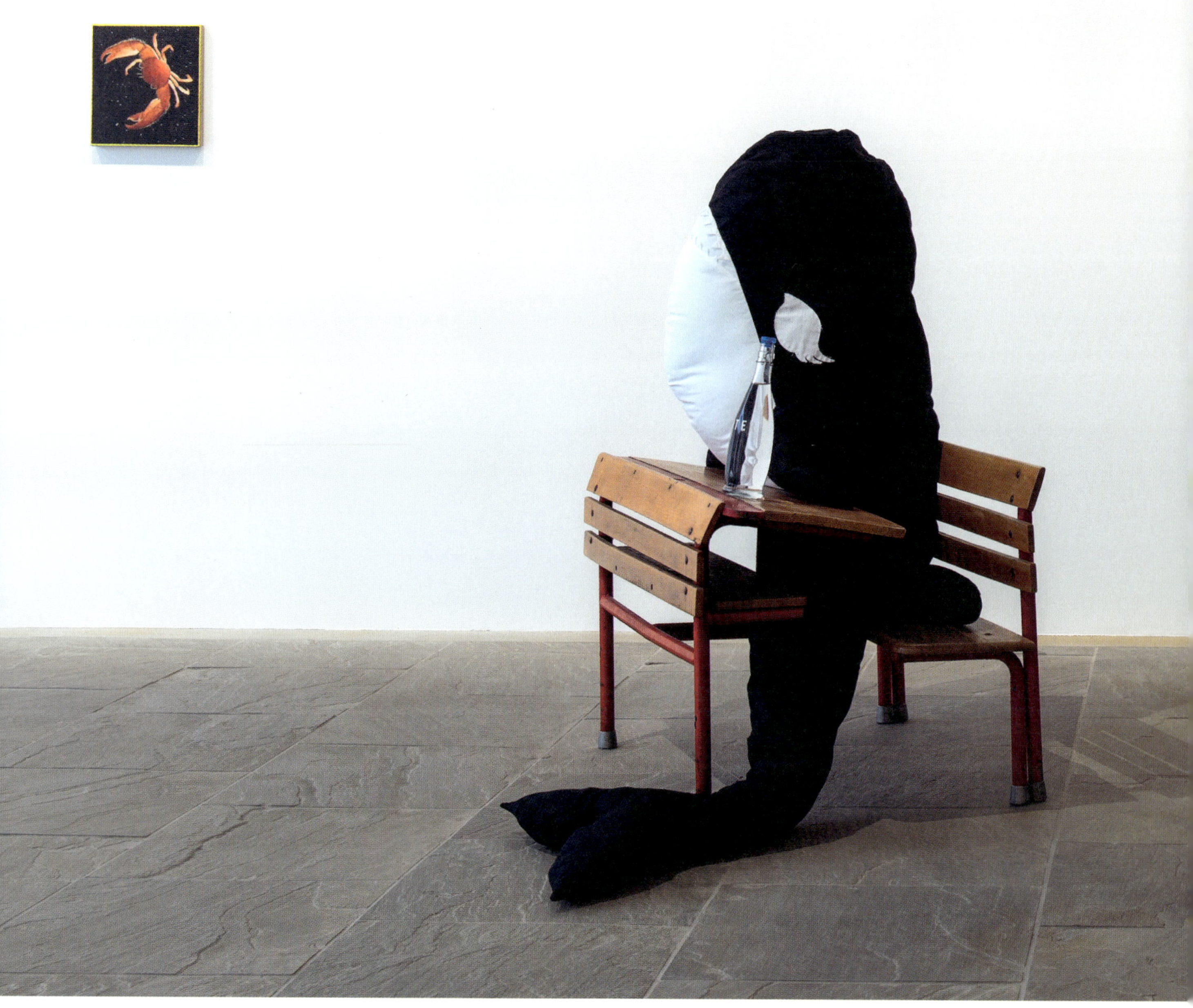

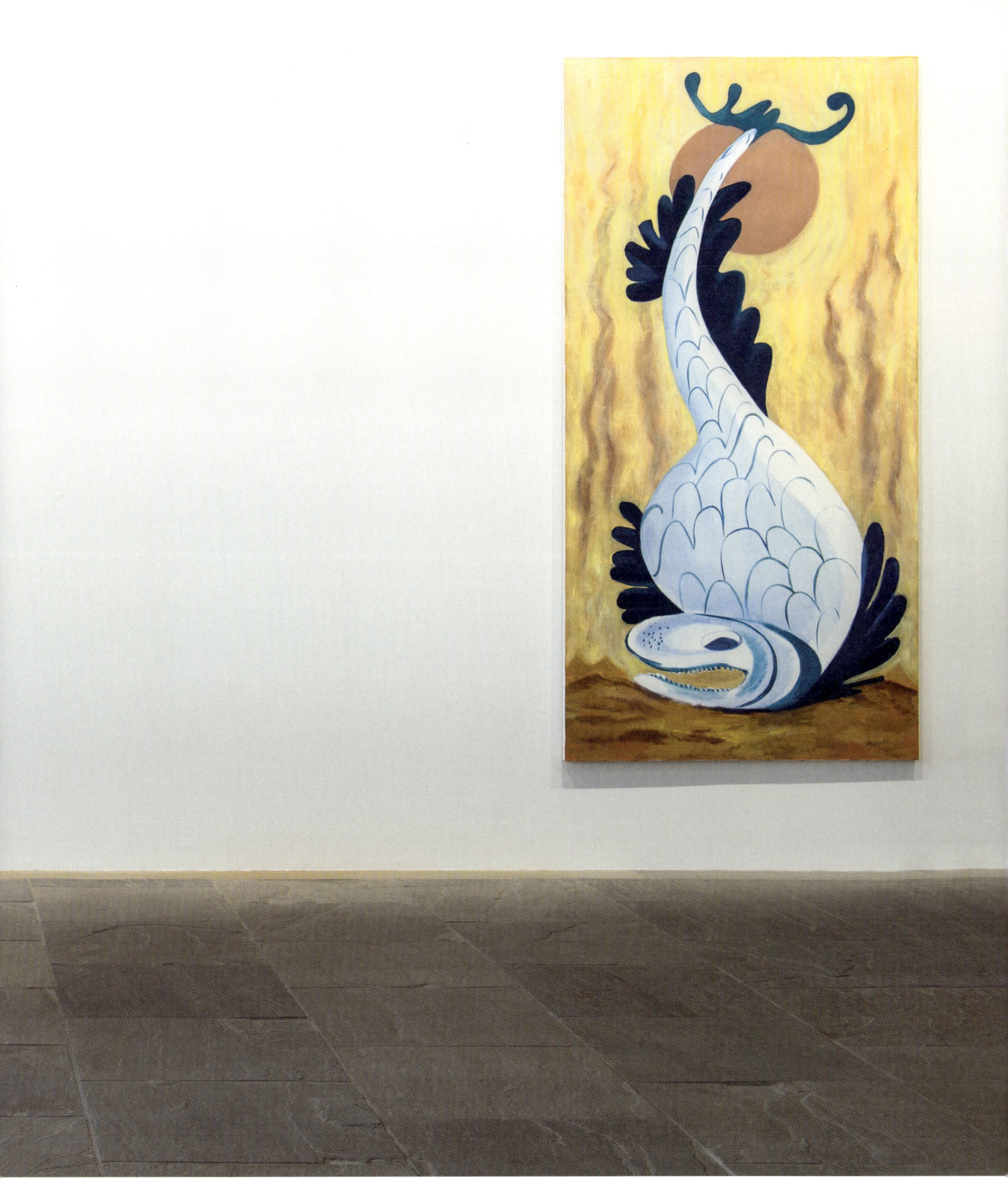

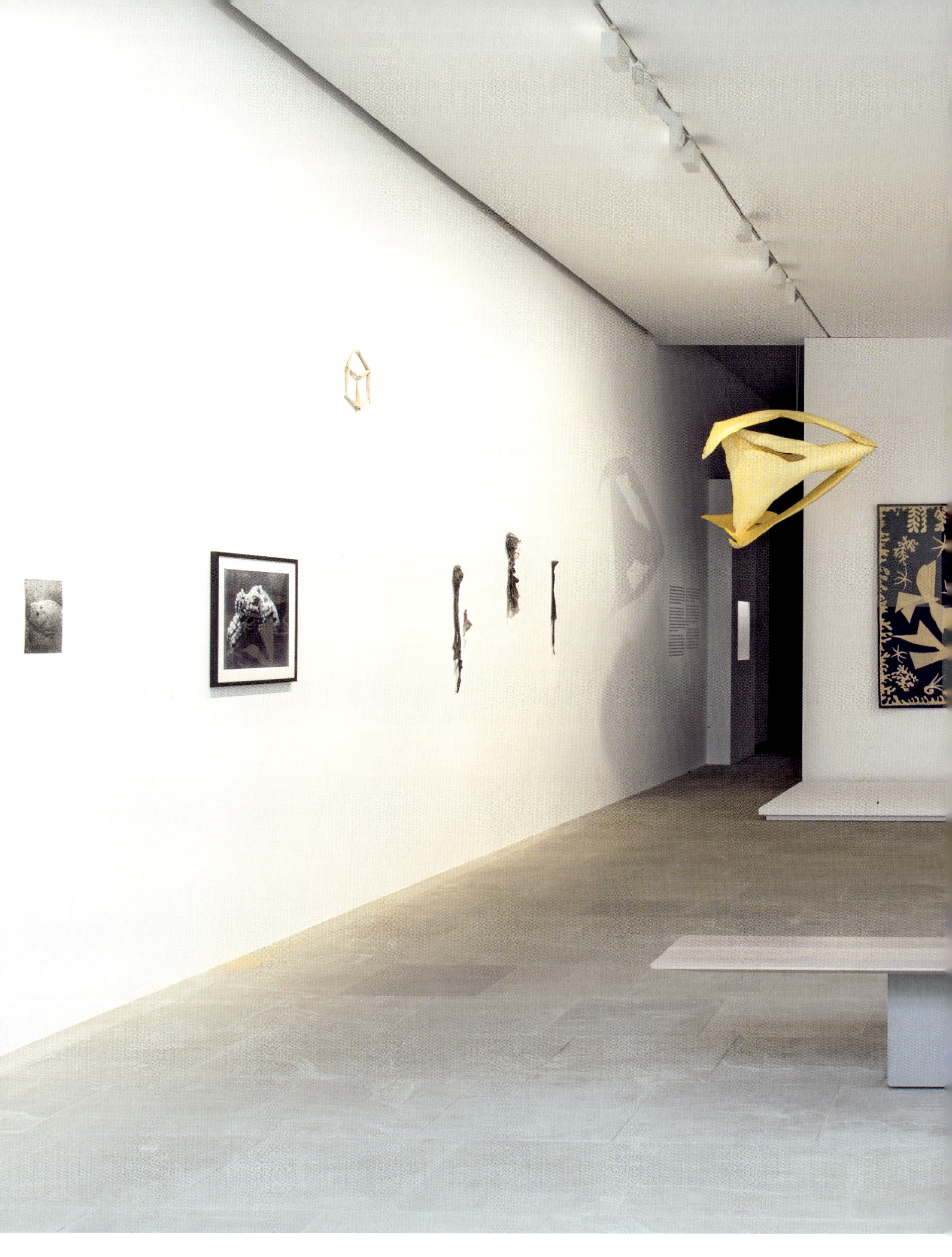

Jochen Lempert Jean Painlevé Michael E. Smith Yuji Agematsu Gabriel Orozco

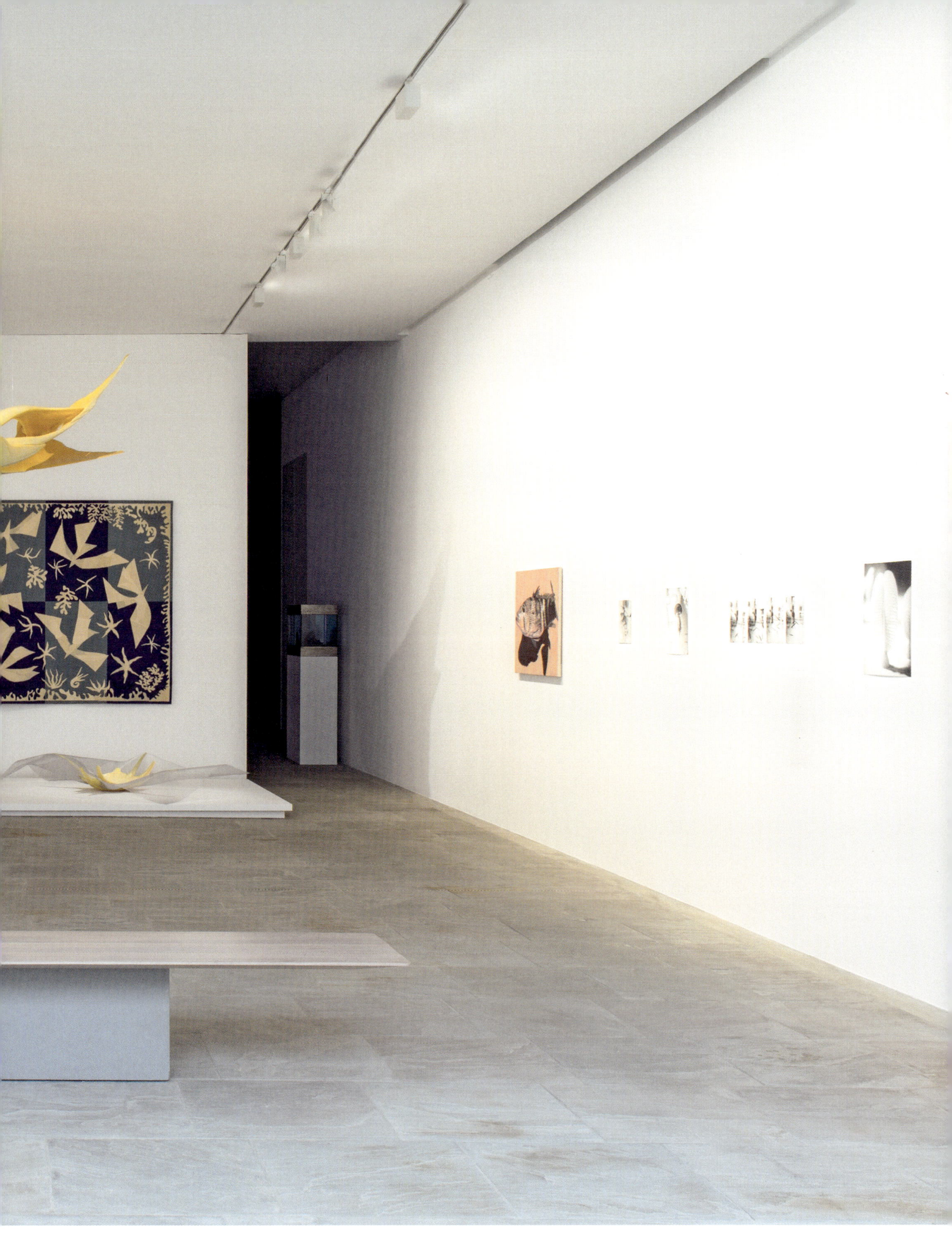

Henri Matisse Adam Higgins Jochen Lempert

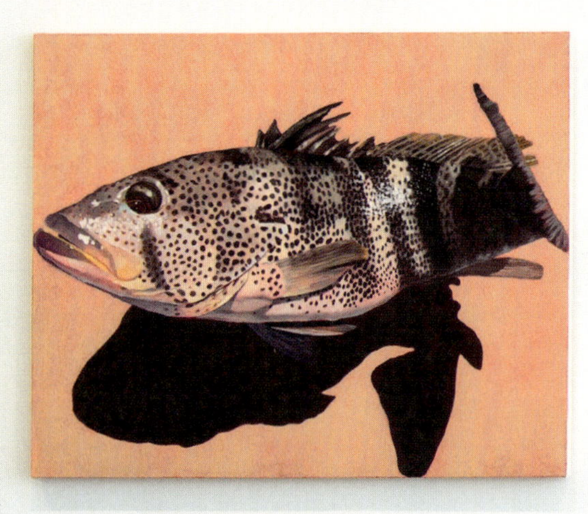

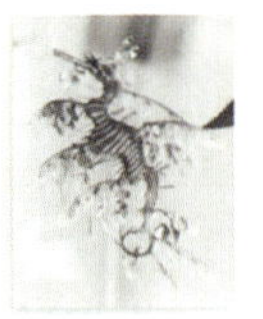

Adam Higgins

Jochen Lempert

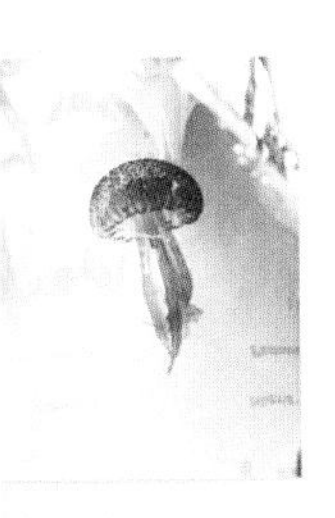

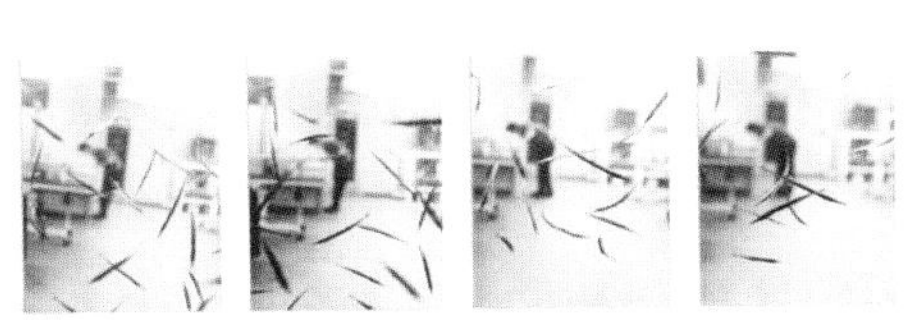

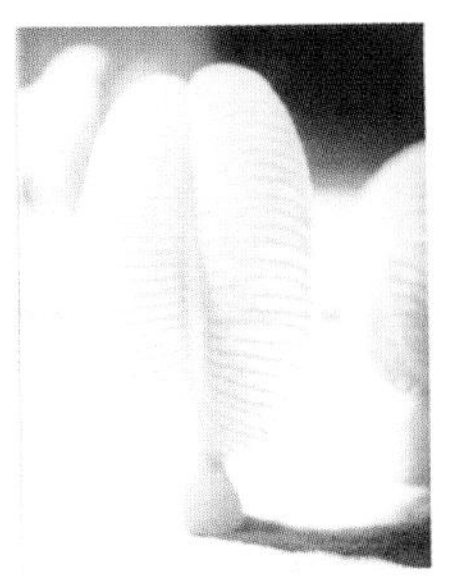

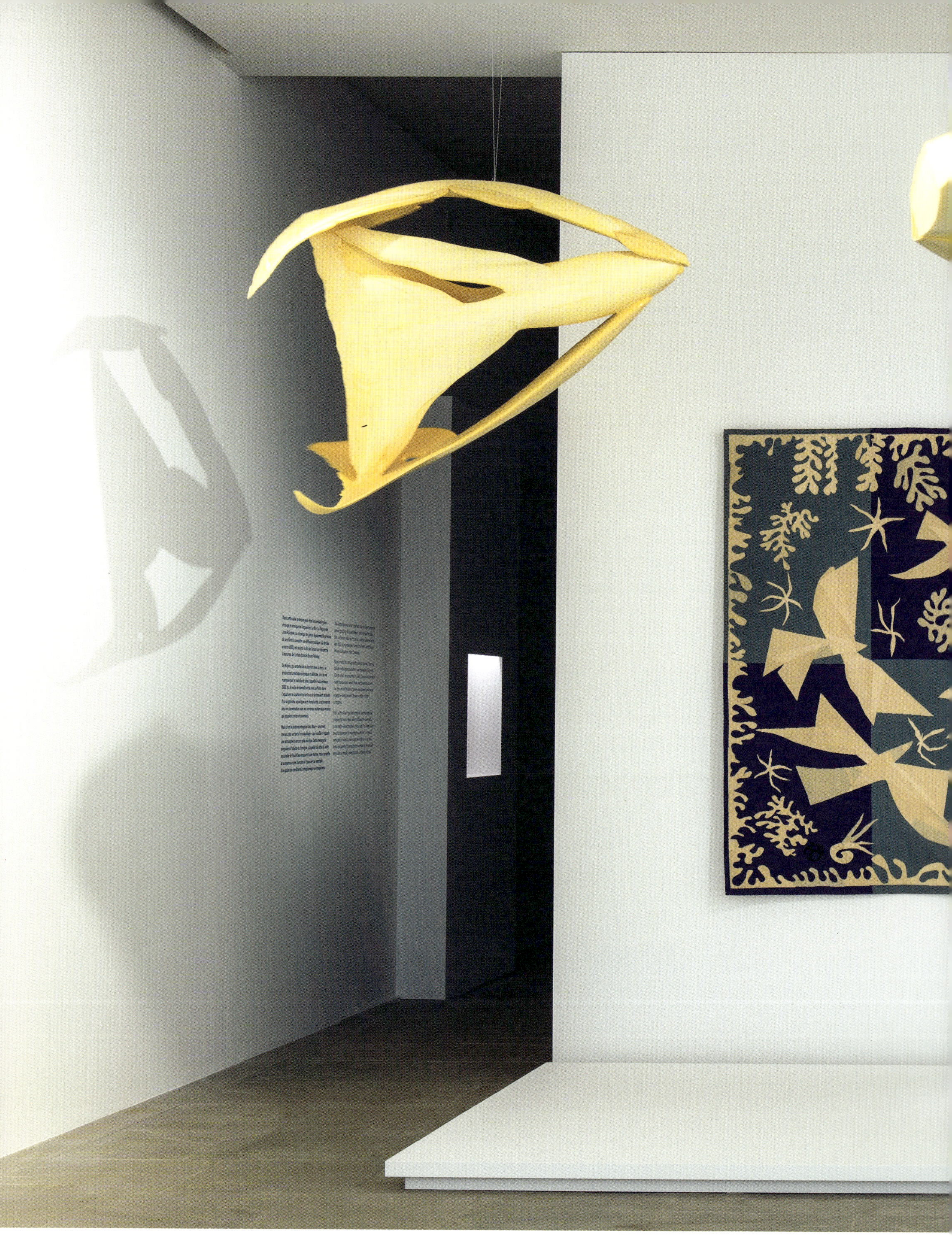

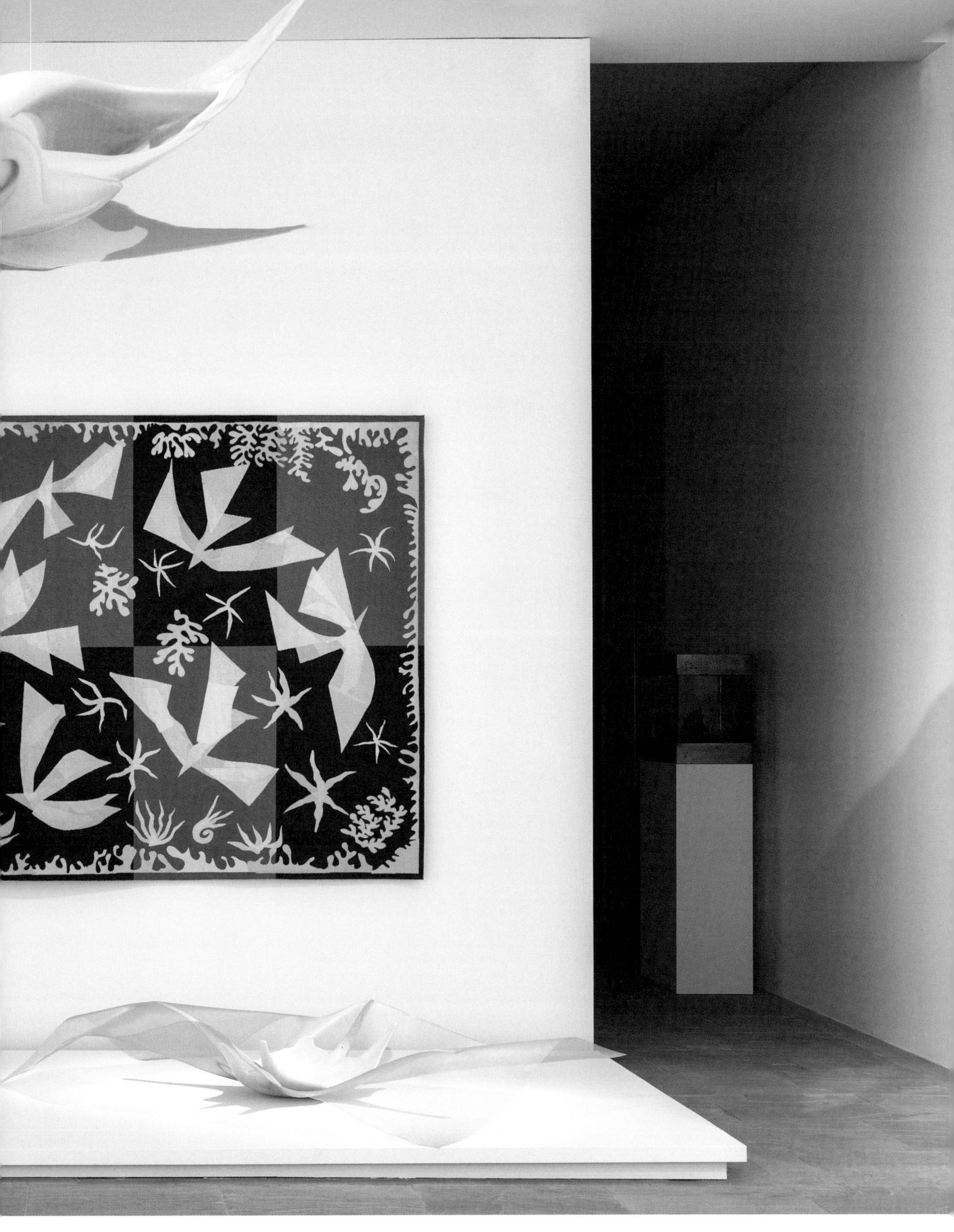

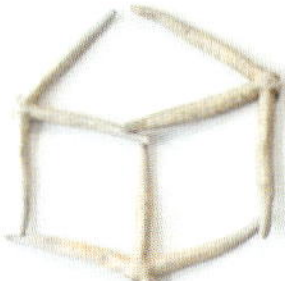

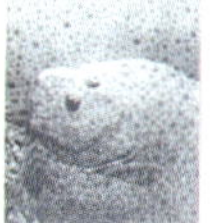

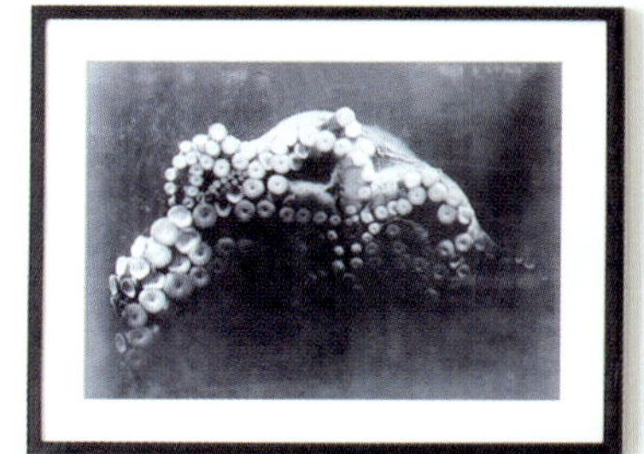

Jochen Lempert Jean Painlevé Michael E. Smith

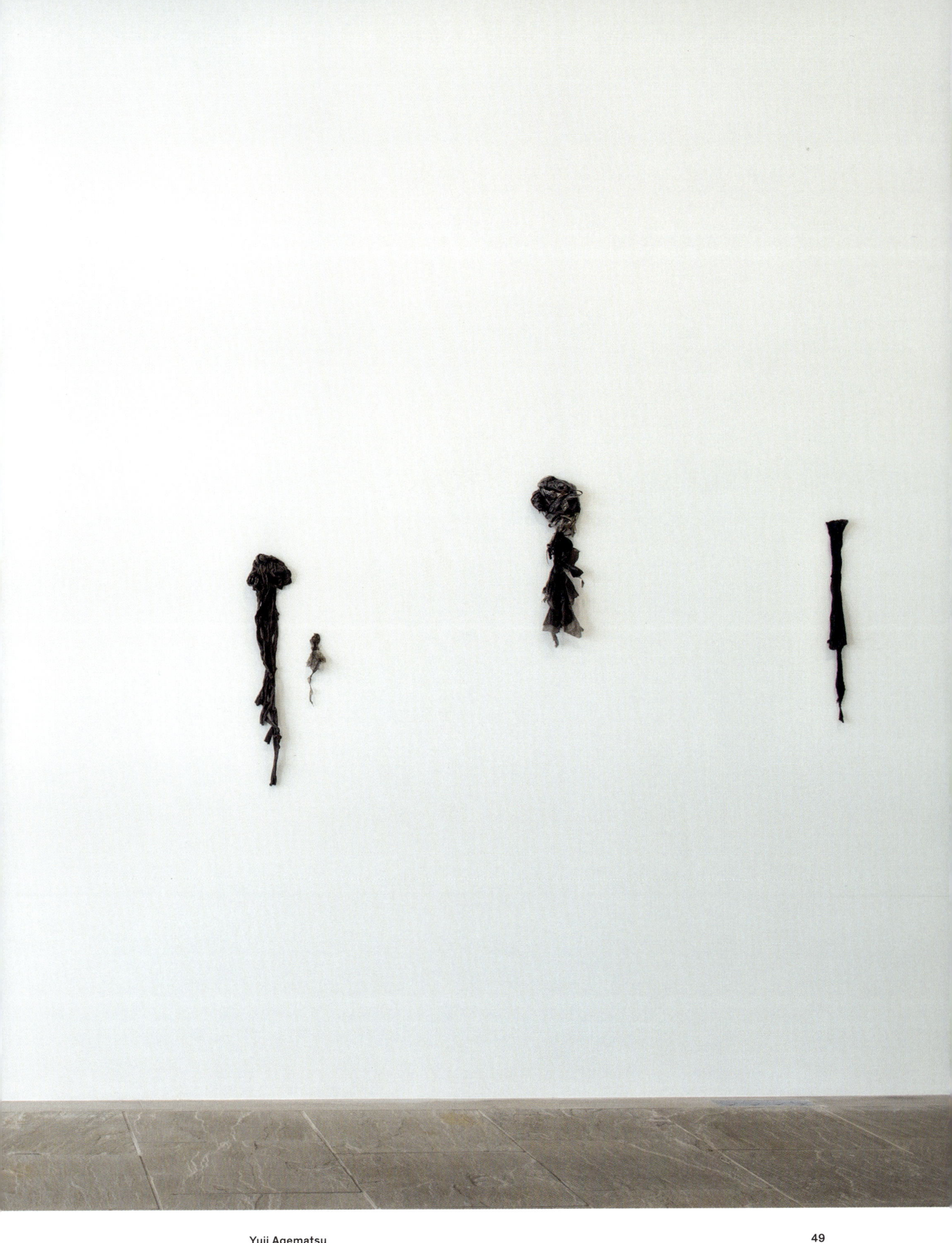

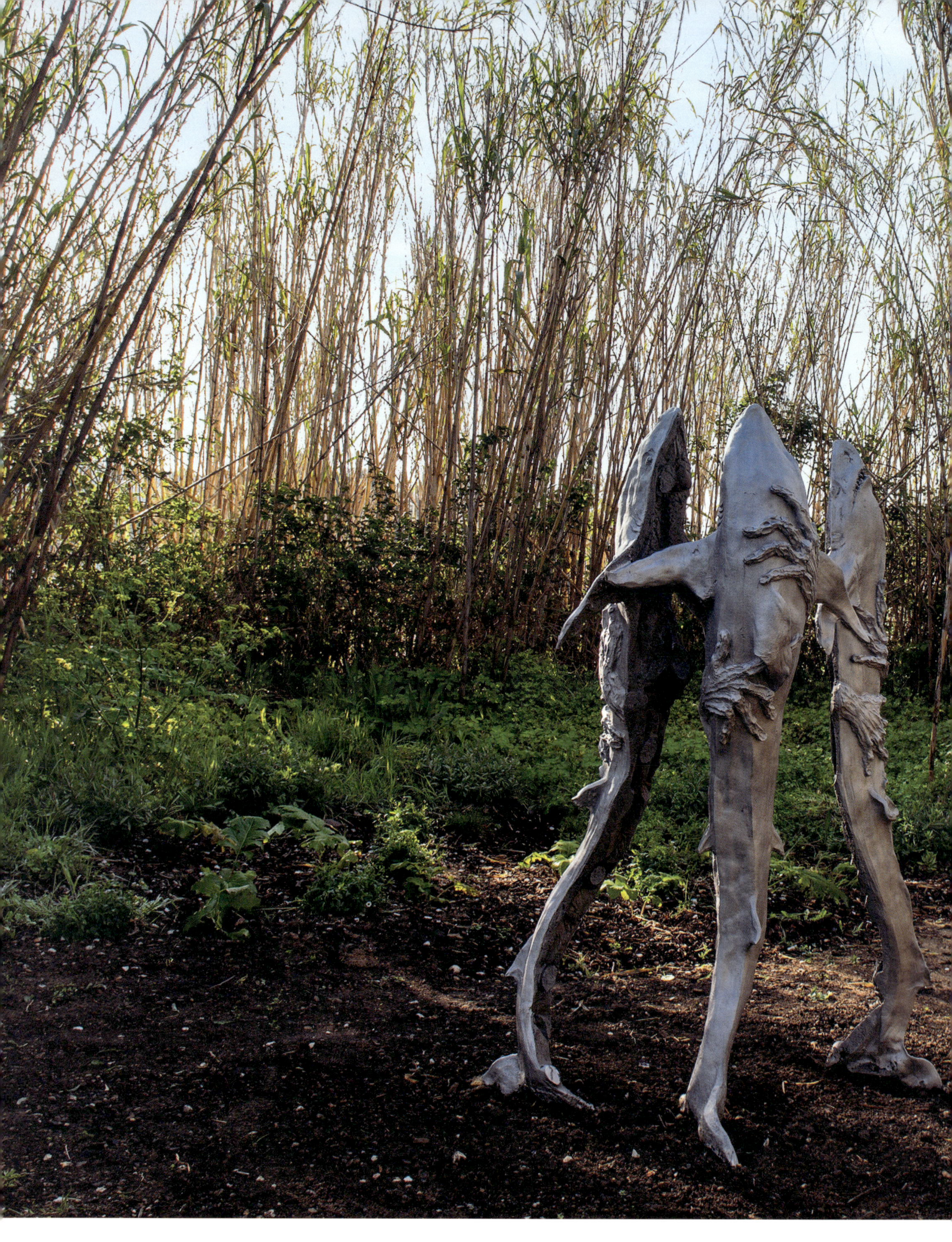

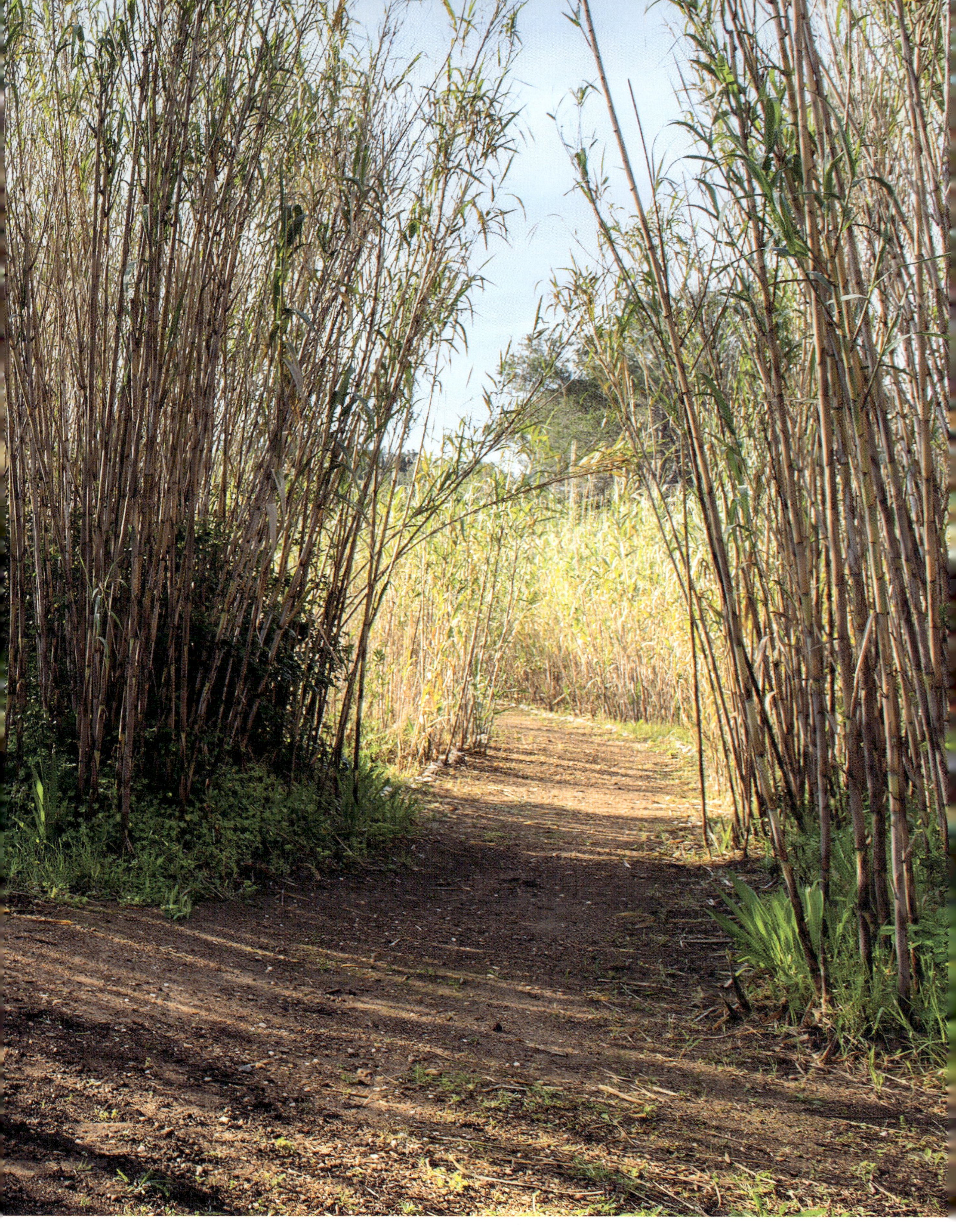

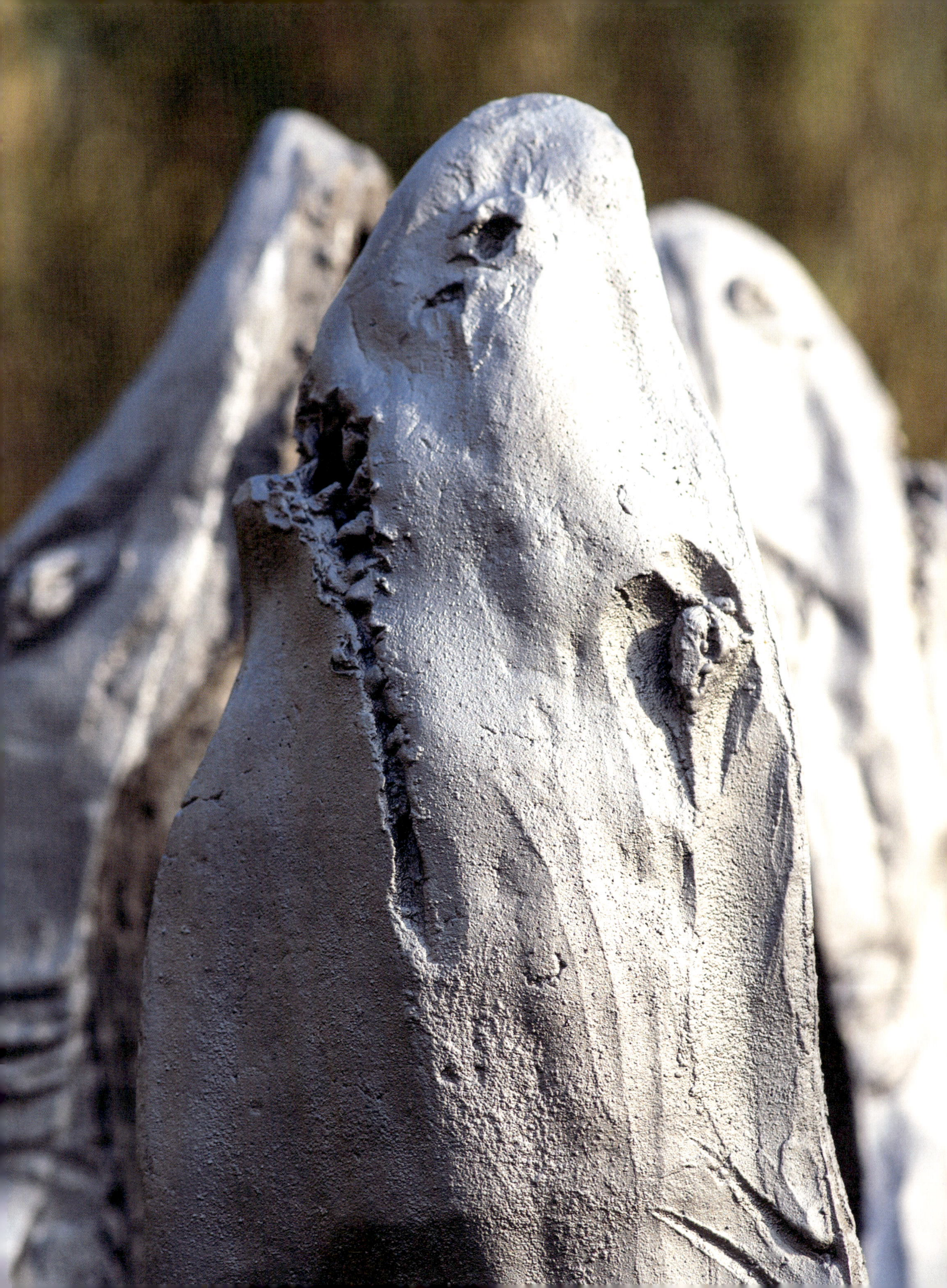

Essays

The Elephant in the Room — **Filipa Ramos**

A young girl, maybe five or six, peeps into the tall vitrines of a vast exhibition hall, an elegant building from the late 19th century. Traversing the main floor of the *Galerie de Paléontologie et d'Anatomie comparée* (the Paleontology and Comparative Anatomy Gallery) of the National Muséum of Natural History of Paris, she slowly walks from one display to the next, following the grid-like system in which the vitrines, armoires with well-locked glasses instead of doors, have been arranged for the last 120 years, since the *ménagerie* first opened in 1898. If her steps were visible, we could see how she spontaneously traverses each row from the beginning to the end, describing precise parallel lines in a sequence that seems entirely natural to her.

She is not alone; her grandmother, who bought her there, occasionally bends down to get closer to her, whispering into her ear, pointing towards a figure or detail, transforming her curiosity into attention. Just like the girl, and despite their age difference of more than sixty years, the grandmother was also brought up in a context in which the museum and the exhibition had been established as institutionalized systems to provide access to unique visions and learning experiences of the world. The old woman is so familiar with exhibitionary logics, including those that comprise the display of death, that it didn't even occur to her that she was bringing a child to a hall populated by the bones, skulls and formalin-kept organs of dead animals, most of them killed for the sole purpose of being exhibited. Museums want animals but they want them dead. Both child and adult seem to be enjoying this experience: of being trained to turn horror into discovery for the girl and of teaching how to suspend empathy, anesthetize fear or suppress disgust through erudition for the woman. Surrounded by all those dead wonders of the natural world that have been killed; sanitized; stripped of their skin, hair and fur; and spectacularly displayed for their pleasure, they are not having a traumatic experience. Those creatures they observe have been physically and perceptively turned into objects and subjected to the gaze of others.

The museum isn't the sole location where operations of this kind take place. A similar intentional lack of empathy for the feelings and experience of those exhibited could have also happened a few meters away, at the *Ménagerie du Jardin des plantes*, the first public zoological garden of Paris (and the second oldest in the world, after the Tiergarten Schönbrunn in Vienna). Established in 1794, the zoo was made to host the animals of the baroque *Ménagerie Royal de Versailles*, desired by Louis XIV and conceived by architect Louis Le Vau in 1663. Its star-shape configuration allowed the various animal environments to gravitate around a central tower which provided an elevated and panoptical view of the garden. A cosmic glimpse of the garden of Eden for the privileged few. During the Revolutionary period, when many of the royal animals were killed by the enraged mob, symbols of aristocratic power as they were, the surviving specimens were rescued and taken to the *Jardin des plantes* in Paris. France's main botanical garden, it was first called *Jardin royal des plantes médicinales* and commonly known in the 17th century, when it was originally founded, as the *Jardin du Roy*. The Paris *ménagerie*'s planning allowed for the circulation of visitors within the park, the individual animals being located in separated and individual cages and pens that could be accessed and observed from various points of view. Such transformation of the menagerie into the zoological garden by a decentralizing spatialization signed the switch of the private animal collection to the public zoo at the same time as it marked the change of visitors from the aristocratic elite to the bourgeoisie, which could now access previously denied visions.

Coinciding with this period of social and political transformations, public zoos came into existence at the beginning of an epoch that corresponds to the reduction of frequent contact with all sorts of non-domestic animals, as authors such as John Berger (*Why Look at Animals*, 1981) or Akira Mizuta Lippit (*The Electric Animal*, 2000) have sustained. The zoo became the place where city people would go to see those animals that were temporally or geographically inaccessible. To a certain extent, the zoological garden was turned into a monument to the disappearance of such encounters or even the apparatus to assure that such encounters would cause thrills with no spills: no risk should be involved in entertainment and learning. It was the Paris *ménagerie* that allowed someone who would never leave France throughout his entire life, like painter Henri Rousseau, to dream the jungle through the cage bars. Indeed, the interconnection between the public presentation of culture and nature became such that a trip to the zoological garden was similar to an art museum visit: individuals, either alone or in groups, moving from one space to the other and observing one specimen after the other, traversing temporalities and geographies that could never correspond to the actual ones. And just like in a museum, visitors were also able to program their excursions according to an itinerary of highlights and not-to-miss items. The large elephant being for the zoo what the ambiguous Mona Lisa is for the Louvre.

It is thanks to this socio-political transition of the access to the collections of wild animals that the girl and her grandmother were able to visit the zoo, more than two centuries later. They would have spent time looking through the elegant bay window of the *Fauverie*, the big cat (small) house, located on the extreme of the zoological garden. In order to get there, they would have followed the articulated ambulatory system within which the various dens, pits, aviaries, vivaria and animal houses have been positioned over time.

On the way there, they would have seen the yacks and the rheas and after that, the gnus, alpacas and giant kangaroos. Then, they would have followed a curve bending North, where they would have seen the foxes and, just in front, the *Singerie*, the ape house, where a group of five Bornean orangutans were impossible to miss behind the obsolete if historically relevant 1930s glass and tile pavilion that still hosts them, hopefully not for much longer. One of them, Nénette, the matriarch of the group, was born around 1969 in the island of Borneo, where her species lives. When she was three, she was captured in the wild and sent to the zoo, where she has been living since 1972. Almost fifty years of captivity is a heavy sentence for an animal whose only crime is that of being fascinating for humans to look at. Nénette was also the star of Nicolas Philibert's homonymous film, first released in 2010.

Largely shot from the external glass that separates Nénette from visitors and incorporating the audio of the conversations and comments of those who look at her, the film contributed to expose her condition as a spectacle prop, neither domestic nor wild, neither pet nor pest, de-exoticized and re-exoticized, turned into an objectified body that belongs to the public realm. But the young girl didn't watch *Nénette*. She'd probably prefer to see King Louie, the mischievous orangutan whose name was probably a tribute to Louis XIV, singing and dancing in Walt Disney's *Jungle Book* film (1967). Paradoxically, it's likely that her grandmother considers her to be too young to be subjected to thinking about how the zoo, instead of fulfilling its promise of showing wild animals in captivity, shows captive animals in captivity. After the orangutans, the two would go to see the Przewalski's horses, which they probably thought looked exactly like any other horse they'd seen (some experts even consider them to be a feral variety of domestic horses), then the raccoons and the Malayan tapirs. There were no elephants. The last one, Jenny, had died in April 1976 and was never replaced. Before Jenny there were Bebe, Rachel, Sarrith, Koutch, Jussia, Bangkok, Roger, Parkie and Hans. In 1870, during the Siege of Paris, Castor and Polux, two elephants named after the mythological twins, were killed. Their bodies were sold as meat by the Boucherie Anglaise in Boulevard Haussmann. According to the January 6th, 1871 chronicle by British writer Henry Labouchère, they tasted bad: "Yesterday, I had a slice of Pollux for dinner. Pollux and his brother Castor are two elephants, which have been killed. It was tough, coarse, and oily, and I do not recommend English families to eat elephant as long as they can get beef or mutton". The only elephant to be seen is the one whose bones lie in the room of the Natural History Museum, its presence standing for all those others whose histories are too unnatural to tell, especially to a little girl.

Going back to the *Fauverie*, were we began, it's likely that grandmother and granddaughter would spend some time looking at the beautiful North-Chinese leopard, compulsively pacing back and forward in its few meters-long glass enclosure. Just like during the visit to the museum, the grandmother also didn't take into account how she was bringing a child to a park populated by distressed and alienated animals, bred and captured for the purpose of being publicly exhibited. In doing so she was accustoming the child to a system of torture and a display of violence that have been legitimized by the tradition of integrating nature within a cultural framework that, by bringing the two systems together, perpetuates, if not accentuates, their chasm.

The systems of exhibiting nature provide an ideal setting to understand how the dualistic divisions that shaped the modern subject — namely those between the cultural and natural, human and animal, animate and inanimate, rational and irrational, civilized and brute, to name a few, and also those that concern the gestures of seeing and being seen, consuming and being consumed — have been naturalized by the modes of displaying the living, even when dead. By relying on material supports of separation — cages, vitrines, moats, fences, cinematic mise-en-scènes created by dioramas, and also shelves, crates and drawers of natural history museums and zoology colleges — these archival and exhibitionary modes consolidate an ideological divide. The materials they are made of — iron bars, nets, glasses, real and fake plants, textiles, wooden cabinets and drawers filled with camphor — induce the perception of difference between those who look and those being looked at, those in front of and those kept behind, those who can leave and those who are forced to stay. This relationship shapes the modern spectator and, in a wider sense, the modern individual, differentiated and separated from "nature", which is turned into a system that can be studied and admired with the necessary physical and conceptual distance.

It is worth considering how the public structuring of the institutions that displayed the dead or living "wonders" of the natural world (such as the above-mentioned natural history museums and zoological gardens) was happening in parallel to the academic edification of other disciplinary ambits, such as those of art history. Throughout the consolidation of art history as a discipline and of art as its object of study, the exhibition became the format that naturally fit its public manifestations. In the context of art history, the exhibition — this old system conceived to subject objects, lifeforms and ideas to power, discipline and rhetoric — became property of art. Museums became art museums, exhibitions art exhibitions, galleries art galleries, and so forth. Things changed little with the passing of the times and nowadays contemporary art continues claiming the monopoly of the exhibition as a model, remaining blind to older and different traditions of putting objects and gestures on display. In doing so, it fails to acknowledge the triangular relation between protection, education and spectacle that has shaped the concept of the exhibition and that has also defined the operative logic of the art exhibition.

However, there is hope for change. While being so attached to their exhibitionary logics, artistic practices also bear a unique possibility for change and regeneration. The methods and methodologies of art serve artistic research and artistic production alike; they are ultimately undifferentiable and exist in a unique symbiotic relation in which research and outcome are undistinguishable from one another. These methods and methodologies are often not exclusively directed to the making of art per se but also towards the re-invention of the modes in which art is exhibited. While relying on the exhibition, art is also actively thinking about the exhibition. By potentially deconstructing and re-writing the politics of display, contemporary artistic practices have a remarkable capacity to mend the above-mentioned dichotomies between subject and object, exhibited and spectator, producer and consumer and, why not, culture and nature. Or at least, they can provide an important contribution to make audiences aware of these biased divisions.

It is perhaps irrational to believe that a major limit for contemporary art (its arrogant claim of a logic of exhibiting that is historically rooted in ancient practices of display) can become a propeller for a major cultural change (the revision of the whole logic of the exhibitionary complex and the exposure of its limits). However, this optimism is rooted not in a rational standpoint but in an affective reasoning. Art explores unusual forms of embodied meaning that have the potential of turning knowledge into comprehension and perception into affects. It's not so much the tautological and meta-reflexive aspects of contemporary art that are relevant here (those remain as valid as other discipline's solipsistic efforts of self-legitimization) but the speculative potential of art. In being speculative, art relies on intuition, imagination and risk. It goes off-track and gets lost, it is not disturbed by failure and it pairs disparate elements whose assemblage shatters conventions and generates new meanings and realizations. Art is capable of seeing itself in that exact speculative matter — after all, the term speculation originates from *speculum*, mirror in Latin — and of allowing others to see things from a different perspective. This is not about defining art as a sophisticated illustrative tool that documents what otherwise can't be seen nor about considering it a bearer of distinctive ethics or moral standards that provide a new judgment to what was previously deemed innocuous. Art potentially disturbs the real, in indiscriminately fastidious and pleasurable manners: it seduces and hurts, it shocks and soothes, it freezes and transforms. By offering speculative visions, it allows us to feel and experience things in non-conventional ways and to think in different terms. The historic exhibitionary systems from where the display of art derivates are in need of more art to rethink and re-feel themselves. It's the only way to shake their dusty coatings, to shatter their vitrines, and to create new desires, for little girls and grandmothers alike.

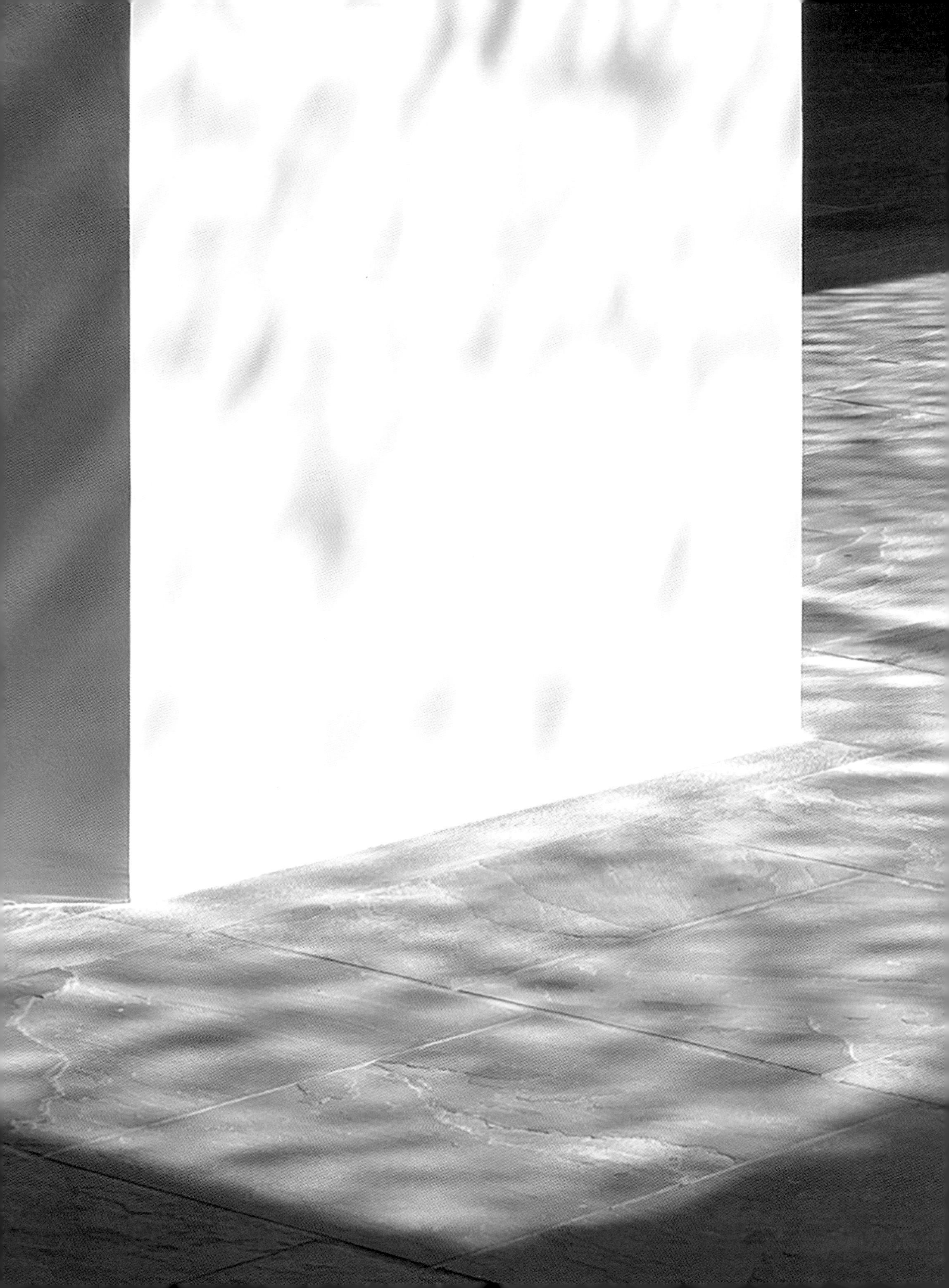

The Nature of Artifice — **Vincent Normand**

From botanical gardens to natural history collections, anatomical theaters to zoological gardens up to the advent of the museological apparatus, institutions for the exhibition of Nature were, specifically within the context of the advent of "natural sciences" at the beginning of modern Europe, crucial sites for the production of scientific facts. Therefore, these institutions were a central means in the constitution of our representation of Nature itself. Founded on the spatial display of classificatory categories, these institutions are places in which objects have been integrated into the taxonomic organization of the natural world, forming a "cosmography" endowed with new symbolic weight. In fact, these spaces lead us to the foundations of what we could call the "ontological engineering" of humanist modernity: its demarcation of the boundaries delineating its "world", its symmetrical production of subjects and objects, people and things, spectators and artifacts, at the heart of which the image of the human subject emerged against the backdrop of a Nature conceived as the background of human thought.

In his archeology of knowledge project, Michel Foucault inaugurated his study of the order of pre-modern knowledge by exploring the naturalistic practices of collecting and exhibiting natural specimens in Renaissance Italy|[1]|, thus highlighting how much the constitution of knowledge by the collection, identification, description and classification of its objects has imposed itself, during Western modernity, as the universal form of knowledge. As proposed by Paula Findlen, in the 15th and 16th centuries collection indeed became common practice, participating in the desire of an elite to know the past, in all its forms, through the possession of its vestiges|[2]|. In parallel, the appearance of natural science and of naturalists wishing to articulate the collection in their cabinets with the interrogation of the natural world, aroused a new attitude towards Nature, then conceived as a readable and decipherable entity, a series of case studies, generating new investigative techniques which, therefore, have transformed the writing of the history of Nature itself.

This process of defining Nature through its exhibition is at the foundation of modernity itself, so that it undoubtedly constitutes one of the most determining aspects of it. From the museum of Ulisse Aldrovandi in Bologna (where the collections of the founder of Natural History were

1
Michel Foucault, "La Prose du Monde", in *Les Mots et les Choses* (Gallimard, 1966).

2
Paula Findlen, *Possessing Nature. Museums, Collecting and Scientific Culture in Early Modern Italy* (University of California Press, 1996).

gathered in 1617), passing by the museographic translation of the encyclopedic nomenclature of Georges-Louis Leclerc de Buffon to the Cabinet of Natural History in Paris in the middle of the 18th century, until the stabilization of the museological system in the middle of the 19th century, and the gradual adaptation of the theory of evolution in modern collection and exhibition practices (of which the Pitt Rivers Museum of Oxford is an archetype), the process of cutting Nature into objects of knowledge (what, with Foucault, we could call the *episteme* of Western modernity) has been closely linked to the practice of conservation and public exhibition.

The museum transforms the classification table into a three-dimensional spatial map. In other words, it *spatializes* it. It thus gives objects the possibility of being "graphs," materializing epistemological categories; that is to say, objects of knowledge which, by charging things with meaning, make them, so to speak, "speak". By uprooting specimens from their environment, and encasing them under glass, like a symbolic "quarantine" situation, the modern museum essentially consists of a Cartesian interface between *res cogitans* and *res extensa*, the observer and the world: it is a place where a categorized projection of the world is made available for inspection by the mind.

The modern museum is therefore a place where the typically modern division between the optical and haptic dimensions of sight (i.e. its scopic and tactile dimensions) has found both a dramaturgy and a scenographic morphology. This separation of sight and touch in exhibitions shows a limit guaranteeing the integration of objects into a specific symbolic regime, divorced from the domain of goods: that of the artifact. It constitutes the exhibition as a means of normative inscription, as a privileged site of modern, positivist and objectivist forms of mediation between the artifact and the subject observing it. The morphology of this separation, in the context of a museum exhibition, is created through distancing effects: sight from touch, intention from corporeality, judgment from interest, contemplation from manipulation, performer from observer. These distancing effects are the interfaces and mediators of sensory and hermeneutic access to the exhibited object, of which the glass display case is undoubtedly the canonical form.

The museum therefore promotes sight as the cornerstone of the experience of objects, and as such represents a concrete archetype of what Martin Jay has called the "scopic regime" of modernity[3]. The fundamental element of this scopic regime is the notion of virtual pyramids anchoring the spectator as the central agent of all that is visible. As Jay has shown, this scopic regime is typical of the modern polarity between subject and object, visually based on the placement of a detached observer, a subject, at the top of a perspective cone whose sides lead to an infinity of objects against which the subject is measured. As such, the museological apparatus is a space for configuring the mediation chain between the object and the viewer, it's the vector of a symmetry between "subject" and "world", the medium of an apparition between "consciousness" and "form".

3
Martin Jay, "Scopic Regimes of Modernity," in Hal Foster (ed.), *Vision and Visuality* (Bay Press, 1999).

This is why the dramaturgy specific to exhibitions leads directly to the concepts that delineate the world of the moderns, what we could call the "ontological matrix" of Western modernity. This apparition between consciousness and form articulates the ontological categories against which the museum has historically been deployed. It is the spatial translation of what, borrowing the system of four ontologies formalized by the French anthropologist Philippe Descola in his enterprise of describing various ways of relating to Nature, we could define as the "naturalist flaw". This flaw designates the dichotomy between "people" and "things" which characterizes the cosmography of Western modernity: a cleavage that, historically, has traversed the modern world, postulating the continuity of physicalities (Nature, matter) on the background of which the discontinuous field of subjects, social constructions and interiorities (Culture, spirit) emerges. To understand more precisely the economics of grand ontological divisions specific to Naturalism in Western modernity, let us recall that Descola makes Naturalist ontology intelligible by describing it as the structural inversion of animist cosmography. Where Naturalism supposes the continuity of physicalities (postulating a "Mononature") and produces discontinuities at the level of Culture (postulating a "Multiculture"), Animism supposes the continuity of culture, or of the "soul" (Monoculture) and sees discontinuities in Nature (Multinature). In other words, the Naturalist perceives the world as an uninterrupted material chain against the background of which the autonomous field of the mind/spirit, the subject and the individual stands out (and within this frame, therefore, what could connect a human with a jaguar, for example, is the shared biological reality and the evolution of the species), whereas the Animist perceives the world like the incarnation, in the form of multiple bodies, of the same spirit (and where, therefore, that which connects the human to the jaguar is the sharing of a soul). As Eduardo Viveiros de Castro suggests: the European praxis "produces minds" on the background of a given material continuum, and the Native praxis "produces bodies" on the background of a given socio-cultural continuum[4].

The museum is the site where the Naturalist ontology is reiterated and re-staged with each encounter of a spectator and an artifact. The genealogy of this "Naturalist flaw" finds what is probably one of its most intense expressions in a founding text of materialist thought, the « Entretien entre D'Alembert et Diderot » (1769), in which Diderot puts his encyclopedic program to the test by imagining a scene resembling an exhibition situation. Imagining coming face-to-face with a stone, the philosopher wonders what the classifying attitude of the materialist thinker before the inert object should be. Should the stone be imbued with the qualities of life and seen as part of a larger sentient being, potentially integrating into a domain shared by humans, or should it be reduced to a mere game of matter and quantity, thereby denying, by extension, the possibility of considering human beings themselves as sensitive and qualitative beings? This historical distinction within materialism between "petrified" life and "vivified" stone is a distinction in which modern exhibition apparatuses, because of their specific dramatization of the link between consciousness and form, are deeply rooted. The spatial functioning of the museum, and more generally of modern exhibition institutions, make them mechanisms largely dedicated to the social translation of this ontological matrix into sensory experiences and means of knowledge.

The museological apparatus is entirely shaped by the symmetrical relationship between objectification and the formation of subjects: here, the manufacture of objects is simultaneously the manufacture of subjects. As such, it can be seen as a site within which the ontological boundaries traversing the modern world have been materialized, made palpable and explicit. The canonical example of the symmetrical production of subjects and objects in the museum is undoubtedly aligned with the concept of the "exhibitionary complex" that Tony Bennett developed in 1988[5]. Largely based on the Foucauldian concept of "dispositive" (or

4
Eduardo Viveiros de Castro, *Métaphysiques cannibales. Lignes d'anthropologie post-structurale* (PUF, 2009).

apparatus), Bennett's argument proposes that, historically, modern exhibition spaces have been intimately linked to a wider network of technologies and institutions (Natural History, dioramas, panoramas...) which, together, define modernity as a reformation of vision, allowing for the emergence of new disciplines (history, biology, anthropology...) as well as their respective discursive objects (the past, evolution, man...), just as the institutions described by Foucault have shaped the modern experience of knowledge in general. Thus, the dispositives constituting the modern exhibition complex can be understood as *biopolitical* spaces where the organization of objects implies an organization of the subjects included in the spectacle of contemplation, where the uprooting of the exhibited objects from their surroundings implies the uprooting of vision itself, and its projection into an artefactual space where perception is constrained and directed.

5
Tony Bennett, "The Exhibitionary Complex", *New Formations*, no. 4, (1988).

The museum, and by extension the exhibition dispositive and the Cartesian space of the gallery, is therefore a site based on a concept of Nature that the museum itself contributes to forging by offering it to perception. Modern exhibition institutions of Nature have thus been central institutions in defining our concept of non-human Nature. As Emanuele Coccia proposed, "they have been the mirror, the reflection of our way of thinking about non-human species, their millennial history, the way they are linked to each other and to space."[6] The implicit agenda of these institutions is to present everything from Nature, and nothing from humanity, as if they were simply archives of a Nature which, at a time when the Anthropocene is a palpable reality, becomes irretrievably absent, thus becoming nostalgic evocations of a world made of cosmic niches in which humanity has not yet set foot, a kind of archeology of a wilderness made more of dreams than reality.

6
Emanuele Coccia, "What is Contemporary Nature?", *KLIMA*, no. 2, (2019).

The Anthropocene is what Mikhail Bakhtin would call a *chronotope*: a tool proposing to align a set of truths produced within a defined place in order to support its chronological division and its narrative. By making explicit the productive continuity between human actions and the environment in which they are performed, the Anthropocene reveals that the age of extraction of the historical subject of Nature that defined modernity was simultaneously the age of the relegation of humanity as a geological stratum. So this *chronotope* makes a modern gesture of separation between Nature and the humanist subject transcending a process that is inseparable from the "erosion" of the soil from which it operates. The Anthropocene exposes the movement by which human history meets geological time, where the historical future of humanity, which has animated Western modernity, crosses paths with that which humanity had set its movement against, exposing the human figure and the backdrop of Nature to their mutual ontological instability: here the history of Nature and that of civilization merge. By revealing that "background" and "figure" enter into an unstable relationship, and that the modern discontinuity between these two planes of representation of existence is dissolved in socio-technological structures and environments, the Anthropocene consists of a techno-ecological discourse of reconceptualization of *anthropos* as planetary relation.

The Anthropocene therefore introduces a new precariousness in the great divisions that modernity has imprinted onto the world. By noting the fact that modern tools of knowledge and appropriation of Nature have not only contributed to recomposing an *analytical* image of Nature, but also to produce it in a *synthetic* way, this *chronotope* acts as a central tool in the critique of the anthropocentrism characteristic to modern thought, and has therefore crystallized various currents of contemporary thought proposing a broadening of what we could call "the circle of humanity" and within which it is necessary to distinguish different horizons: an "antihumanist" vein (in which the human subject, in its classical sense, is not necessarily the privileged holder of rationality), a "transhumanist" vein (in which humans are not the only rational agents), and a "posthumanist" vein (in which rationality extends beyond the biological and symbolic terms of the human).

In this context, it seems that the exhibition-form itself, heir to the modern dualisms shattered by the Anthropocene, faces its own obsolescence. Yet, fortified by its power to produce symmetries between objectivity and subjectivity, it may very well find in this the opportunity for its political relevance. For that, the exhibition-form will have to be invested in such a way that its capacity for producing forms of mediations first turns on its own foundations, so as to plunge into the fabric of the categories of thought which are lodged there, in the very texture of the borders which delimit and articulate them, in the depths of the engineering of the limits by which our very concept of Nature was constructed and collapsed, so as to restore it to its artifice or, even better, to its *artefactuality*: a Nature that is closer to human art than to Natural History.

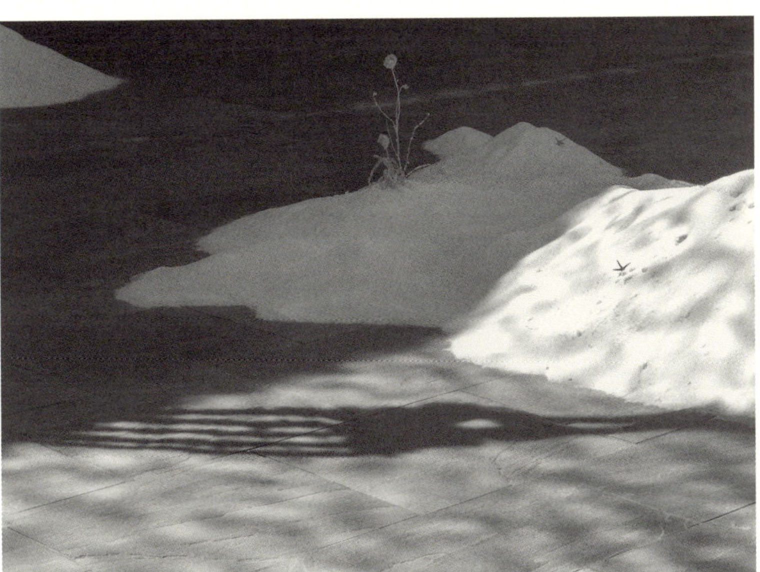

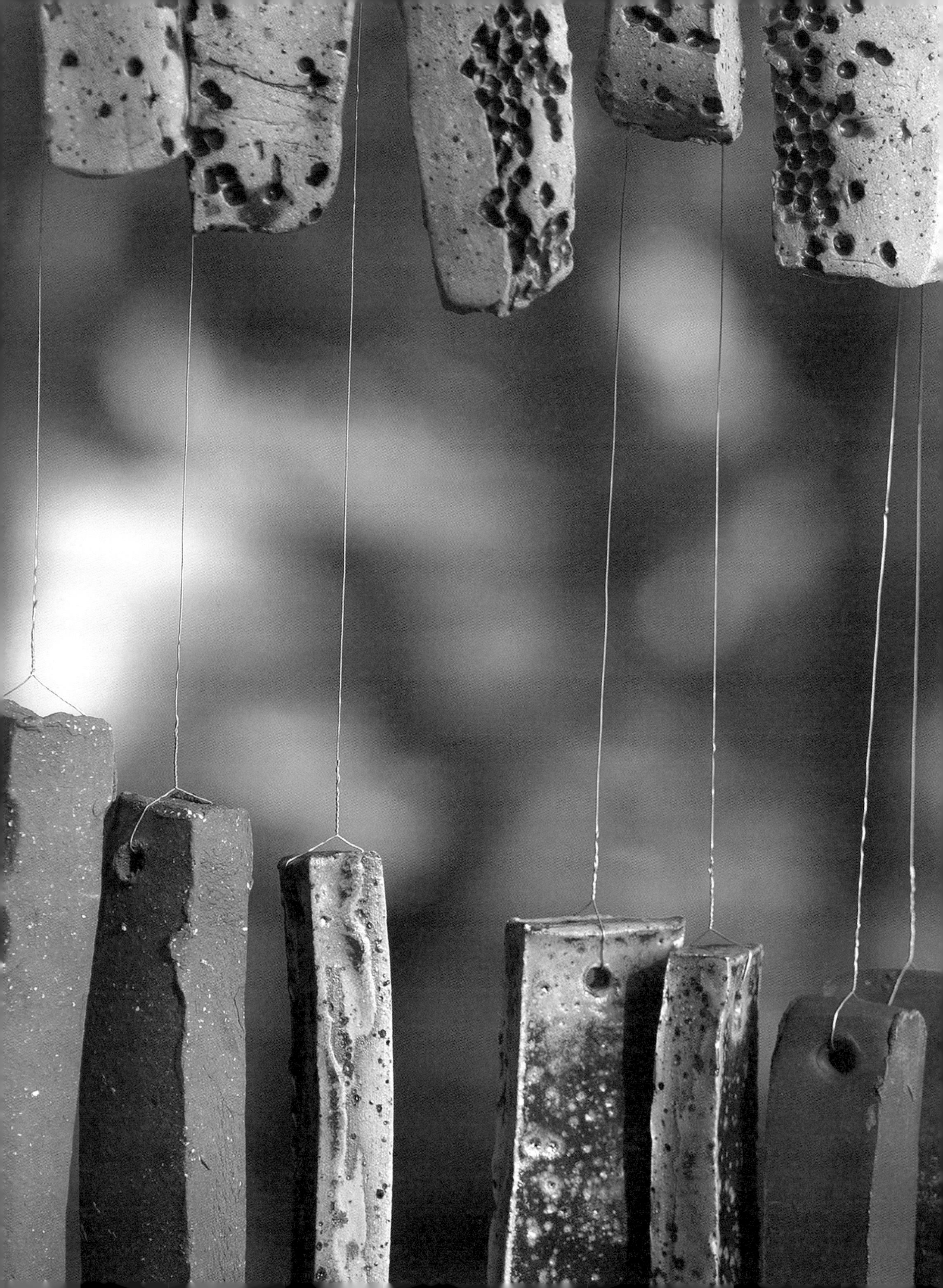

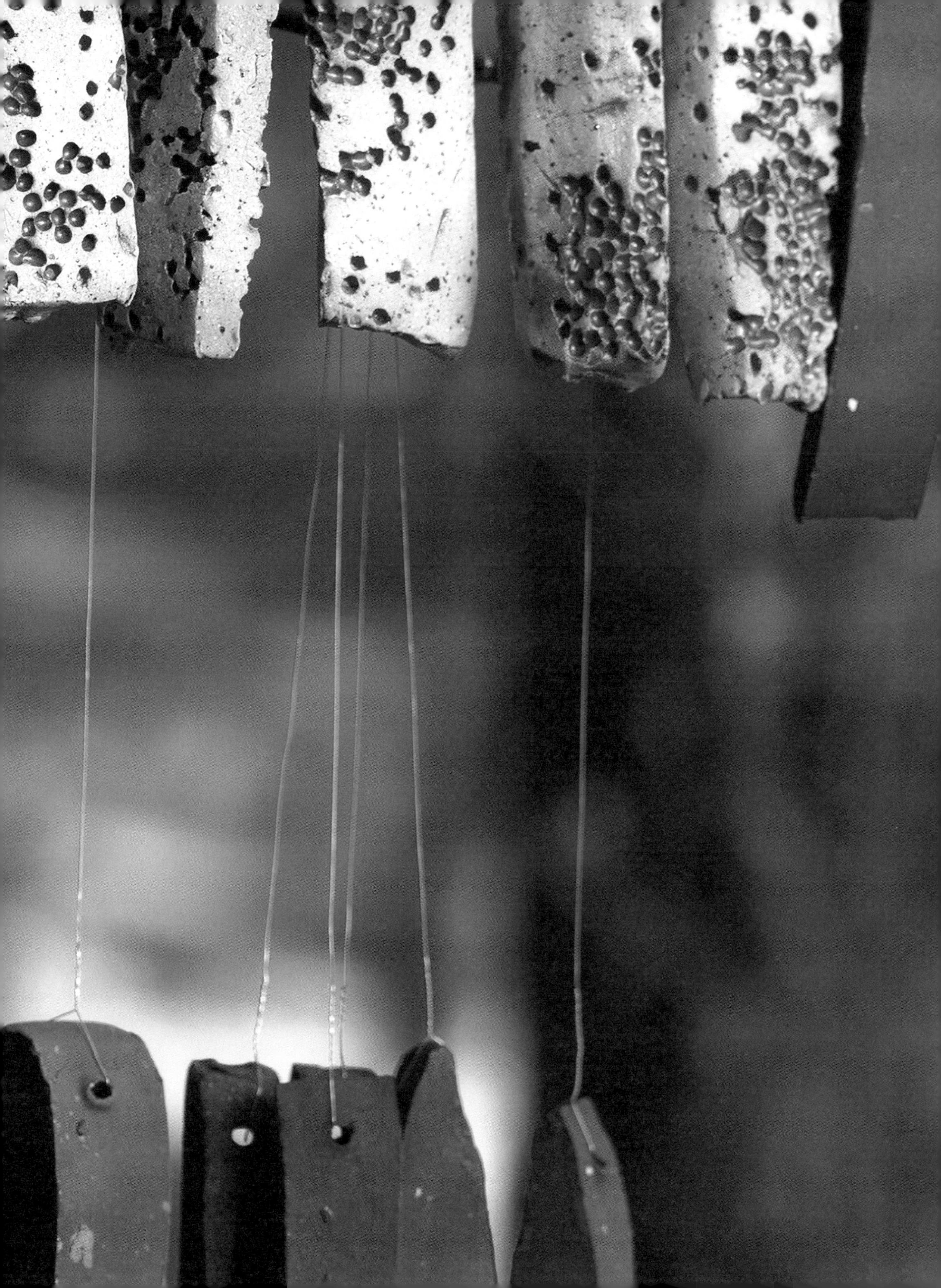

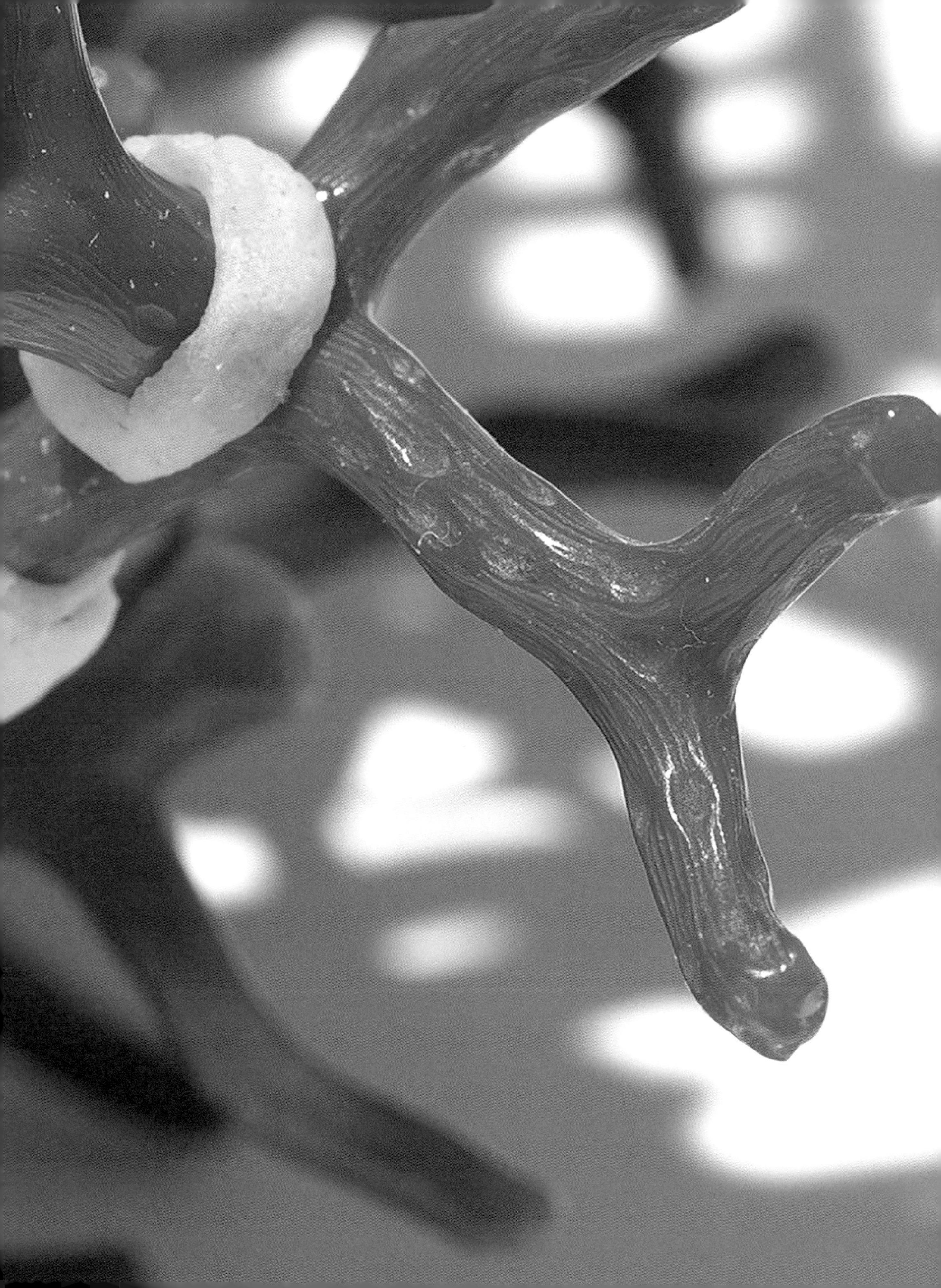

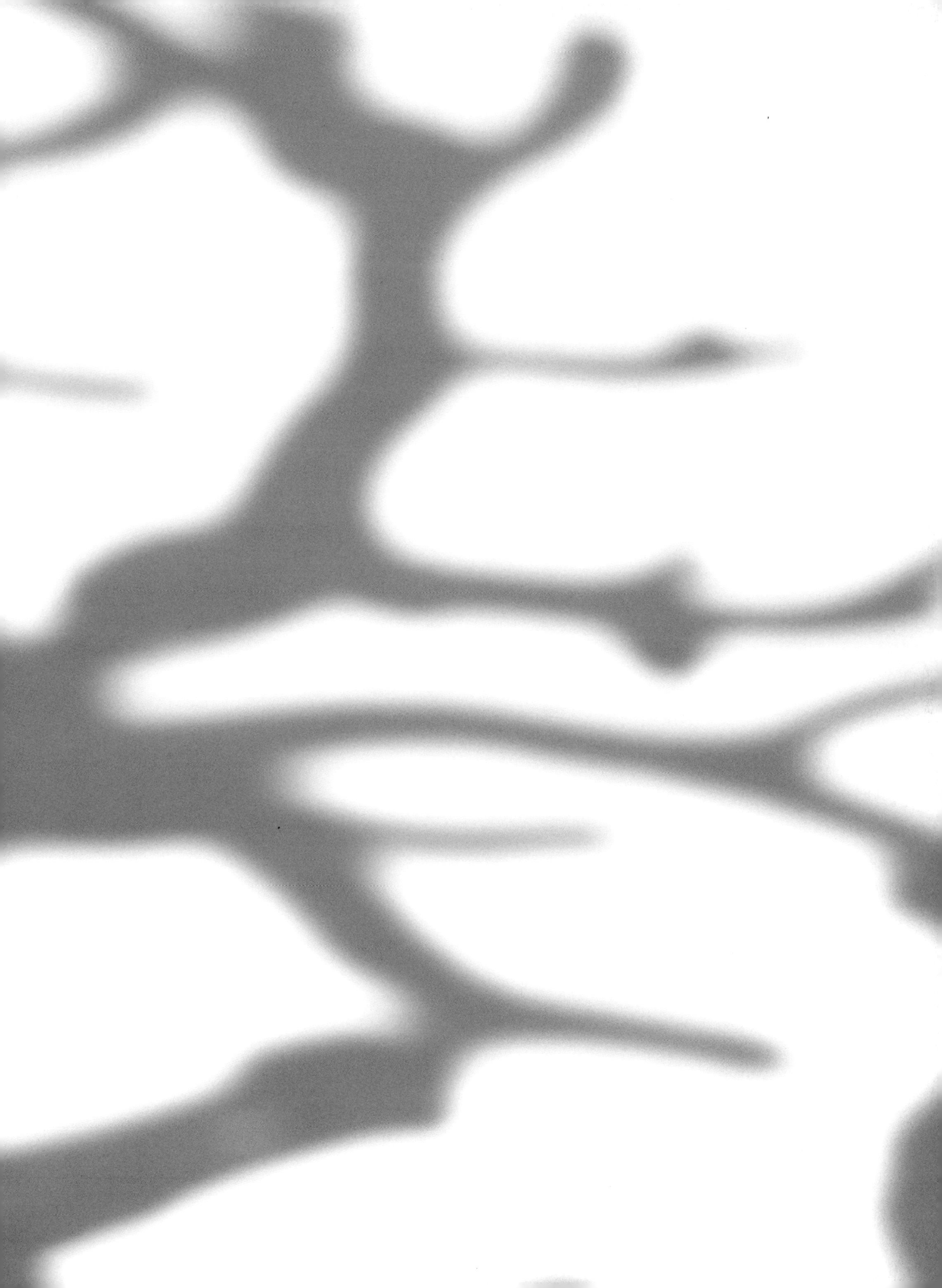

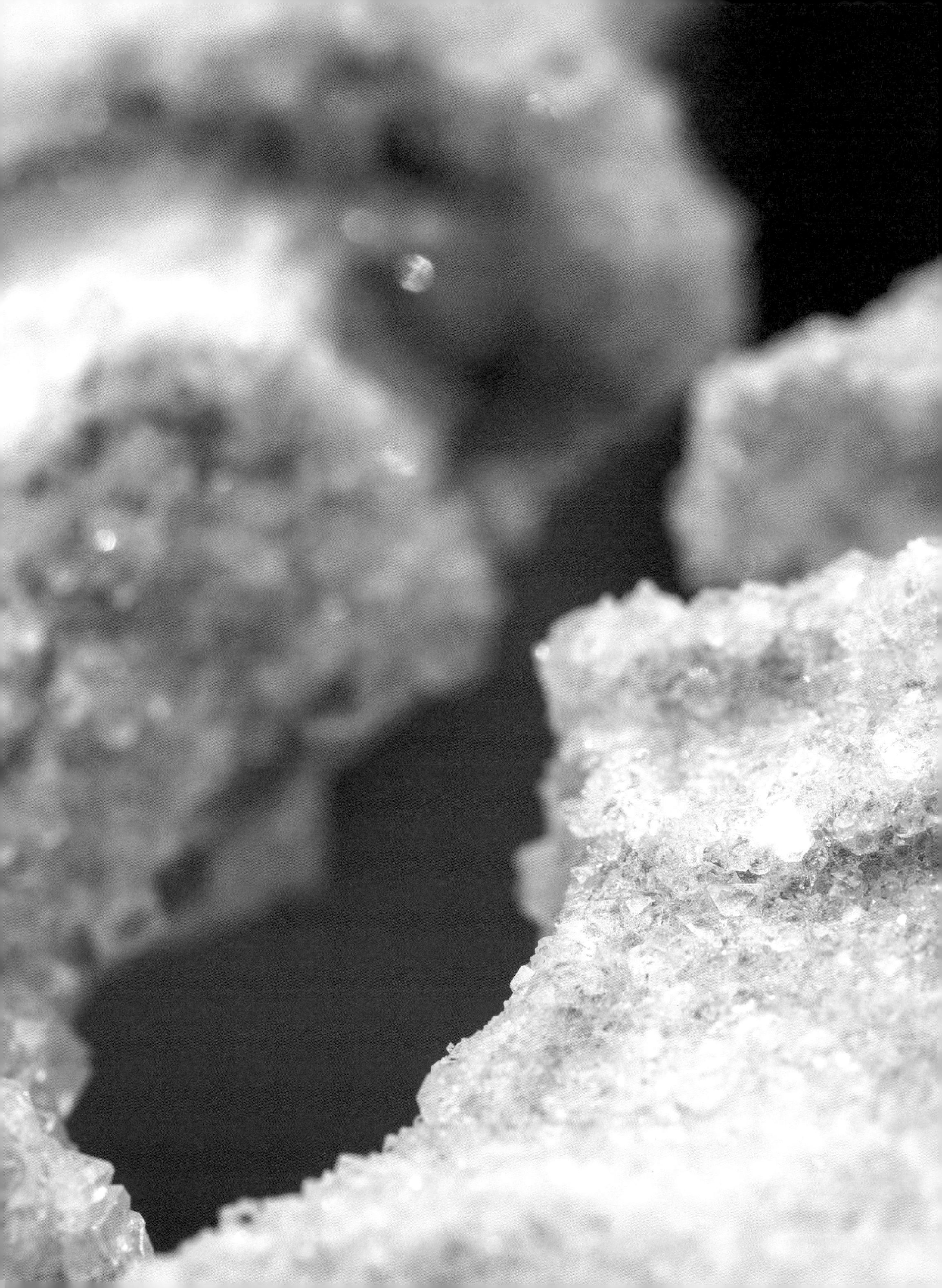

Artists

2019.04.03. PM 12:37
Tepito, Aidal Alcocer
2019
Cloth and polyethylene wrap
Two parts: 83.8 × 16.5 cm
and 19 × 9 cm and
7.5 × 3.5 in

2019.04.03. PM 12:37
Tepito, H. de Granadita
y Aidal Alcocer
2019
Plastic bag
75 × 7.6 cm
30 × 3 in

2019.04.01. PM 3:21
La Merced, San Miguel
and Jon Hormiguero
2019
Plastic, cloth,
paper, adhesive tape
63.5 × 17 cm
25 × 7 in

Yuji Agematsu

Yuji Agematsu (b. 1956, Kanagawa, Japan; based in New York) is known for creating sculptures out of the seemingly insubstantial urban debris of everyday life. A long-time resident of New York City, Agematsu walks its streets gathering up everything from tiny wrappers to chewed gum to modest flotsam and jetsam of unidentifiable origin. Each *trouvaille* is notated in a small notebook, in which the artist records the time, place and date of the find in a combination of English and Japanese. If the debris is small enough, it is inserted and amalgamated into what he calls "zips" — the small cellophane wrapper from a pack of cigarettes which he fills from material only on the day it is found and then eventually collects into months. Or if what he finds is too large to fit in a plastic sleeve, it is liable to enter other sculptural configurations which might be placed on a plinth or pinned to white foam-core board or directly to the wall like so many entomological specimens.

His contribution to *The Imaginary Sea* comprises three discrete works which consist of plastic bags and scraps of packaging melded together to the point where their forms evoke underwater sea creatures, possibly even jellyfish. It is hard to say if these are somehow the organic byproduct of an ironic, man-made nature of refuse, or if they are willful approximations of a form of sea life which may no longer exist. C.S.

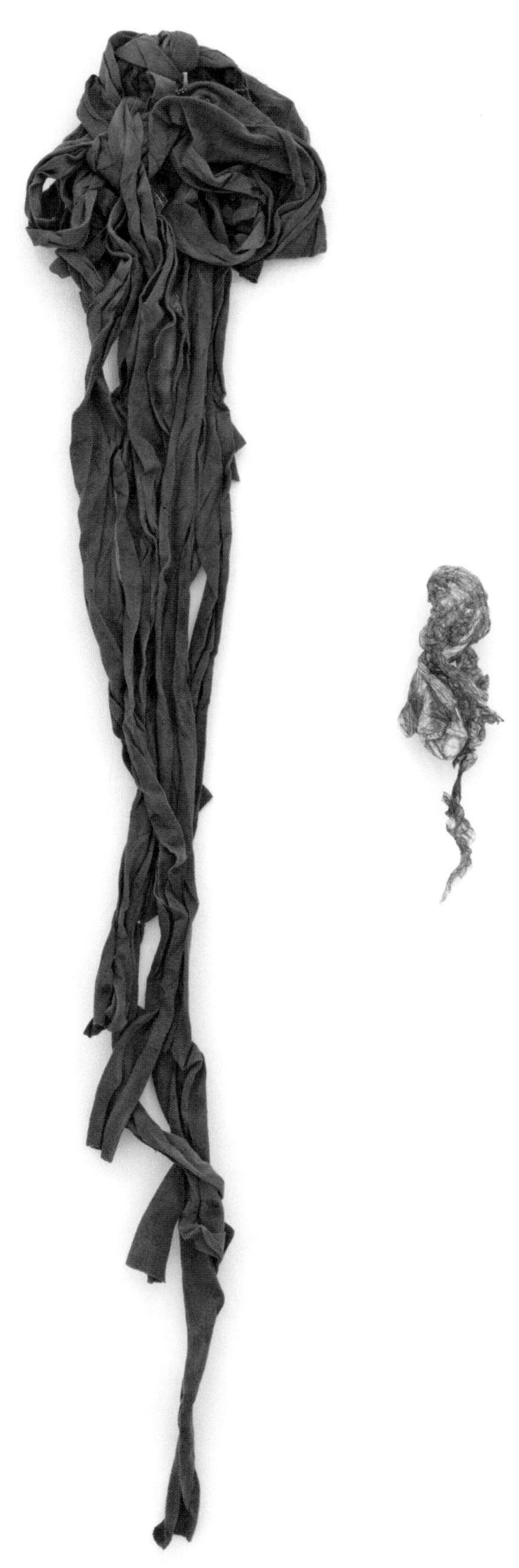

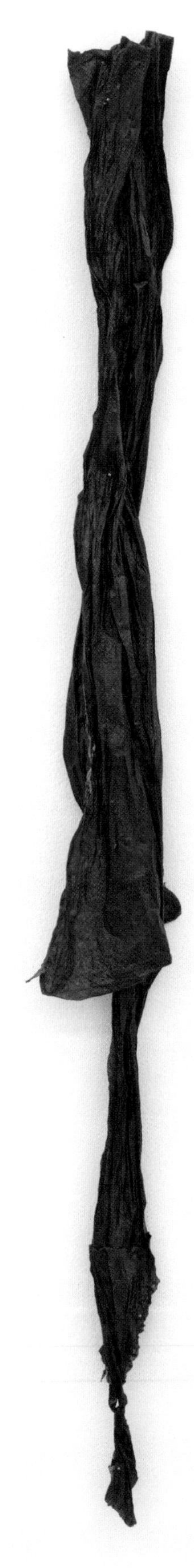

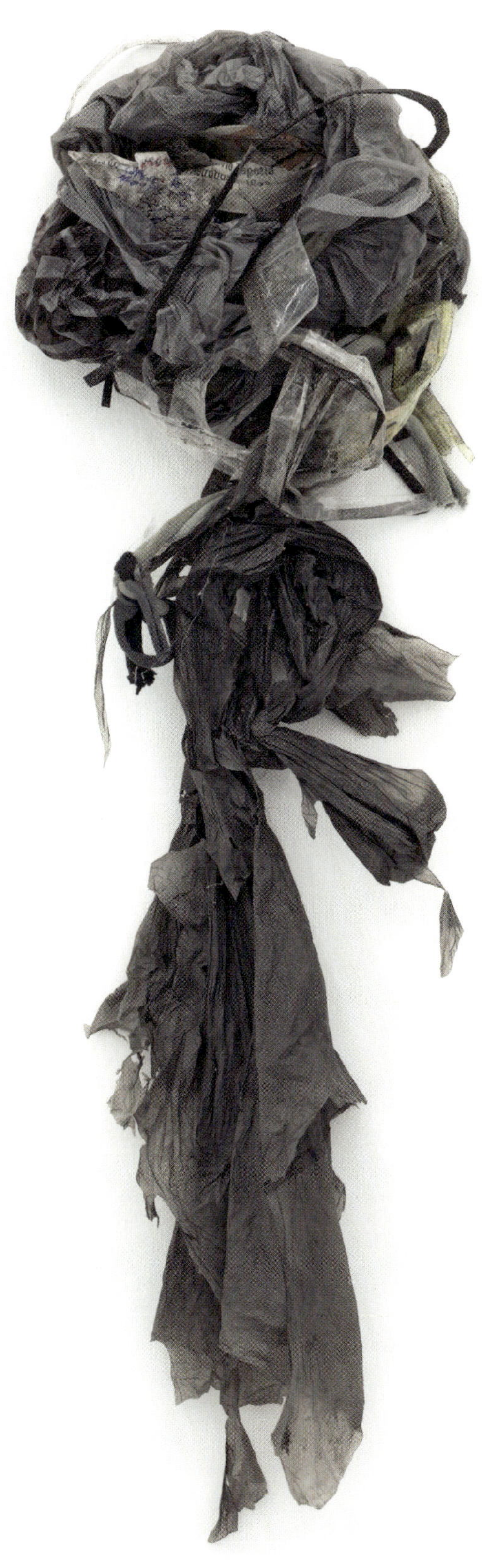

Aquarium demi plein
1976-1982
Oil on canvas
146 × 89 cm
57 × 35 in

Gilles Aillaud

"Is the glass half empty or half full?" Ostensibly there is no right answer, only ones that betray pessimism or optimism. In *Aquarium demi plein* (1976-1982) the half-full tank is not a mere subjective point of view, but a fixed circumstance, one that emanates a sense of unease and alienation: the very half-fullness of the tank undermines the optimism of seeing it as such. This subtle lyricism is characteristic of the politics of Gilles Aillaud (1928-2005) — writer, painter, set designer, political organizer, and one of the main proponents of *Nouvelle Figuration*, the return to figurative and representational art following decades of abstraction. Aillaud studied philosophy before turning to art, and his Marxist influences seamlessly inform his aesthetics. Themes of animals in captivity dominated his work throughout the politically turbulent 1960s and 1970s, articulating a critique of late capitalist culture. Zoos are the perfect analogy for these lines of thought, where display is also a kind of prison. Among the moody, blue-gray palette of the fish there are hopeful swipes of yellow, perhaps suggesting a whisper of optimism after all. C.C.M.

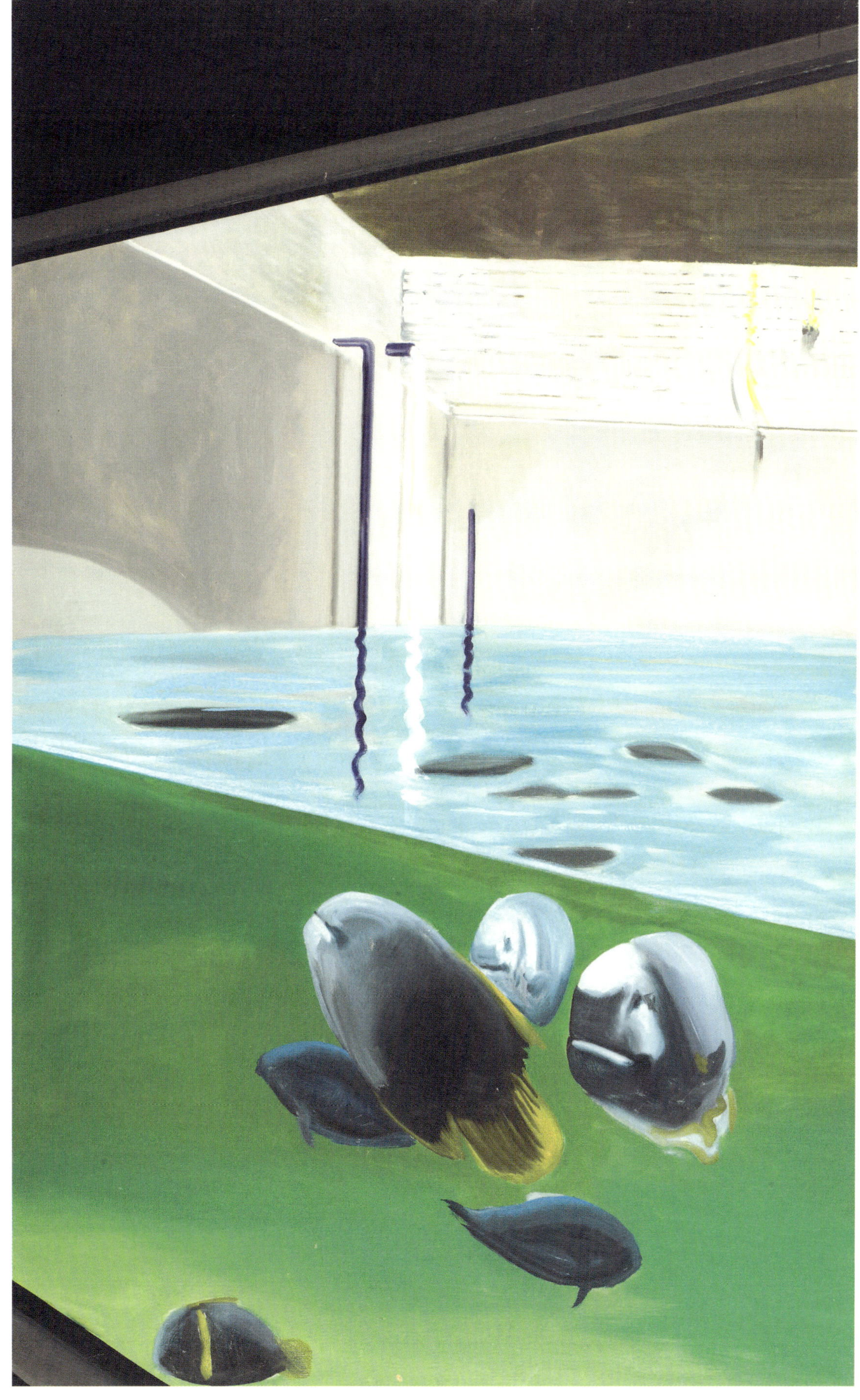

Crab n°2
2018
Aluminium
90 × 90 × 14 cm
35 × 35 × 5.5 in

The Dance
2018
Aluminium
183 × 90 × 110 cm
72 × 35 × 43 in

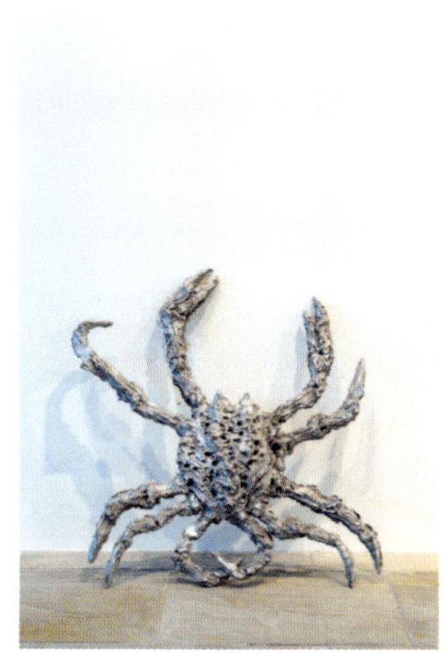

Jean-Marie Appriou

Jean-Marie Appriou (b. 1986, Brest, France) sculpts wild bestiary and dynamic characters that equally absorb the mythic ethos of his homeland in north-western France, and references ranging from space travel and Greek mythology to pop music and Romantic poetry. Appriou works with traditional materials like bronze, ceramic, glass, and marble, often beginning with his own hands in the studio, then working with foundries to scale and produce his objects, humbly preserving thumbprints, rough edges, and other all-too-human slips for all to see.

Crab n°2 (2018) is a life-size aluminium sculpture of a spider crab. The weathered finish results from the idiosyncrasies of the foam and clay Appriou uses for the model that are retained in the final casting; giving the creature the look of a living fossil, having crawled from the ocean floor to take its final place among the recorded annals of history in the preservation of the museum. *The Dance* (2018) is another welter of reference harnessed by Appriou's marriage of handcraft and fabrication. The title and composition call to mind Matisse's joyous and iconic 1909 painting *La Danse*, yet the allusion is unclear, as Appriou's flayed sharks seem bound by malignant appendages, or else by the desire to surround some invisible prey. C.C.M.

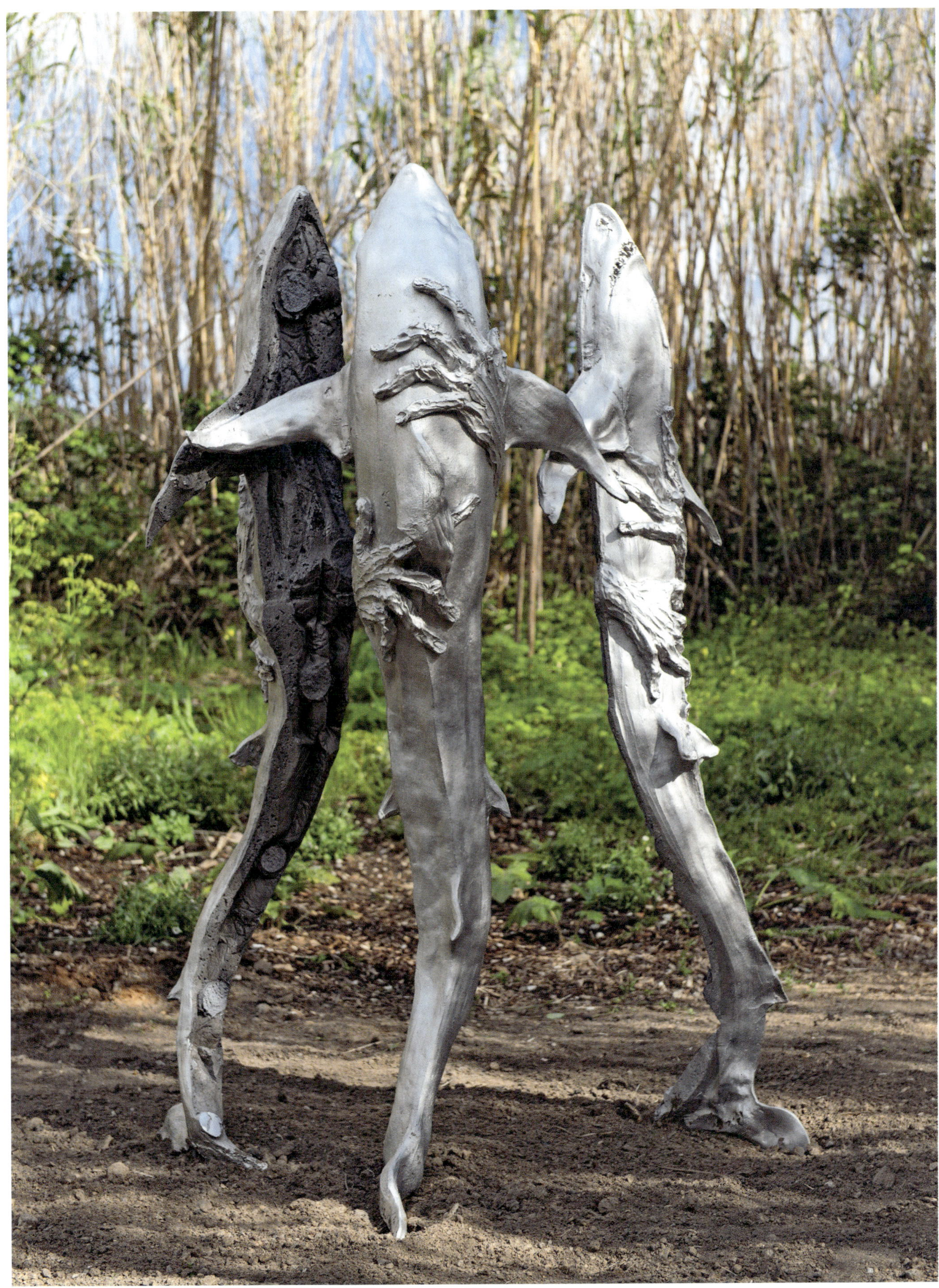

Encéphalogramme de la mer
2006
Mixed technique on canvas
200 × 300 cm
79 × 118 in

Miquel Barceló

"... a sea-change / Into something rich and strange" wrote Shakespeare. Descending through each oceanic atmosphere, the water strips away more light and we lose the sun entirely in the darker depths. To hold off the black weight at the bottom of the sea, the creatures there make their bodies glow. No human can really know what the sea looks like to a clownfish, an octopus, or a mantis shrimp whose eyes contain twelve rods for color compared to our measly three and can see five shades beyond ultraviolet. "As a child I was often afraid to open my eyes under water; I still can't tell you why except the chlorine of public pools and the menacing mysteries of what lies beneath the froth of heaving oceans." Miquel Barceló grew up next to the sea in Spain and dived deep into that floating world for squid and octopus and fish. "For me, diving is very close to painting", said the artist in 2013. The sea and its forces haunt the long career of Barceló, the wet paint of his handmade pigments softens into curving visions of wetter water and the creatures that live in it. And while Barceló has often surfed the churning surface, here he reveals what visions the sea can bring if only you're brave enough to open your eyes. A.B.

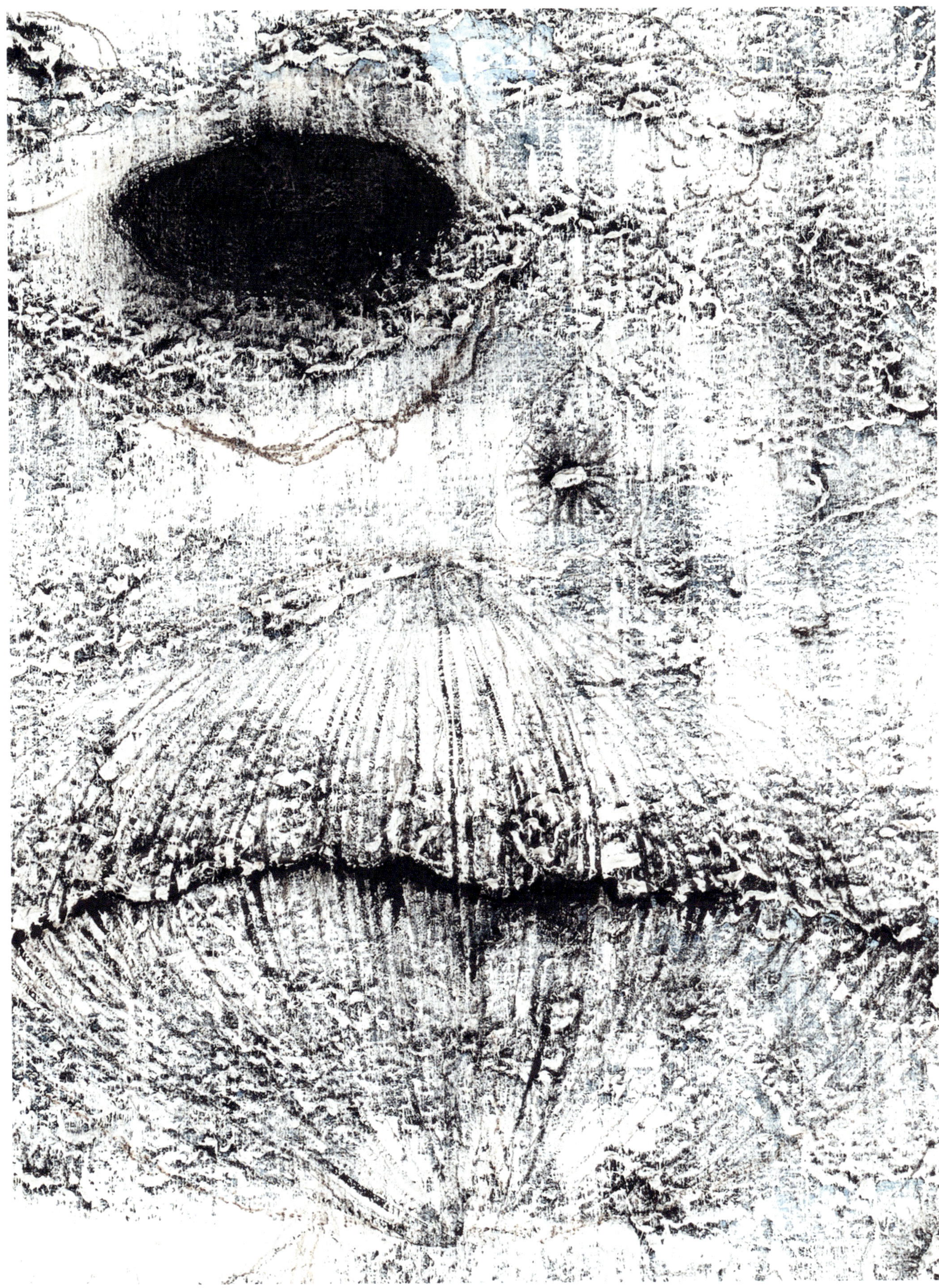

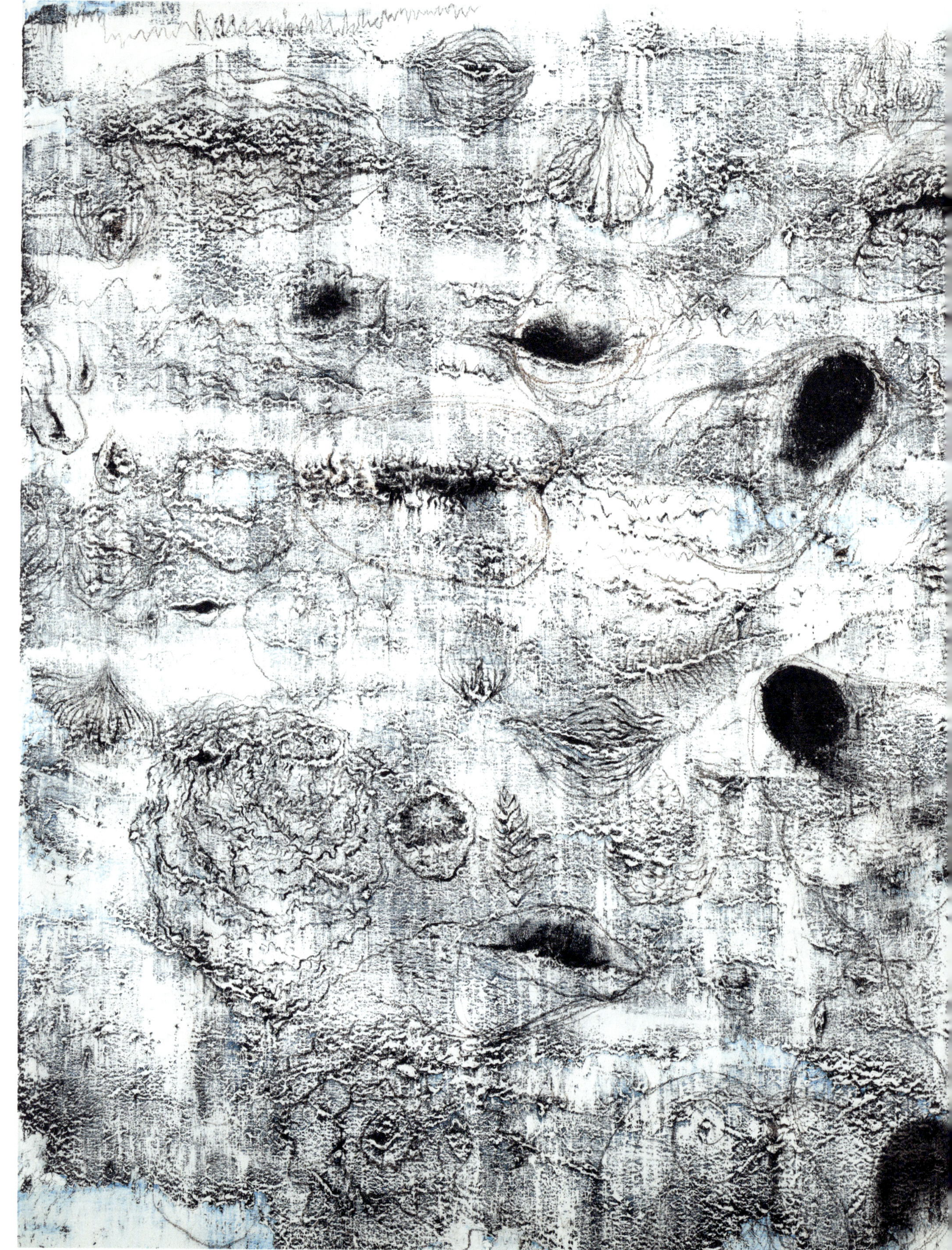

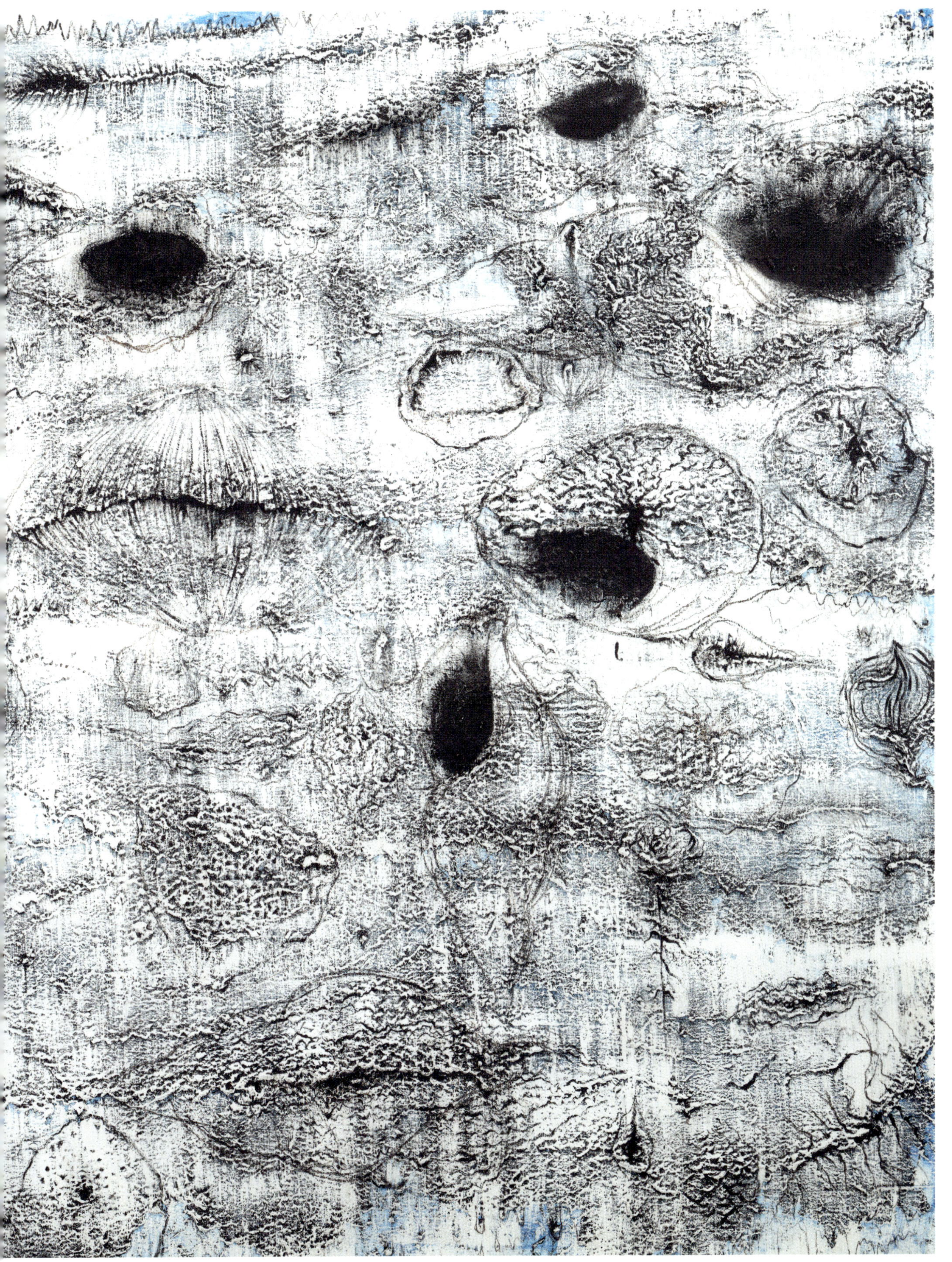

The Fall and Rise
2021
Resin, salt, mixed technique
1300 × 300 × 400 cm approx.
511 × 118 × 157 in approx.

Bianca Bondi

The work of Bianca Bondi (b. 1986, Johannesburg, South Africa) is part science, part sorcery, and grounded in a keen awareness of and concern for the effects of globalized capitalism on our planet and its inhabitants, both human and non-human. Death, rebirth, and the living nature of all matter are recurring themes of her practice. Live plants, bones, decaying metals, spices, and salt all find their way into her sculptures and installations.

When a large whale dies, its body often sinks directly to the bottom of the ocean, especially if the animal is undernourished. Within days, active scavengers converge on the new food source and voraciously remove the flesh from the bones at a rate of approximately 40 to 60 kilograms of flesh per day. A whale can be stripped to the bone in a matter of months, becoming an ecosystem unto itself. For *The Imaginary Sea*, Bondi has created *The Fall and Rise* (2021) a site-specific, 12-meter-long whale skeleton, frankensteined together from several different species, some currently living, others from the dinosaur-era. This chimeric creature hangs upside down from the museum's ceiling, a supine attitude of death but also a suspended position of resurrection — an embodied collapse of the line between life and death, an elegant affront to the linearity of time. C.C.M.

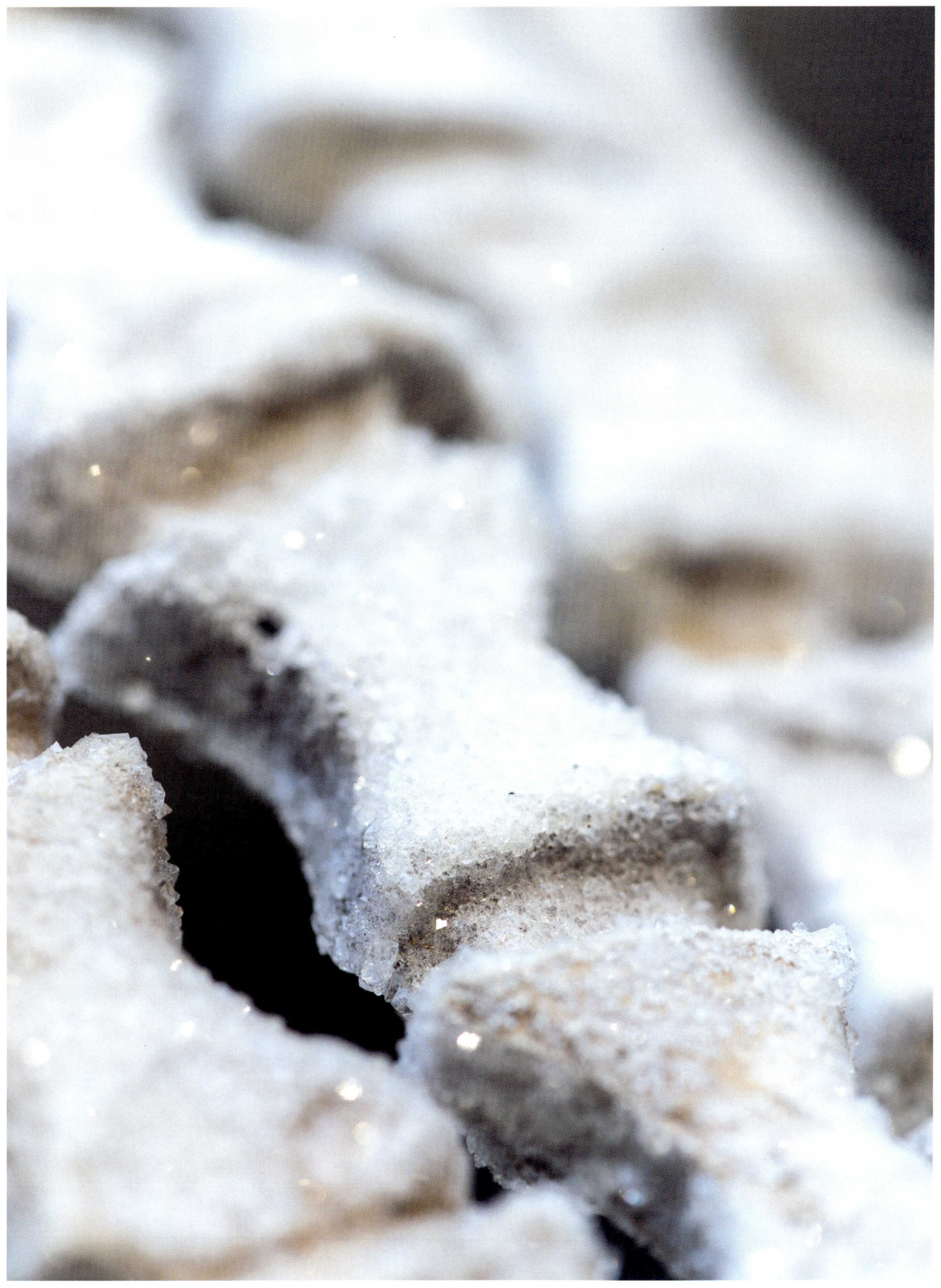

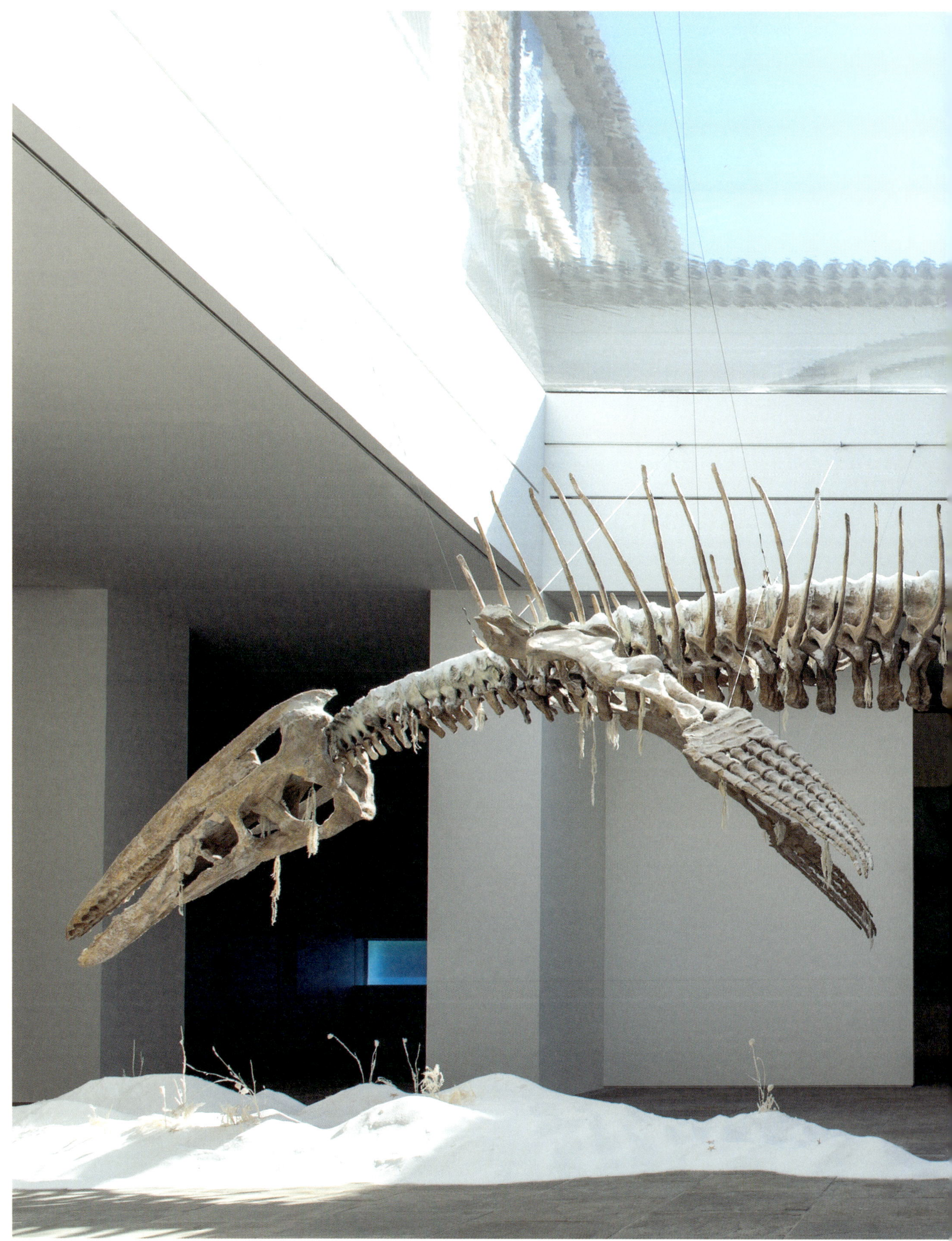

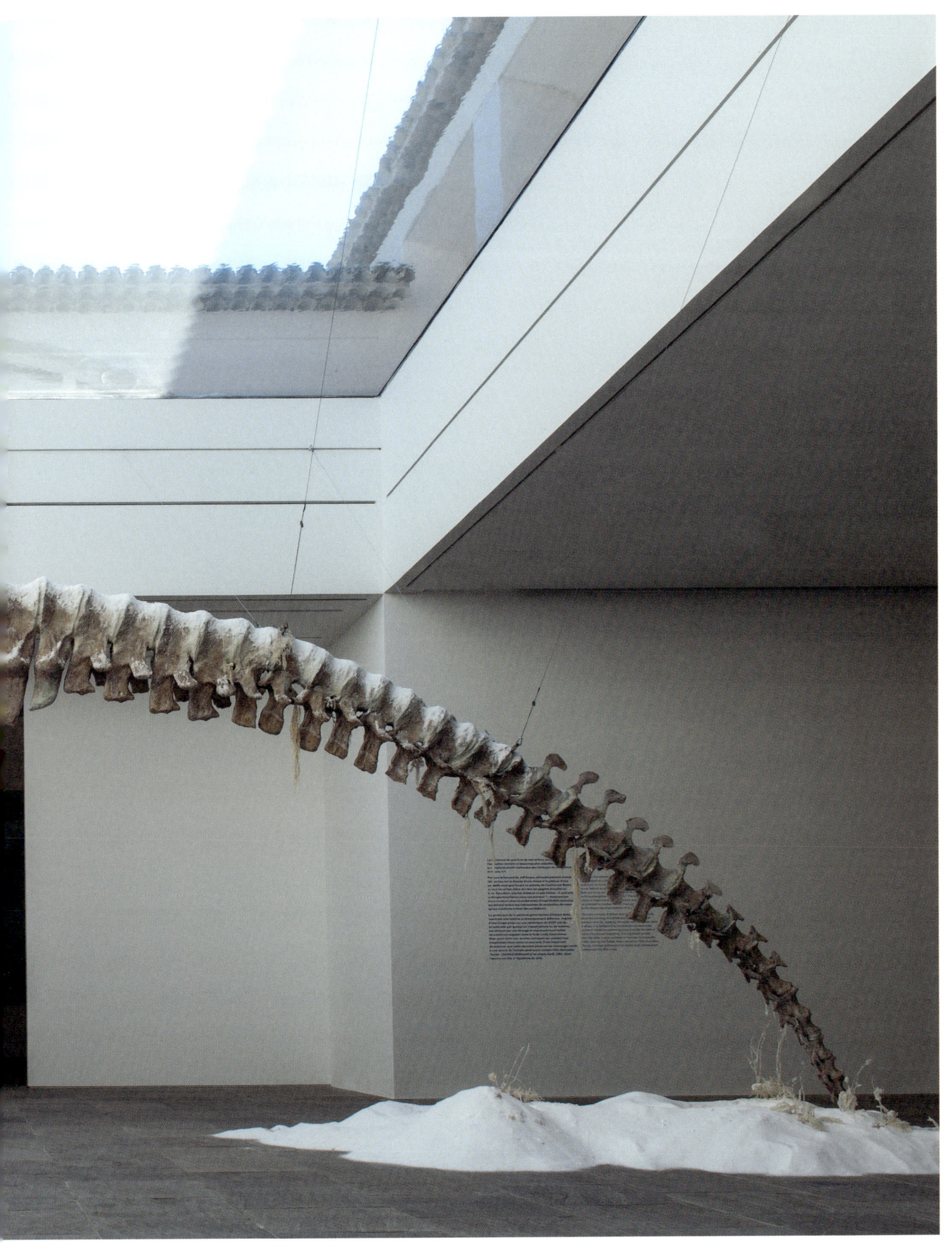

KILLER WHALE WITH LONG EYELASHES 2 (SCHOOL DESK VERSION)
2018
Wood, metal,
glass bottle, fabric
150 × 120 × 120 cm
59 × 47 × 47 in

Cosima von Bonin

With a certain plush cuteness, this stuffed orca with long eyelashes sits at attention at a school desk, a bottle of water ready to quench the thirst of this sea creature far from the sea. "Who's Exploiting Who in the Deep Sea?" German artist Cosima von Bonin asked as the title of a recent traveling exhibition, a graduation of a kind for her long interest in sea creature sculptures. These kinds of goofy anthropomorphic set-ups wouldn't look out of place in any suburban shopping mall or adorning with a blissfully unaware if macabre glee the entrance to any family-friendly seafood eatery. They're a little funny and a little sad. Something fierce and wild and dipping toward extinction made into a cutesy prop. The factories hum, churning out plush marine creatures, which then end up as part of the great plastic garbage patch, another hunk of junk poisoning actual marine life. Just one reading of many and for sure the artist doesn't give anything away. Her sculptures are perhaps more like the absurd magic of French poet Nerval walking his pet lobster through the streets of Paris rather than anything too literal. But Cosima von Bonin did give a hint about meaning in an interview with the Brooklyn Rail in April 2018: "Really it's like Mike Kelley said: It's somehow a making sense of senseless things — you take this and you take that and in the end it's poetry and it's a piece of art. I don't want to refuse to explain my art, but you can stand in front of a piece of art and say fuck you, or it can break your heart." A.B.

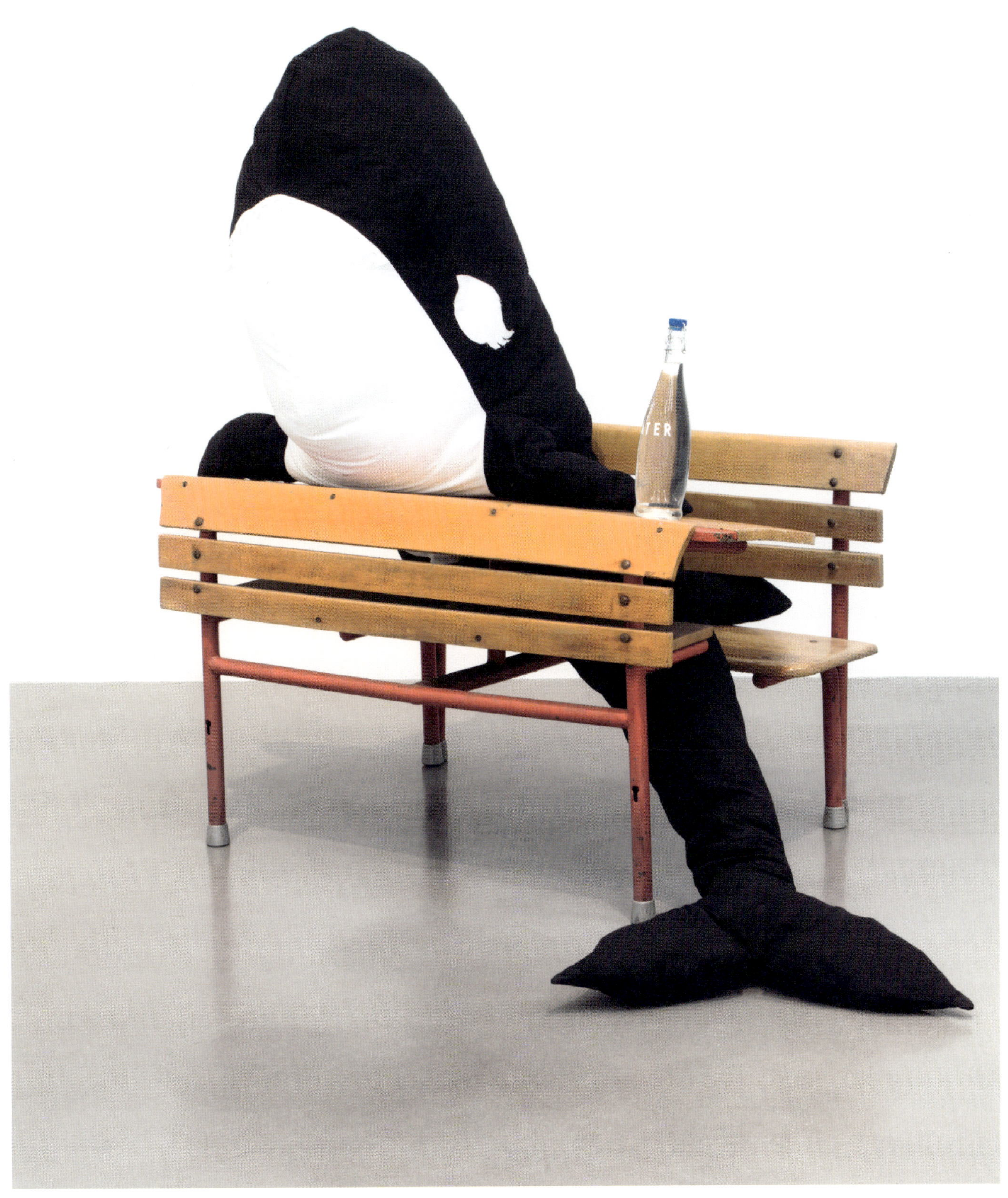

Crab and Plankton
2014
Oil on linen
35 × 30 cm
14 × 12 in

Untitled
2018
Oil on linen
259 × 218.5 cm
102 × 86 in

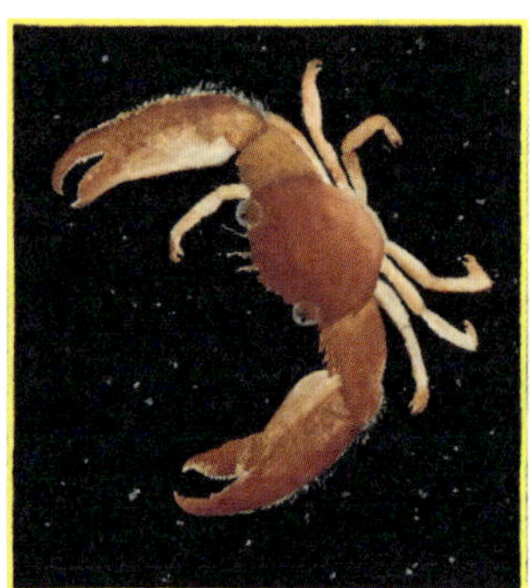

Leidy Churchman

Even given the slow consideration that is canvas-time, the paintings of Leidy Churchman are occasional, almost diaristic, wrought with an immediacy and simplicity that honors the flickering inspiration of its subjects. Churchman is a painter who isn't stuck with the tyranny of narrative or the freight of monumentality. The unreal magic of Henri Rousseau feels easy to invoke, but Churchman's oeuvre often feels much more personal than the Frenchman's exotic fantasies. Churchman can draw from his experiences those images that beguile, compel, haunt without having them have to carry more than the tenderness and consideration he brings them; that weight of feeling we find with empathy, or as the painter says: "It is such a soft sadness, it is beauty". Felix Gonzales-Torres famous billboard of the indented pillows after his lover died of AIDS finds a new form here. But instead of rumpled sheets, the bed is a dark body of water, alive with glistening fish, a gentle dream of life amidst love's mourning. The order of a hedged garden, the flat simplicity of a gravestone, the bathtub of a luxury tower, his sister's research, a menu from a vegetarian restaurant, a single crab wandering amidst a confetti of plankton, a lifetime organized not by stories but by pictures, each lovingly wrought with a gentility and verve that reveals a distinct hand of the thoughtful human behind it. A.B.

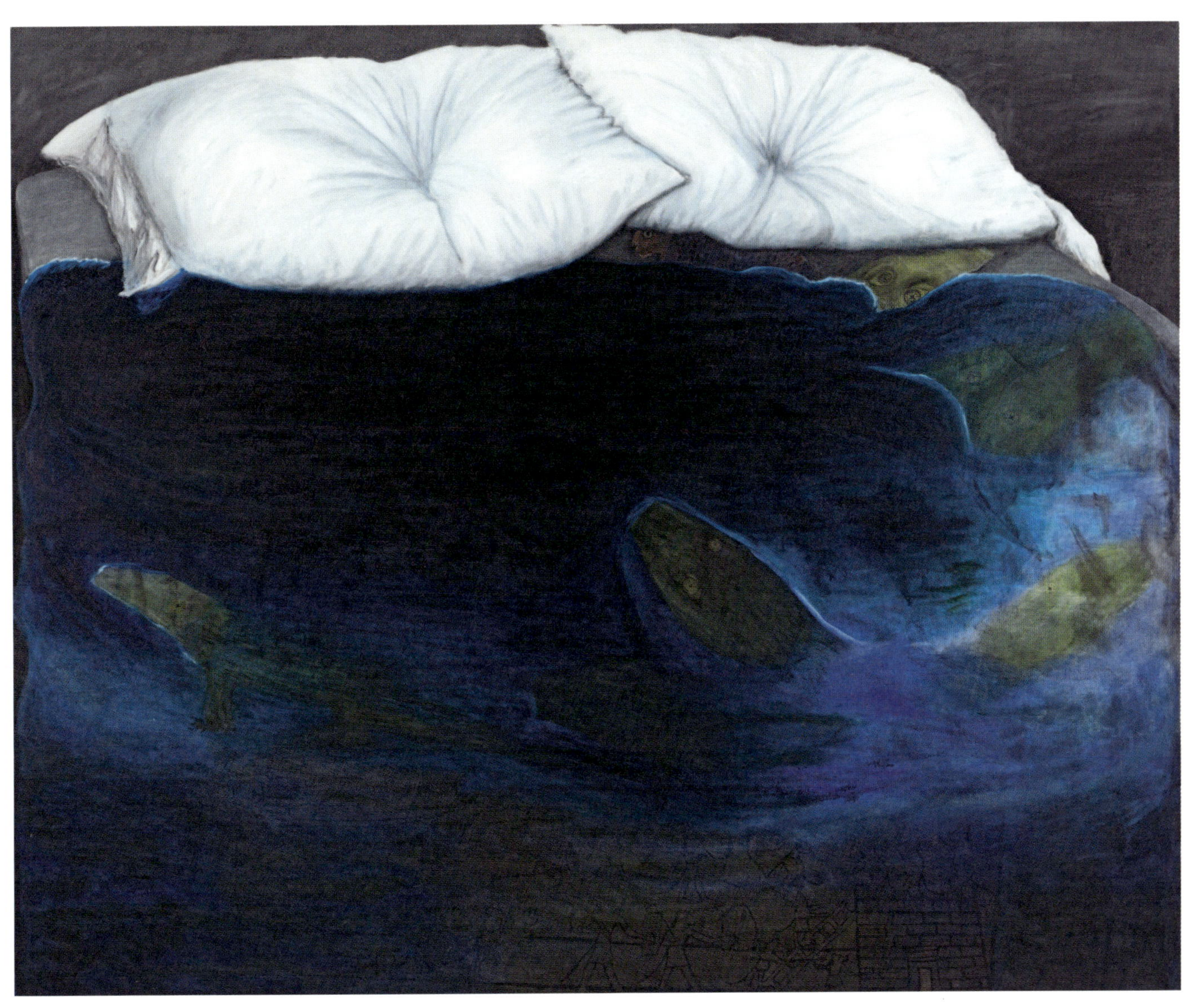

Pierres (Double hélice)
2021
Reconstituted stone
18.2 × 15.5 × 10 cm
7 × 6 × 4 in

Julien Discrit

Julien Discrit (b. 1978, Epernay, France) works mainly in video, photography, installation, and performance. Such ephemeral mediums provide the tension between the forms the works take and his enduring interest in grounded, earth-bound subjects like geography and anthropology. As attempts to describe and in some sense contain the physical world, such areas of study are an important source of reflection for Discrit. Inspired by anthropologist Philippe Descola's inquiries into the relationship between nature and culture, Discrit excavates the assumptions that are the foundation of western scholarship— is the world of culture fundamentally separate from nature, or is the split itself an invention? — studying each like a gem through a jeweler's loupe.

For *The Imaginary Sea*, Discrit presents a work from his ongoing *Pierres* series, depicting human hands holding rocks. The result is an object hovering somewhere between sculpture and fossil. The grip, a desperate gesture signifying an attempt at ownership, seems to be on the verge of melding with the very thing it grips. This deceptively simple sculptural gesture also brings forth the idea of "ruin" as a replicable modern aesthetic, as opposed to a merely inaccessible material past. C.C.M.

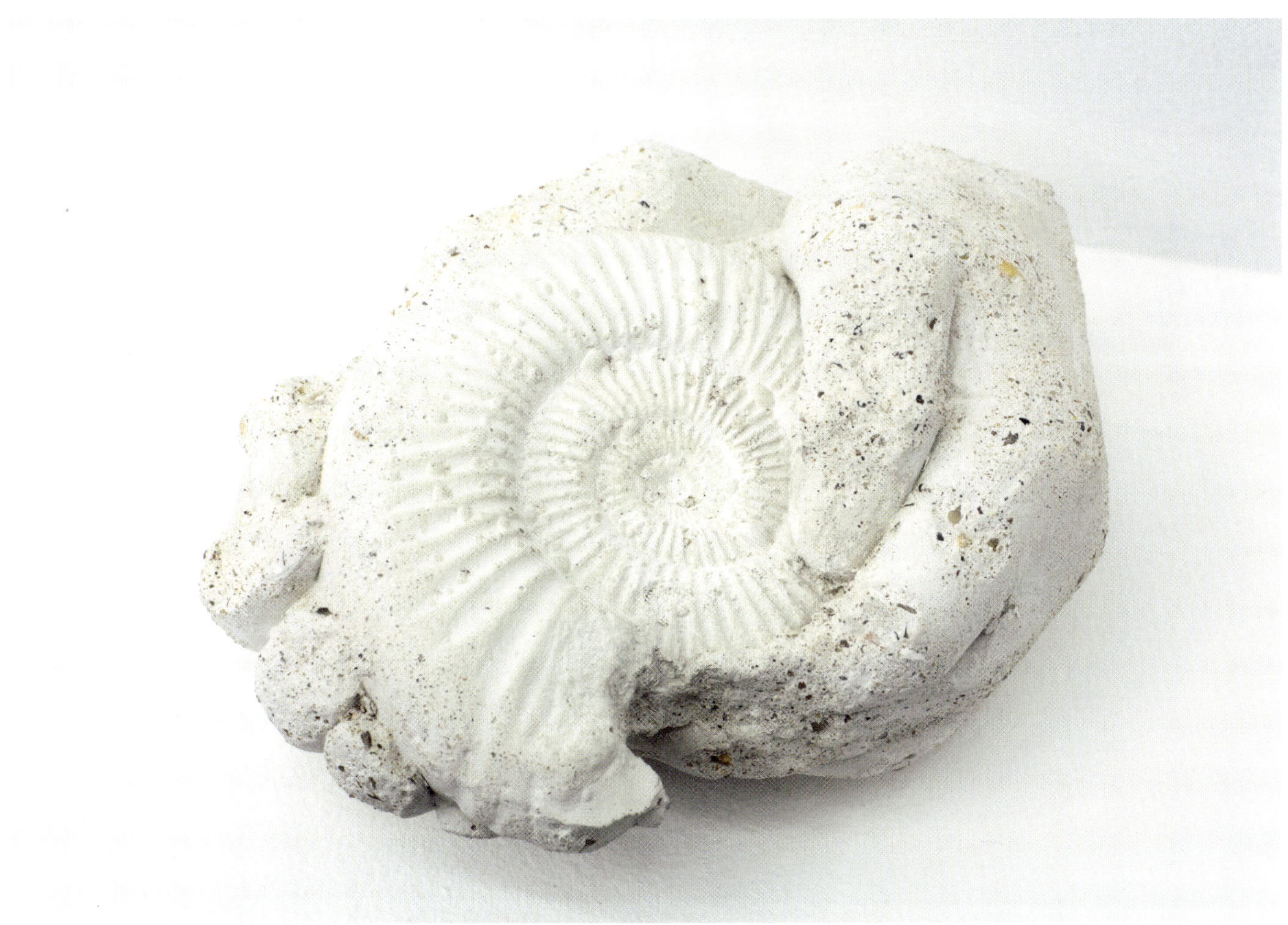

Corail Costa Brava
1994-2020
Mediterranean red coral,
glue and bread crumbs
25 cm approx.
10 in approx.

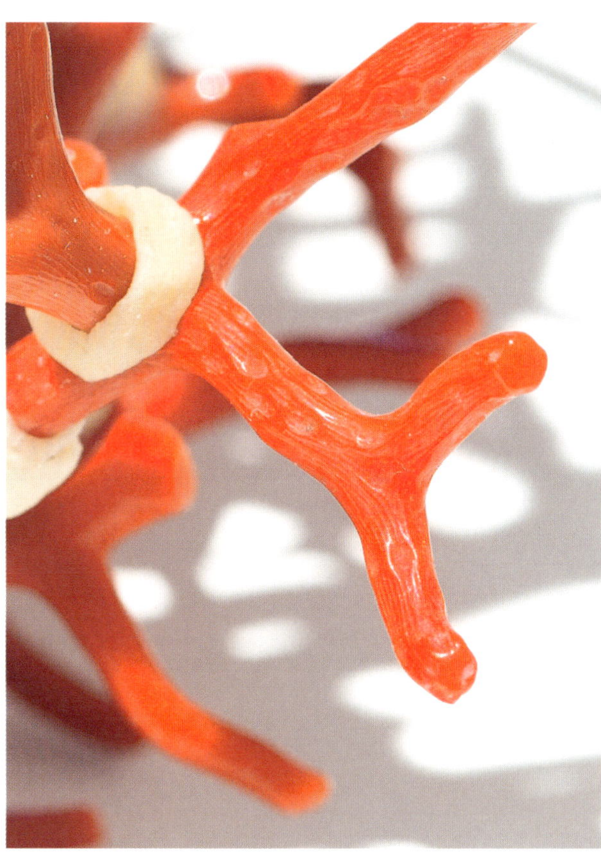

Hubert Duprat

Hubert Duprat (b. 1957, Nérac, France) works in the fissures between nature and culture. The resulting creatures and objects often challenge categories of preservation like the museum, the library, the archive, etc. He is perhaps best known for collaborating with a coterie of caddisfly larvae on *Trichoptères* (1980-1997), replacing the aquatic insects' natural supply of twigs and debris with bits of gold and precious stones, prompting them to cocoon themselves in tiny jeweled sheaths which, when abandoned, remained held together by their silk.

Corail Costa Brava (1994-2020) is another collaboration. The tumbleweed-like arrangement of red coral is held together with bits of pressed and dried white bread, marrying high artisanship with the kind of ad hoc craft children partake in when rolling their sandwich bread into those satisfying little pellets. A man-made gem of organic materials, *Corail Costa Brava* has the quasi-scientific quality of a *Wunderkammer object*, bristling against its patent beauty and enigmatically decorative merit. C.C.M.

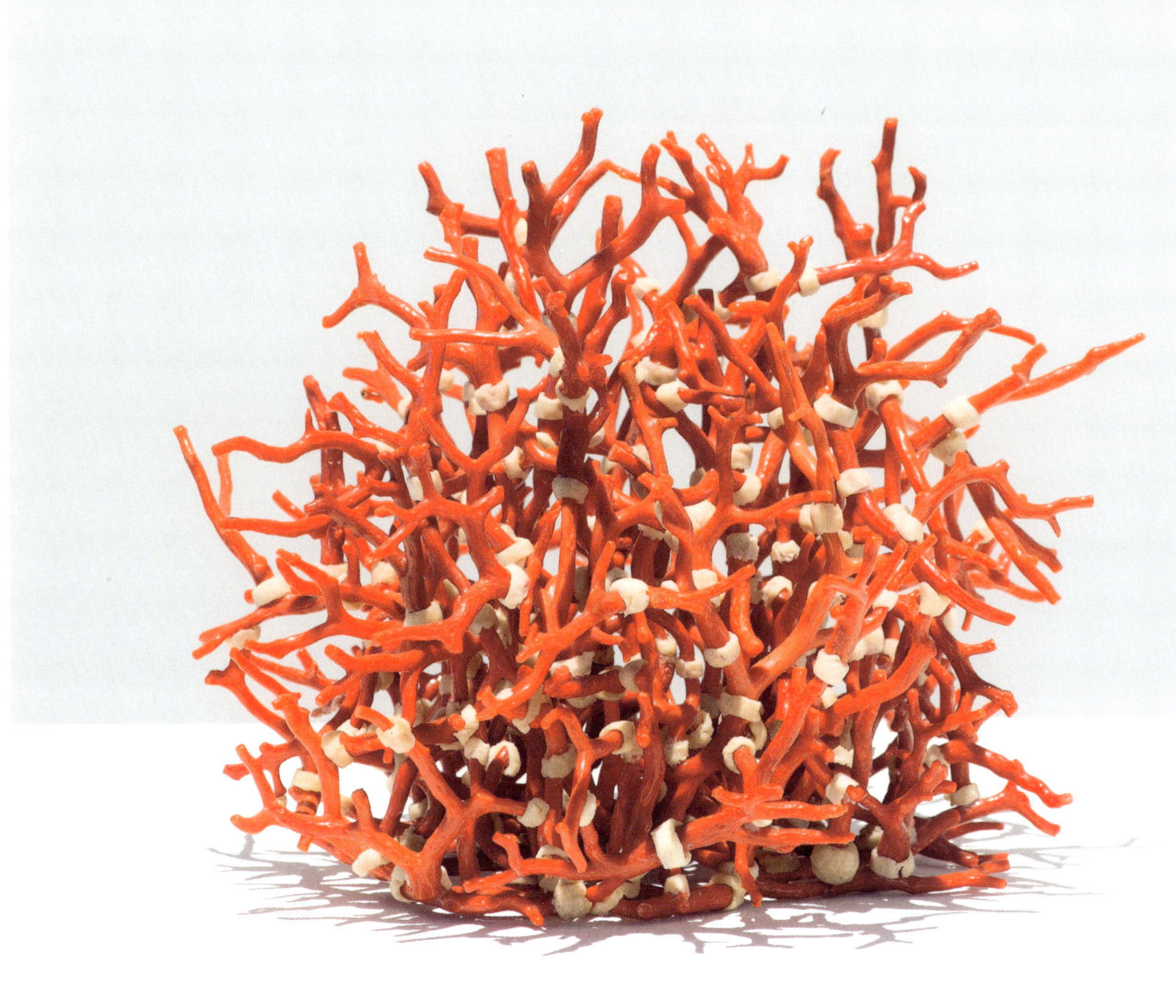

La couleur de l'eau, Porquerolles, -10m
2020
Color photography on adhesive film
Window n°1:
220.5 × 84.5 cm
87 × 33 in
Window n°2:
223.5 × 84.5 cm
88 × 33 in
Window n°3:
221.5 × 84.5 cm
87 × 33 in

Nicolas Floc'h

The work of Nicolas Floc'h (b. 1970, Rennes, France) embodies the romance of marine exploration and the urgency of climate change activism; often all with a click of his underwater camera. The spirits of James Turrell and Jacques Cousteau infuse his multidisciplinary practice — his work marries the cool conceptualism of geometric abstraction and color studies with the warmth of awareness and conservationist efforts. His decade-long explorations of coral reefs recently took him to Japan, where Floc'h dove alongside scientists from the Tara Ocean Foundation to document artificial reefs — giant concrete and metal structures submerged by governments in the hope of rebuilding degraded marine habitats and buoy local fishing industry.

For *The Imaginary Sea*, Floc'h has created a site-specific intervention inside the Villa Carmignac, placing a blue plastic film over the long, horizontal window, turning the gallery window into an aquarium wall. The blue-green *glaz* of the window film is sourced from the color of the water around Porquerolles, forming a conceptual snapshot of the island while capturing its visitors in its watercolor haze. C.C.M.

Born, Never Asked
2017
Watercolor on paper
119 × 89 cm
47 × 35 in

Camille Henrot

With an early background in film animation, advertising, and music videos, Camille Henrot's (b. 1978, Paris, France) voracious and what she sometimes refers to as an "irrational" approach to systems of knowledge, produces delightful and compelling work across film, painting, sculpture, and installation. Her references range from self-help literature and social media, to ethnographic film and *ikebana* — the Japanese art of flower arranging. At the heart of her work is an interest in the physical and psychological spaces where the political and the emotional intersect, and the ways in which language and images help us deal (or not deal) with a rapidly changing globalized society.

Born, Never Asked, 2017 is from Henrot's ongoing *Tropics of Love* (2010-) series, lissome watercolor sketches that use playful and dreamlike imagery to explore unsettling and all-too-human power dynamics. In this drawing, a seemingly full-grown but tiny human appears to be slipping out of a vagina, only to be perilously poised over the gaping maw of a perhaps not-so-friendly fish. The phrase "I never asked to be born!" is often used as a cliché of adolescent angst, but the metaphor Henrot sets up here is both touchingly absurd and unsettlingly universal. C.C.M.

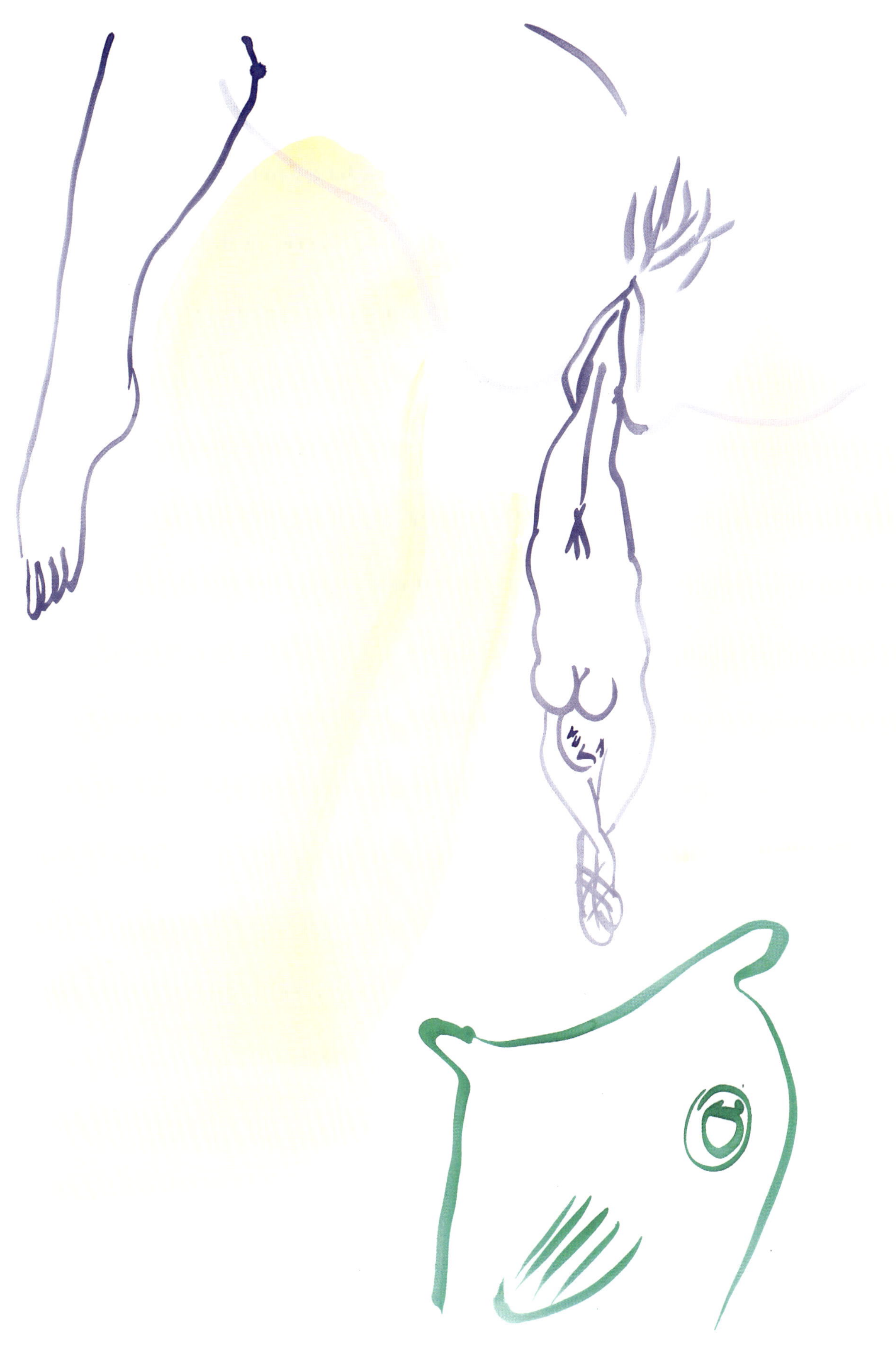

Spotted Bay Bass
2019
Oil on canvas
76 × 91 cm
30 × 36 in

Adam Higgins

In Adam Higgins's (b. 1989, Huntington Beach, California) painting practice, pictures pass through his vision and out his hands like steady melodies. Forrest Bess and Agnes Martin up went to the joke shop, and came out with paintings of fish, flopped onto the ground and were snapped with the artist's cell phone before being thrown back to their watery domiciles. The tightly-cropped pictures in this series, falling somewhere between portrait and zoological study, hem the creatures in on all sides — the edges of the canvas become their own kind of tank for the briefly captive fish. The eponymous subject of *Spotted Bay Bass* (2019) is bent upward like a curl of shaved wood, its eyes bulging in what might be anthropomorphized as existential panic. Higgins plays catch-and-release with this subject, even as he "captures" their image for posterity, wryly reiterating issues of representation and interiority that have occupied painters since the dimmest flickers of modernity. C.C.M.

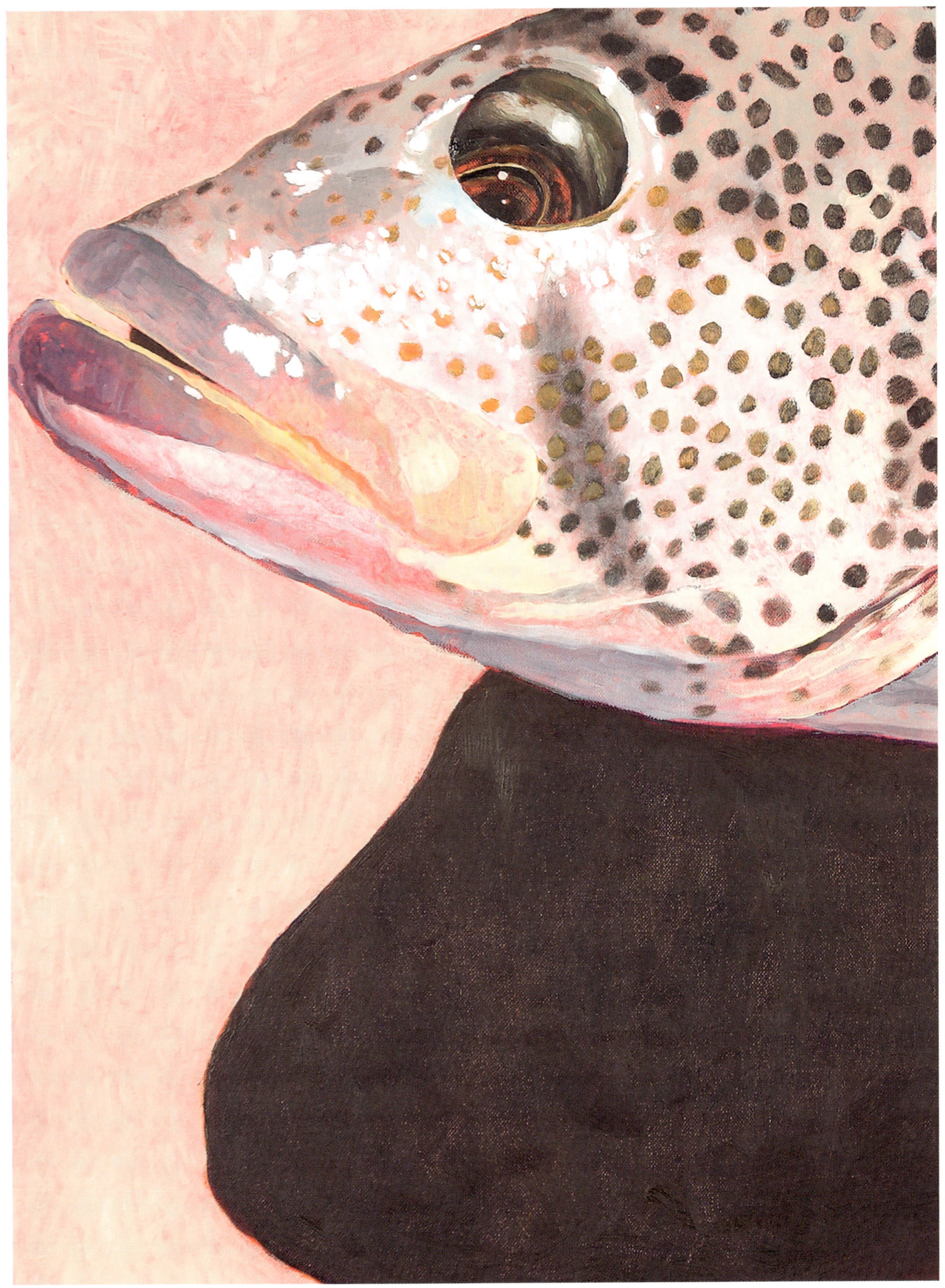

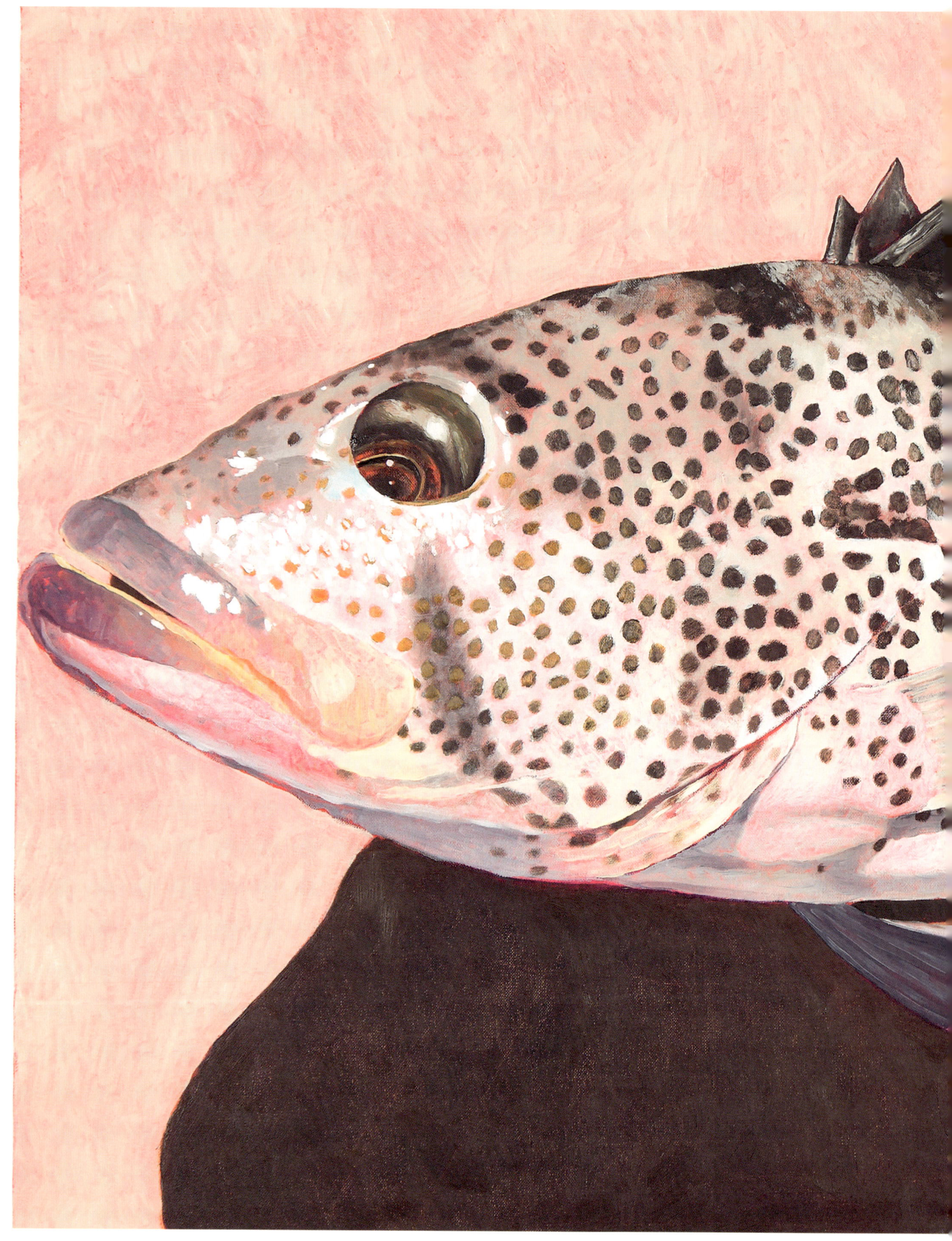

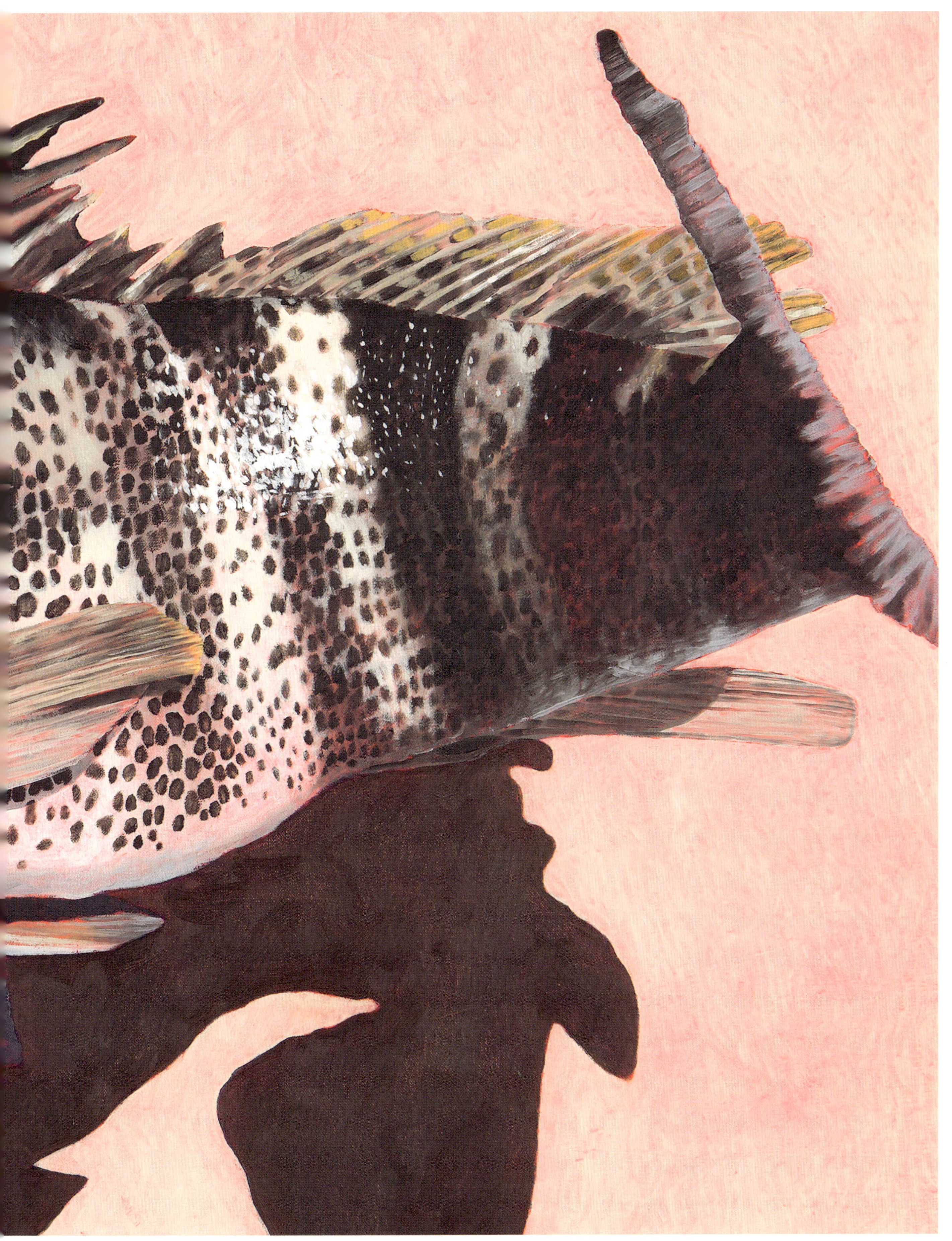

Whale II
2014
Oil on canvas
244 × 122 cm
96 × 48 in

Allison Katz

A lithe fish jumped from a story book, its toothy mouth in a hard grimace. Pounding its head against the ground in an uncomfortable turn, its pear-shaped body bent just so against a dusty world makes this odd creature look almost certainly like a fish out of water. Did someone drop a peach in the water or is it a peachy sun, its celestial luminescence a bruised fruit that our fish can almost slap with its tail? The streaks alongside that wonky bod could either be heat waves or action lines from a bounding wriggle. Truly, Allison Katz found her subject for *Whale II* in an 18th century book, where some imaginative soul attempted to depict the massive sea mammal without ever having actually seen one. Katz paints her curious creatures, scowling faces, occasional abstractions, and giant pears lounging at home in her sly stories with a peculiar palette, the colors always a bit dusky, half-lit and supple. Paintings by Katz always look a little laid-back, effortlessly odd, and invariably tender. Intimacy always takes work, but when you sidle up next to her pictures, they seem to put you at ease, make you smile, cool your anxiety, and heat up your heart. Relax, it's just a painting, they whistle to you, and you do relax, and her visions soften you up, become important without self-importance, moving with deceptive ease and native grace. A.B.

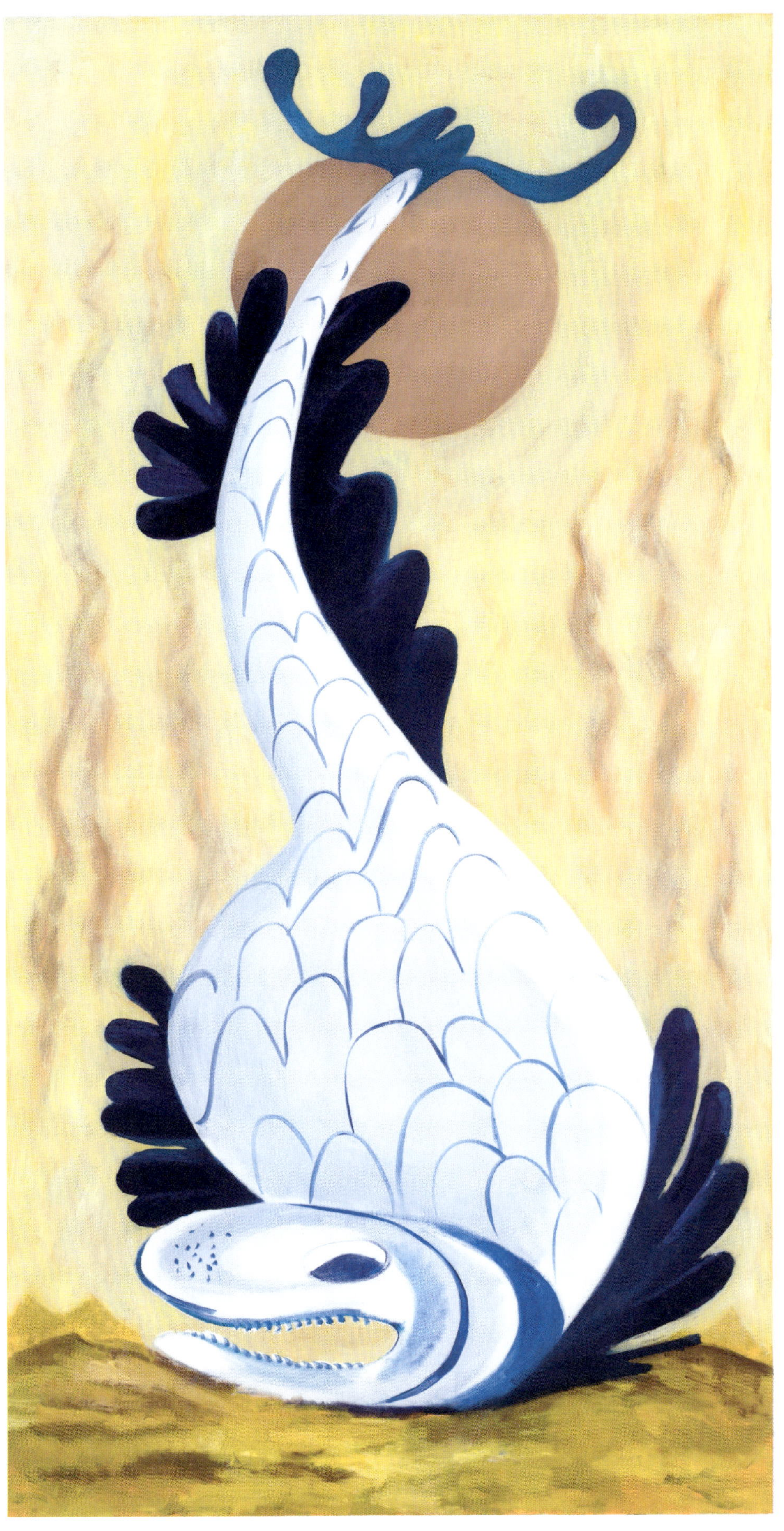

Aquarium, 1921, 99
1921
Watercolor and pencil on paper on cardboard
24.2 × 31.7 cm
9 × 12 in

Aquarium, was made the same year that the Swiss-German modernist Paul Klee (1879, Münchenbuchsee, Switzerland - 1940, Locarno, Switzerland) started teaching at the Bauhaus school in Weimer, Germany. A great lover of nature, Klee, who would later summer on the island of Porquerolles, had an aquarium in his home, which he encouraged his students to study, and which inspired several of his watercolors at the same period.

One particular point of interest with this work, and others like it, was to try to capture and portray the rhythms of nature through the movement of fish in their environment. This is depicted via the repetition of forms, as if their contours were ramifying through water. This same repetition all but submerges the forms in abstraction, demonstrating the extent to which the very origins of modernist abstraction are not distinct from but thoroughly embedded in nature. As such, early European modernists like Klee remind us that contrary to Cartesian systems of thought, nature and culture are directly linked, at least from an artist's perspective. C.S.

Paul Klee

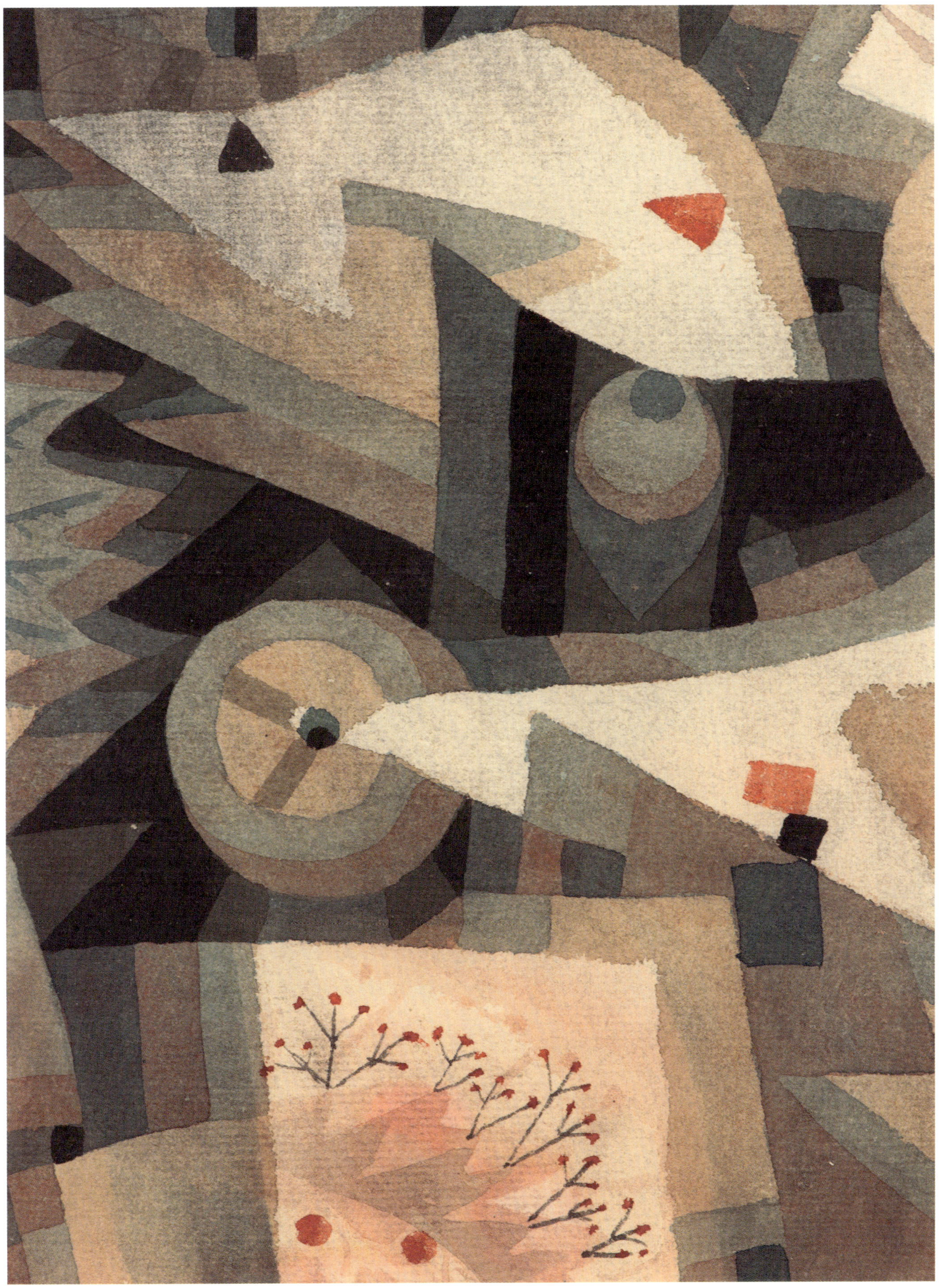

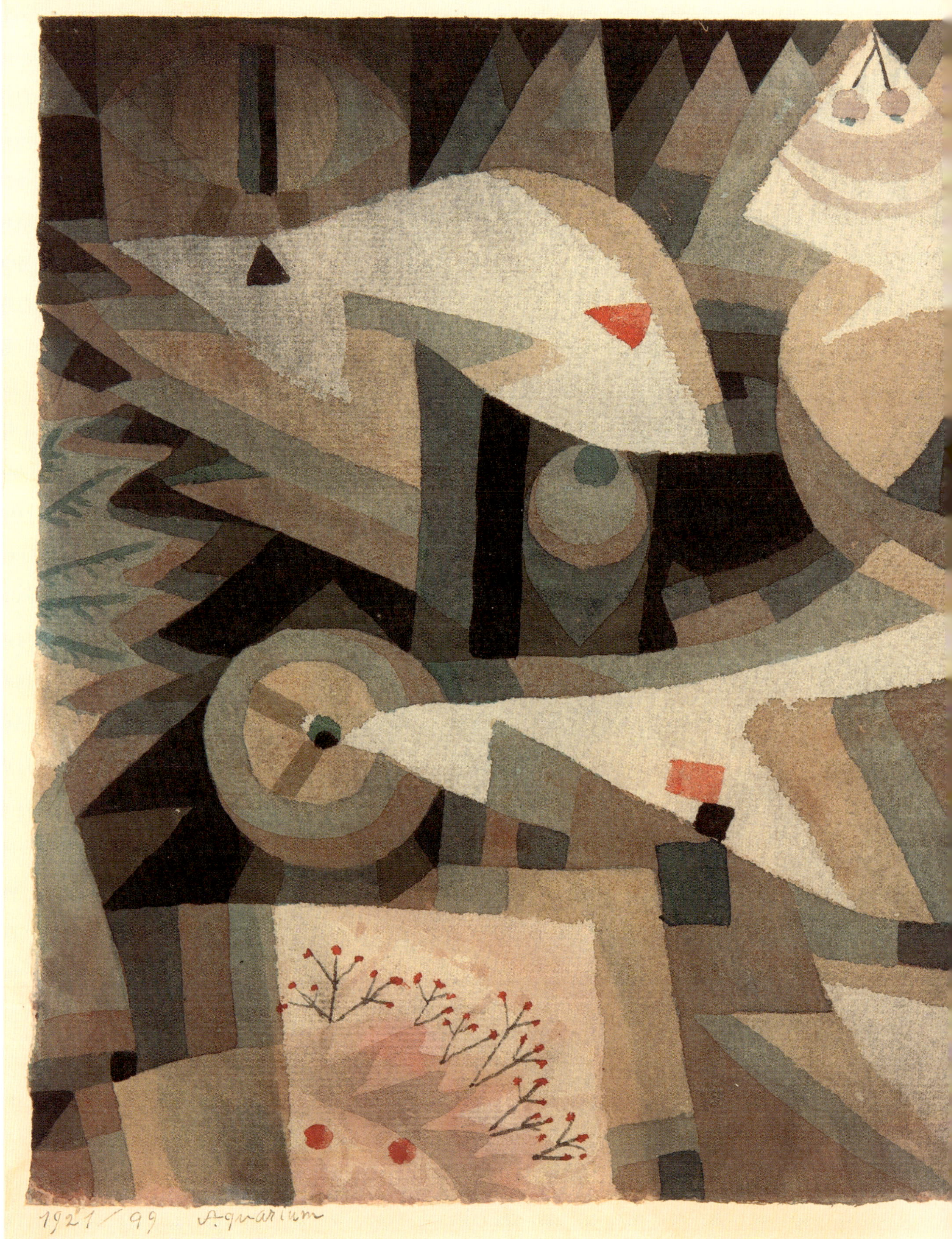
1921/99 Aquarium

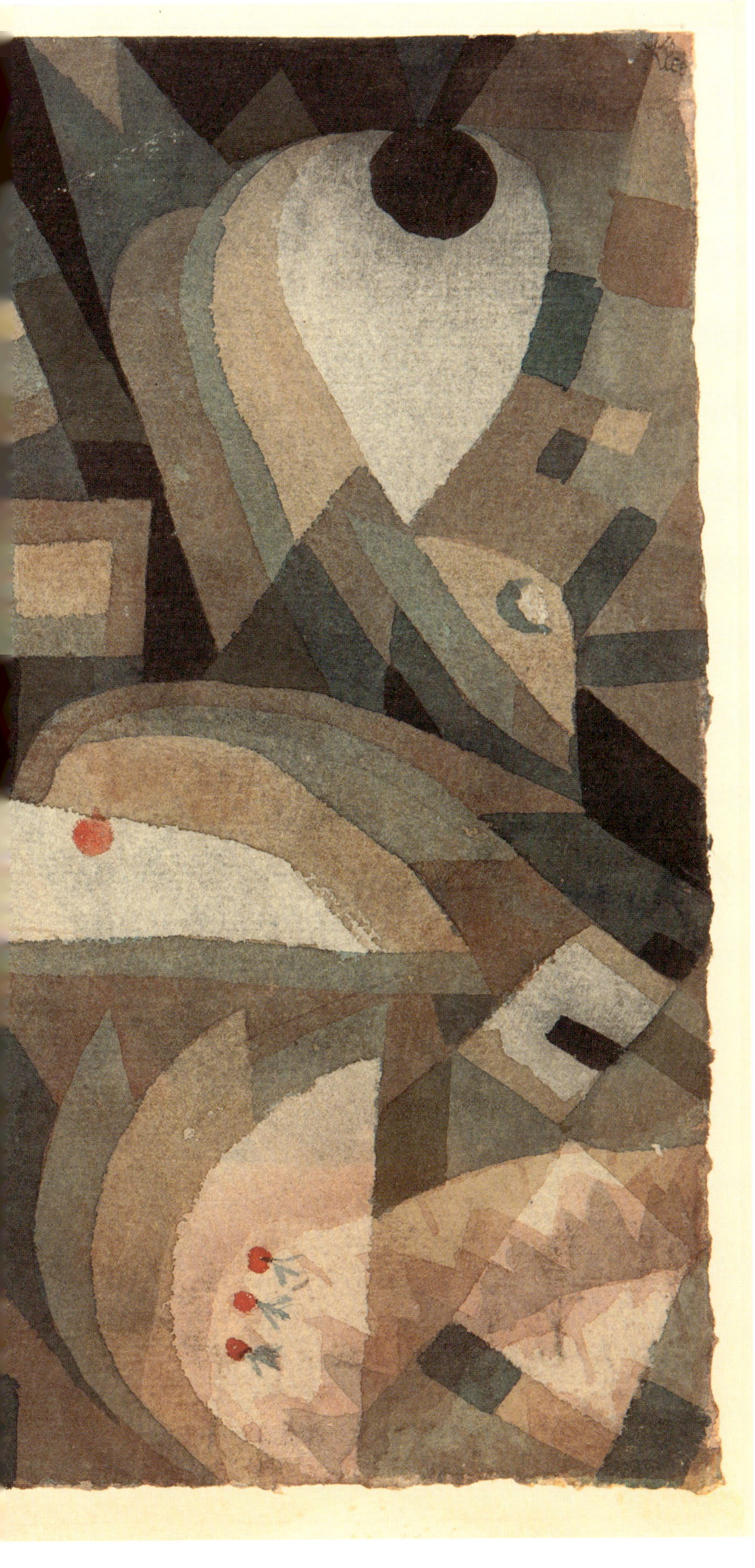

Sculpture éponge bleue sans titre, (SE 49)
1960 ca
Pure pigment and synthetic resin, natural sea sponge
38 × 18 × 7 cm
15 × 7 × 3 in

Yves Klein

Yves Klein (1928-1962) was born in Nice, France and studied judoka in Japan before returning to his home country in 1954 to devote himself to art. His work is a relentless exercise in expanding the field of painting and sculpture by liberating color "from the prison that is the line." To that end he has employed fire, naked bodies, immaterial silences, and choreographed performances, often with his signature, ultra-saturated cerulean hue, known as International Klein Blue.

Sculpture éponge bleue sans titre, (SE 49) from 1960 embodies Klein's revelation that a tool for depositing color can become its own medium for it — working in the studio, he was captivated by sponges's ability to hold color with more intensity than a brush. The destabilizing depth of Klein Blue calls to mind the vastness of the sea; here the sponge becomes an arcane messenger, having traveled into dazzling and murky depths, and returned newly tumesced with the poetic mysteries of the deep. C.C.M.

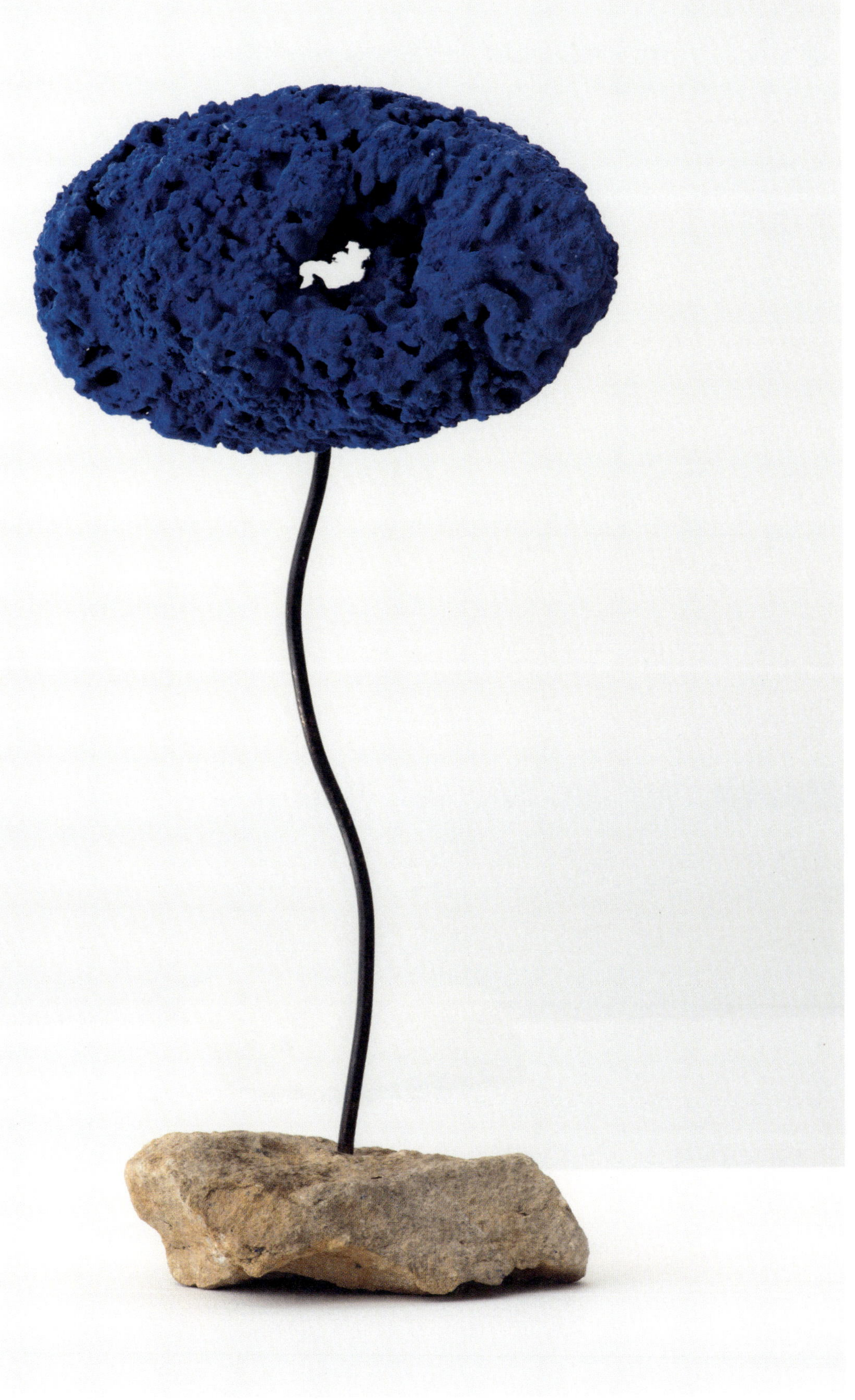

Acrobat
2003-2009
Multi-colored aluminum,
galvanized steel, wood, straw
228.9 × 148 × 64.8 cm
90 × 58 × 26 in

Since the 1980s, Jeff Koons (b. 1955) has pushed the boundaries of sculpture through his treatment of everyday objects, casting the ephemera of mass culture in enduring materials, often at unlikely scale. He drags European avant-garde traditions like Surrealism and the Readymade through the yard sales and rec rooms of broader cultural history, courting controversy and breaking auction records along the way.

In *Acrobat* (2003-2009), a giant inflatable lobster is suspended in a handstand, one claw resting on the back of a wooden kitchen chair, the other on an upturned garbage can. Even upon close inspection it's still almost impossible to tell that the taut, puffy crustacean is actually a weighty aluminum cast. There is something oddly peaceful in the formal harmony of this acrobatic tableau, even as we are tempted to unite the disparate visual elements through narrative or commentary — was there an avalanche in the garage? Does it speak to the precariousness of American middle-class leisure? According to Koons, the work is completed only through the unique emotional or intellectual response each viewer brings to it. C.C.M.

Jeff Koons

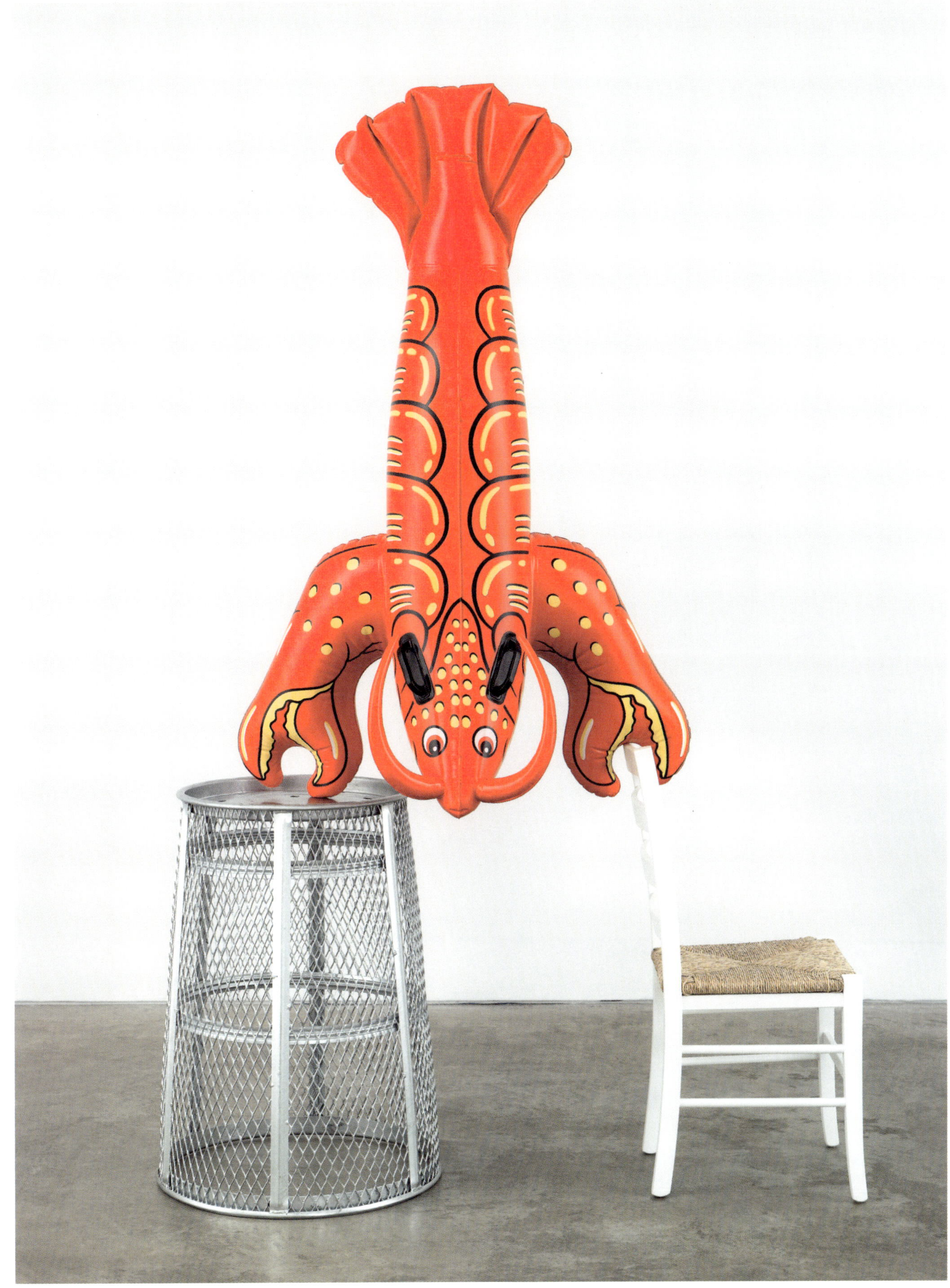

Sans titre (Les Méduses)
2006
Silicone
9 large jellyfish
Diameter 70 cm
28 in
Length 280 cm
110 in
11 medium jellyfish
Diameter 50 cm
20 in
Length 260 cm
102 in
9 small jellyfish
Diameter 40 cm
19 in
Length 240 cm
94 in

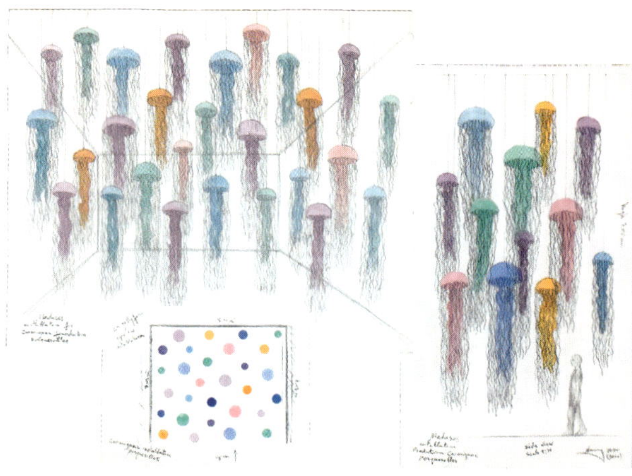

With billowing glowing bells and long tentacles, a swarm of silicon jellyfish find their home out of water with a spectral elegance. Their strange beauty hides a fatal menace, tangle with the wrong jelly and you'll end up sinking from their deadly sting. The Israeli-born, Paris-based artist Micha Laury developed this idea over time but didn't give his drawings their final form until his daughter told him a story in which she witnessed a fatal encounter with these pelagic creatures. As the ocean boils and the oxygen there with it, the jellyfish of the world, around for over 500 million years, have found a fold in space-time for the over two hundred known species to explode in variety. Brainless, bloodless, spineless, their soft symmetries take their shape wholly from the element they swim in. Here, their colors beam with otherworldly force, floating between our world and theirs, giving us space to move safely between the tentacles of these ocean medusae. **A.B.**

Micha Laury

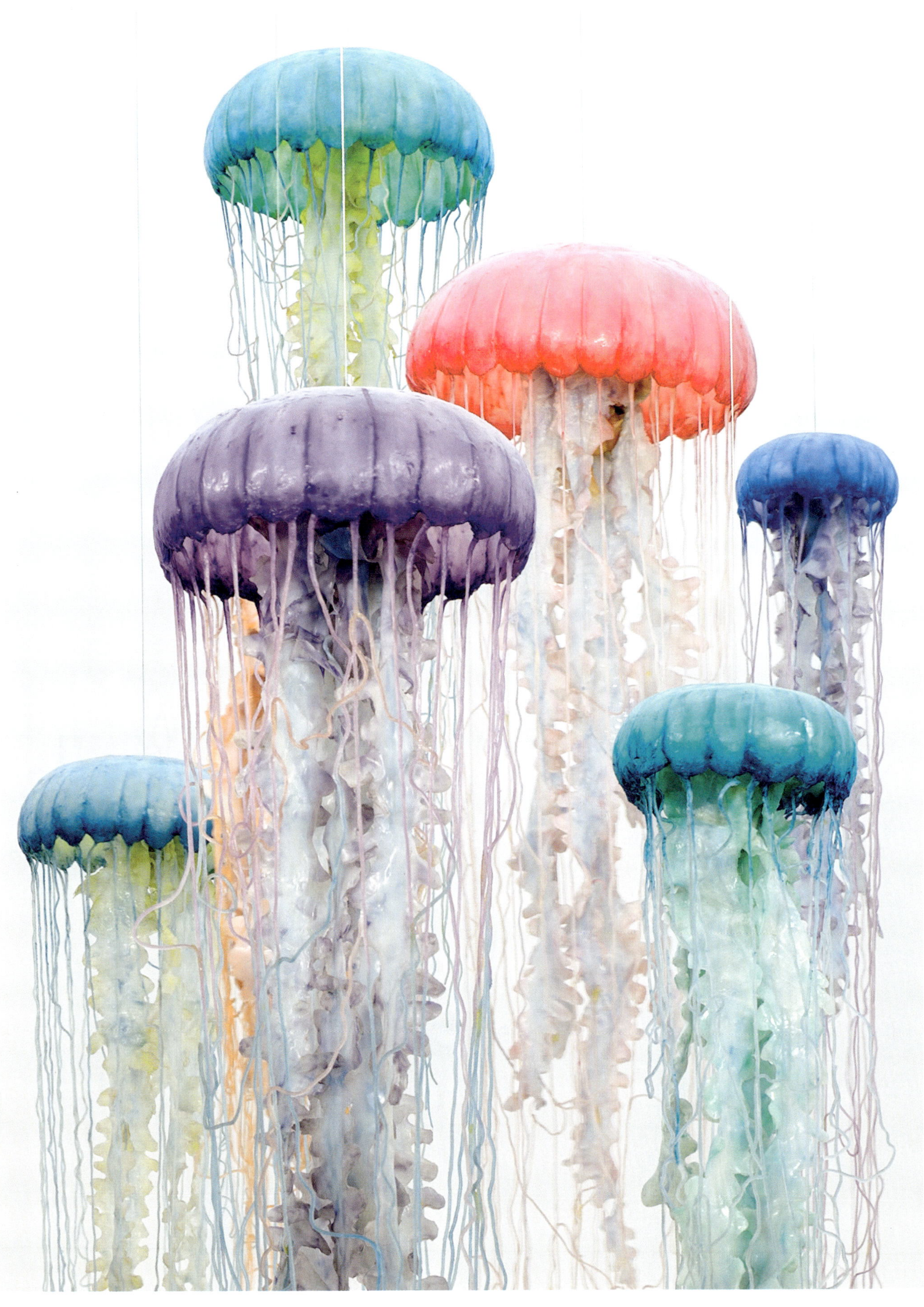

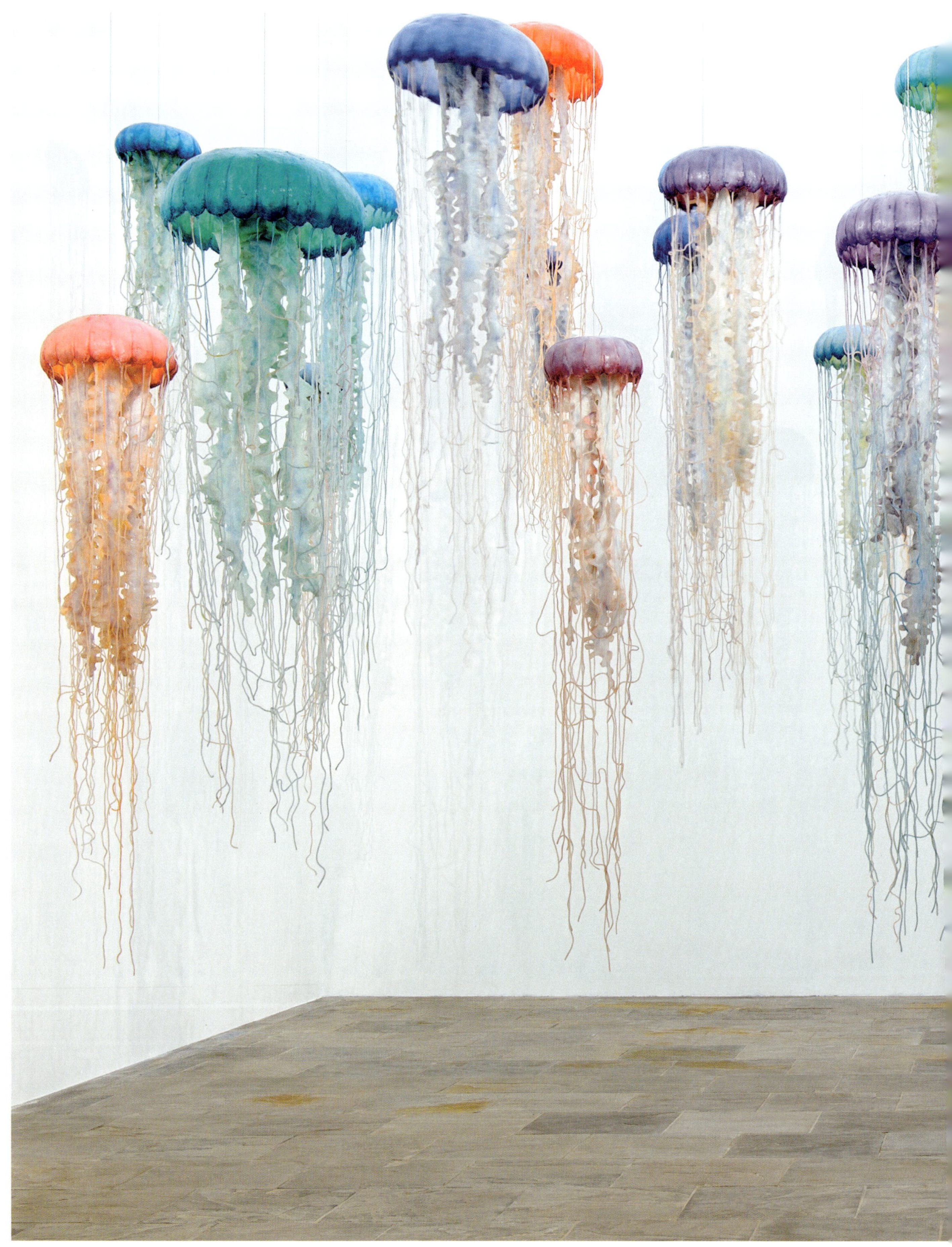

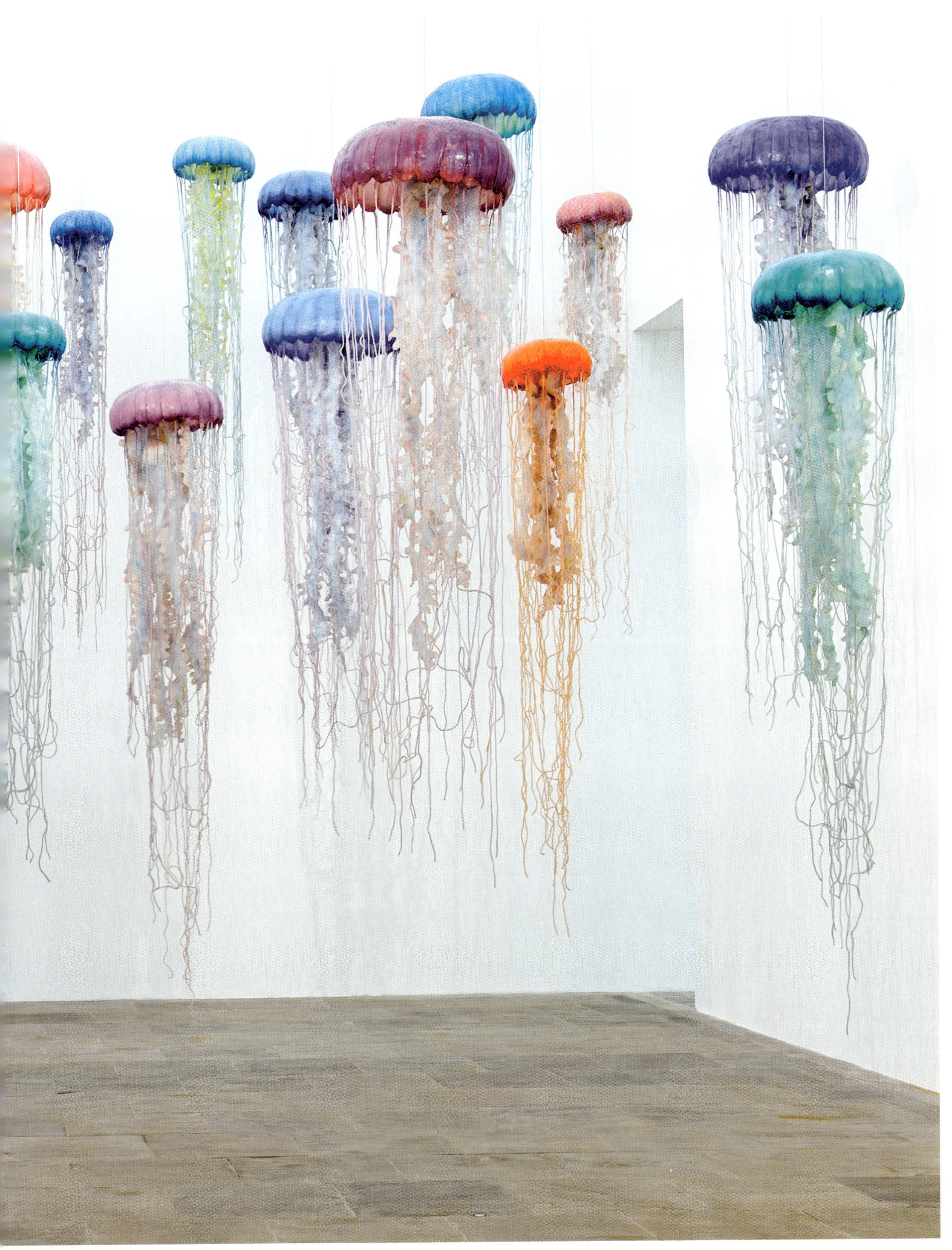

Shells
2020
Oil on jute
23 × 30.5 cm
9 × 12 in

Jennifer J. Lee trawls the abyssal depths of the Internet for subjects, swimming down into archives of stock photography to find which seemingly-generic picture will leap out. Once caught, she hyperealitistically paints each onto a rough netting of jute. Repeated patterns in the images flicker before your eyes, but the rough canvas adds soft noise to the tableau, like the fugitive pixels of a downmarket jpg. Here, she's found a mountain of empty seashells, a whisper of the life they once held, depleted. Shells litter the beaches plentifully; they rarely possess value in the scarcity game of capitalism. A shell, one of billions, can go from life to skeleton to dust so easily. But when you pluck one out, put it in your bag, carry it home and arrange it on your bookshelf as a memento of your day at the beach, this simple act of election makes it special to you amongst all the other shells. The Internet and its endless stream of images is sort of like this. Jennifer J. Lee doesn't pick her images because they are so beautiful, usually quite the opposite. But by choosing them and then carefully painting each, she makes what might have been random detritus into something special, unique, loved. A.B.

Jennifer J. Lee

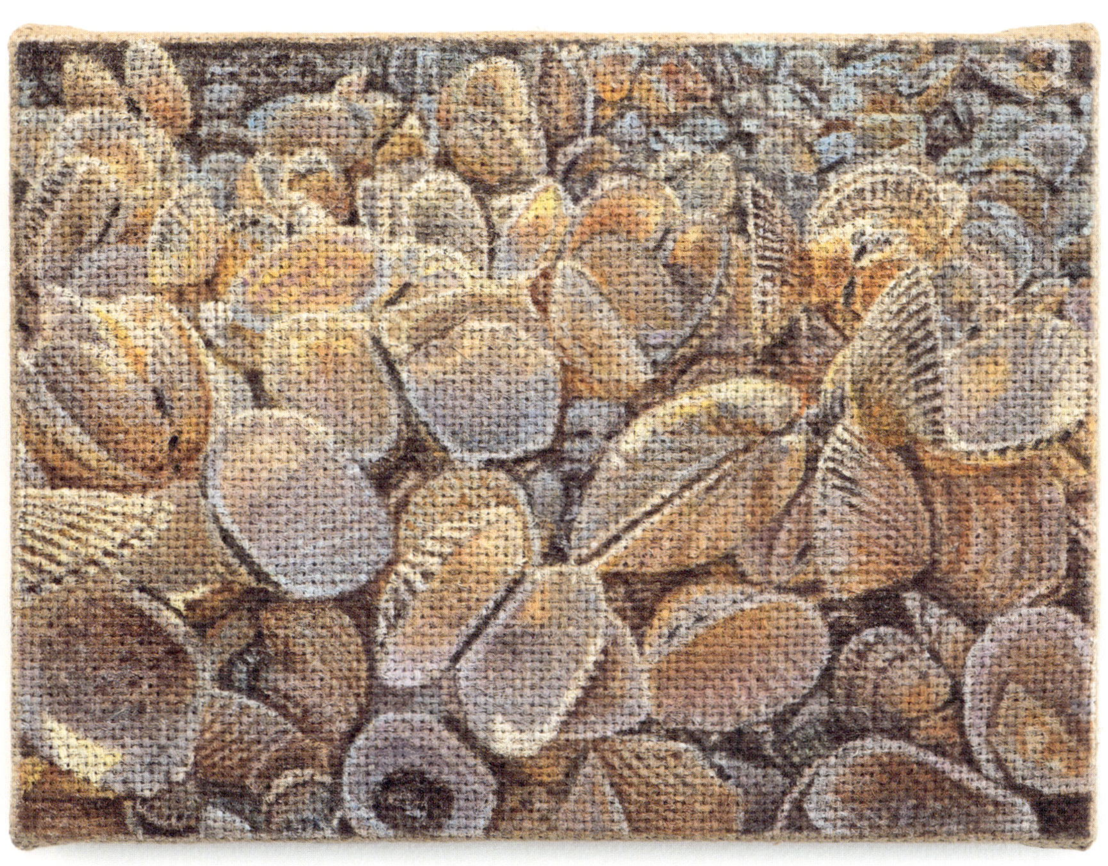

Untitled
(Plastic Bag III)
2017
Silver gelatin print
38.5 × 29.5 cm
15 × 11 in

Jochen Lempert

Jochen Lempert (b. 1958, Moers, Germany; based in Hamburg) is one of the more respected and admired photographers working today. Trained as a biologist who did his field work on dragonflies and who, until relatively recently, also moonlighted as an ornithologist on research vessels on the North Sea, his work is grounded in a deep and broad understanding of natural history. This scientific training is one of the reasons why his black and white silver gelatin photography may seem, at least formally, indebted to the taxonomical modernism of the likes of Karl Blossfeldt and August Sander. But what sets the work of Lempert apart and makes it contemporary is its specific interest in the evolving relationship between the animal kingdom and human civilization, how the two interact, mutually adapt, occasionally mimic one another and, ultimately, synthesize despite humankind's best efforts to distinguish itself from the natural world.

Lempert presents a series of works in *The Imaginary Sea* which all deal with the fauna of the sea. Here we encounter everything from images of a semi-abstract camouflage of a flat fish partially disappearing in a marine environment to a jellyfish floating in a plastic bag to a father and a child regarding fish in an aquarium. The eye of the photographer always culturally and scientifically interprets what is seen as much as human beings marvel at and seek to understand the natural world. C.S.

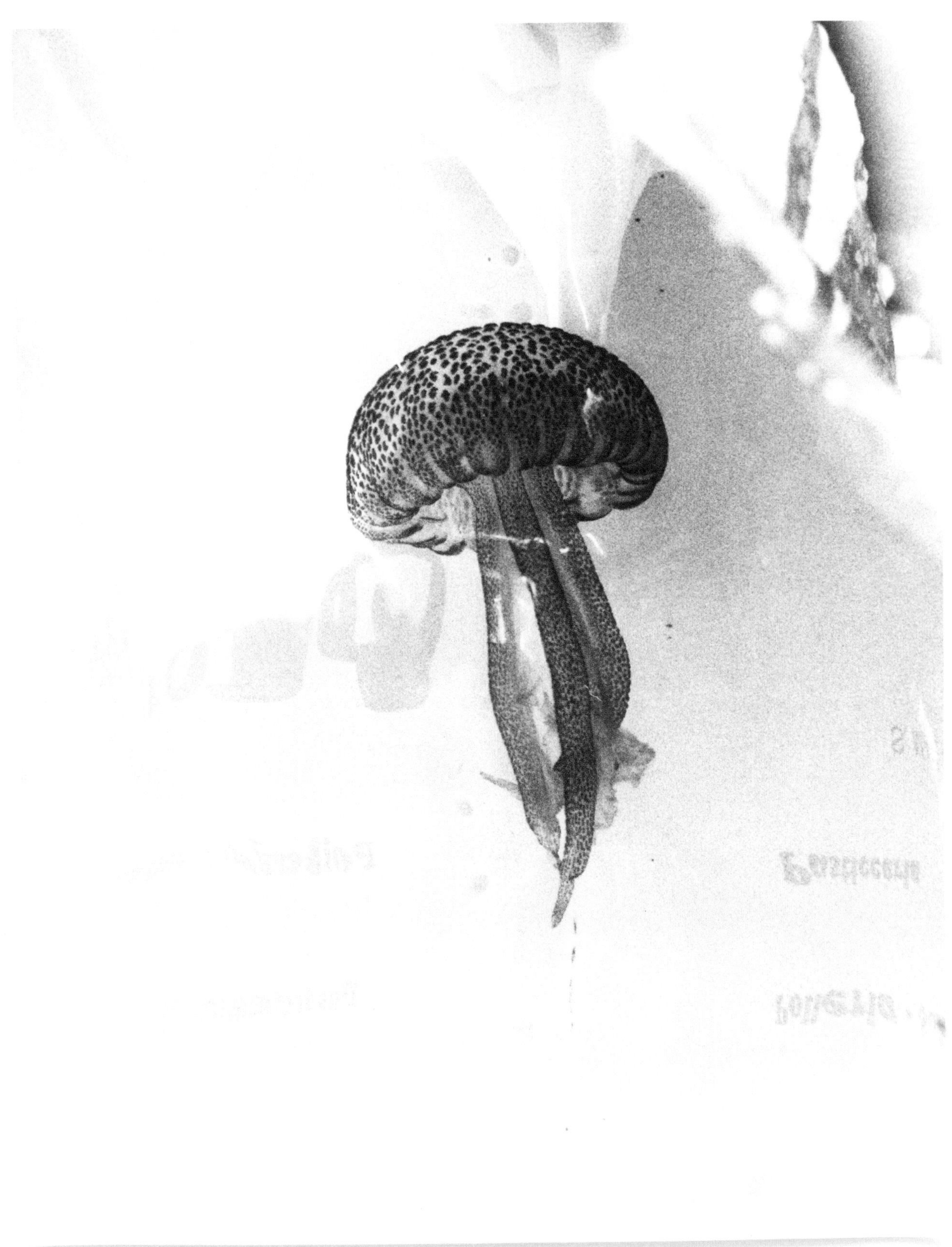

→
Seefeder
2017-2018
Silver gelatin print
50 × 37 cm
19 × 15 in

↓
Untitled
(Aquarium, Toronto)
2017
Silver gelatin print
49 × 38.5 cm
19 × 15 in

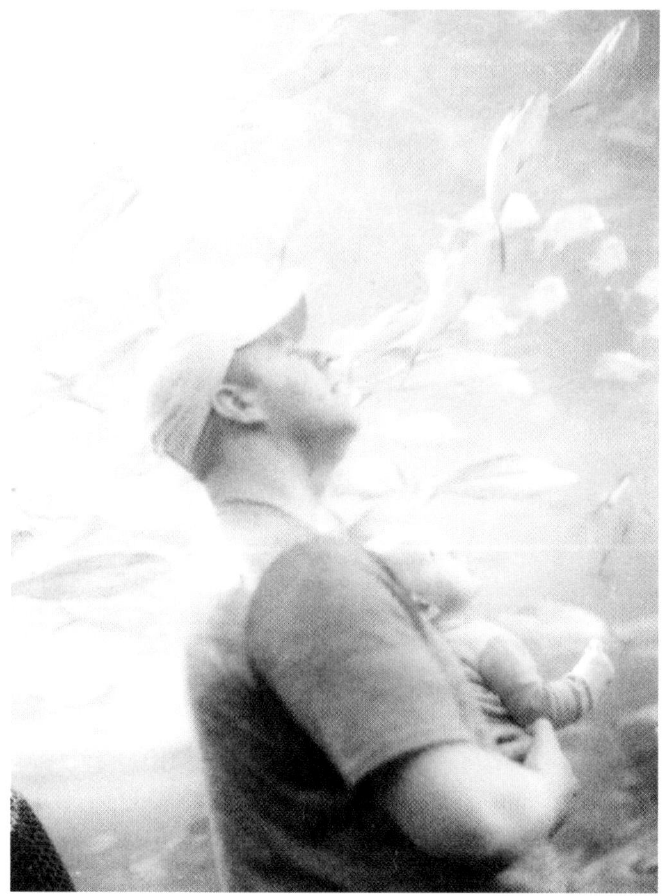

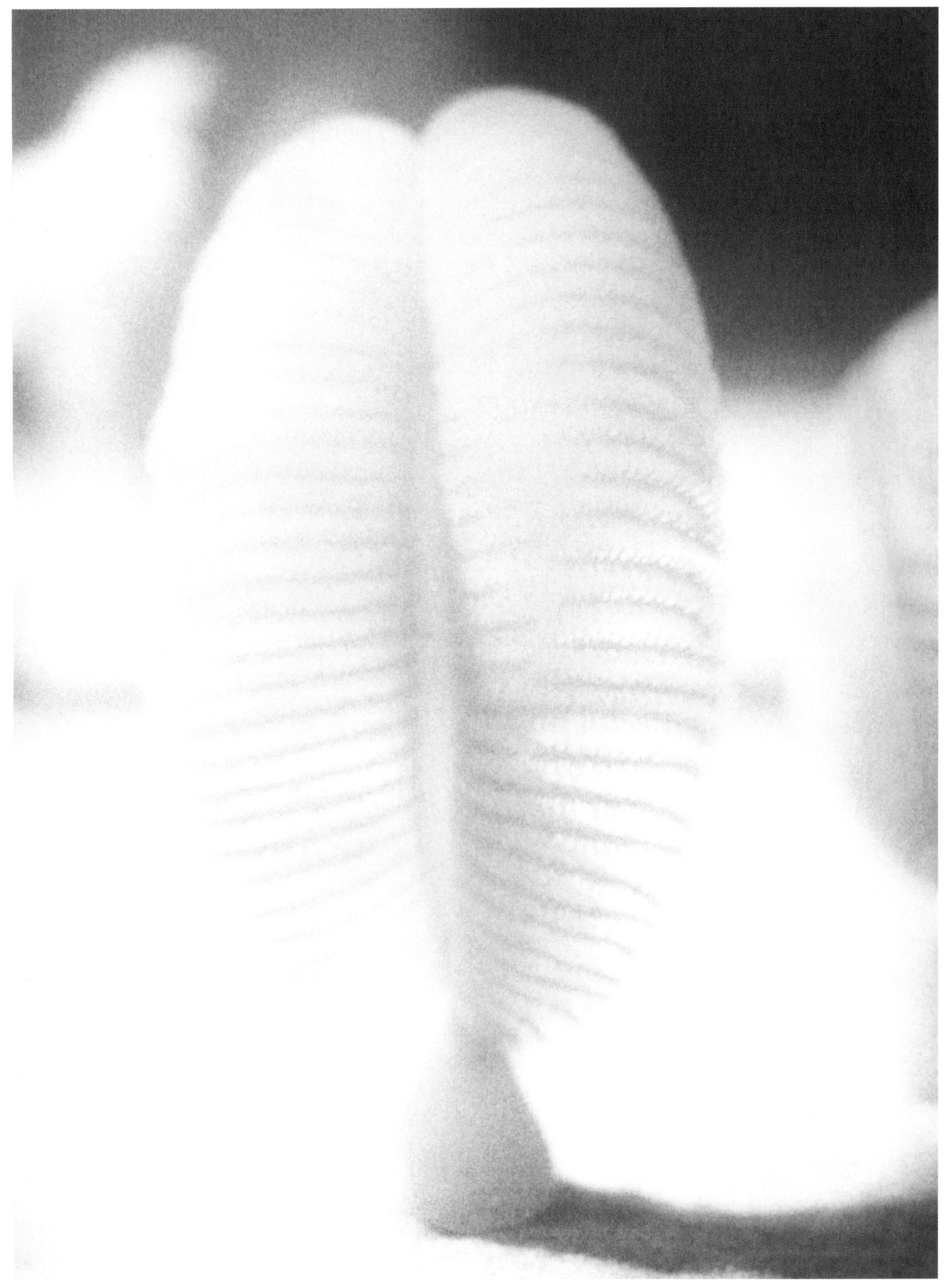

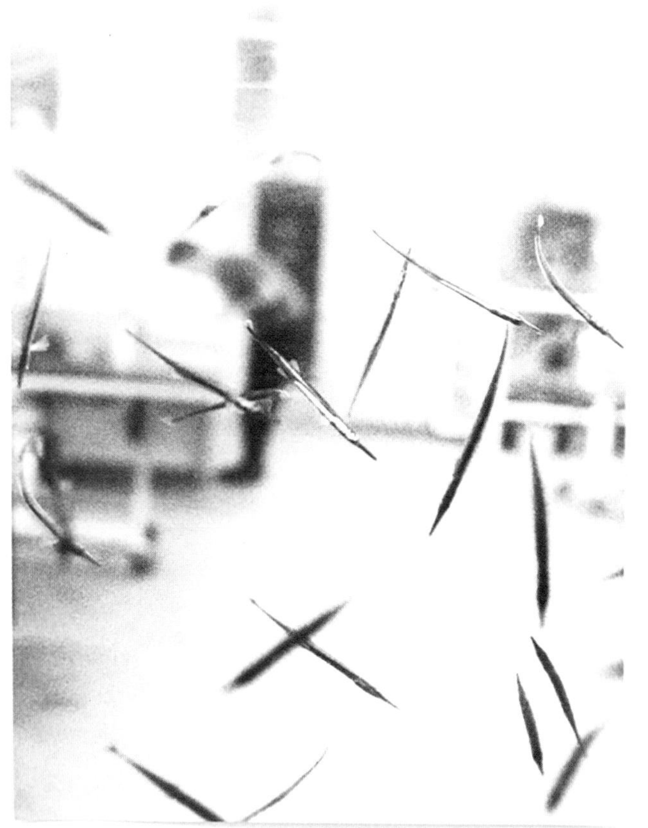

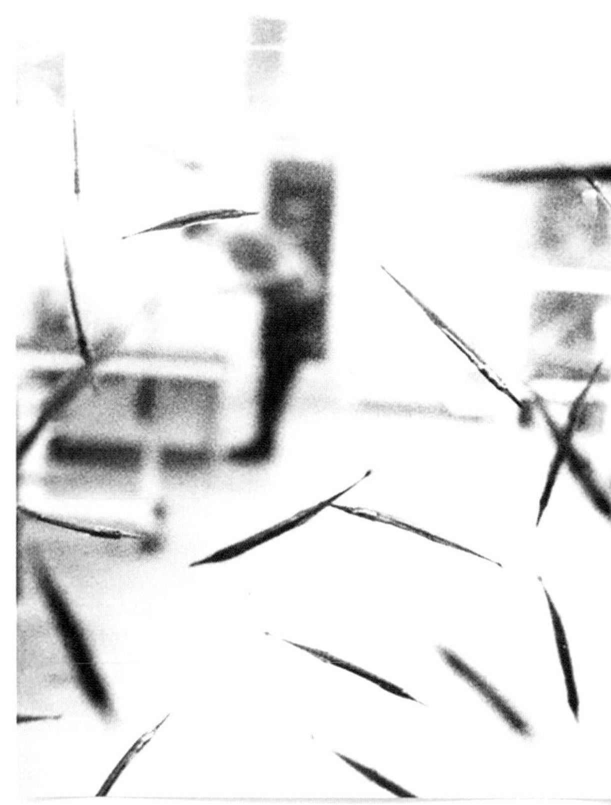

Untitled (Fishes and Human Body)
2017
Silver gelatin print
23.5 × 17.5 cm
9 × 7 in

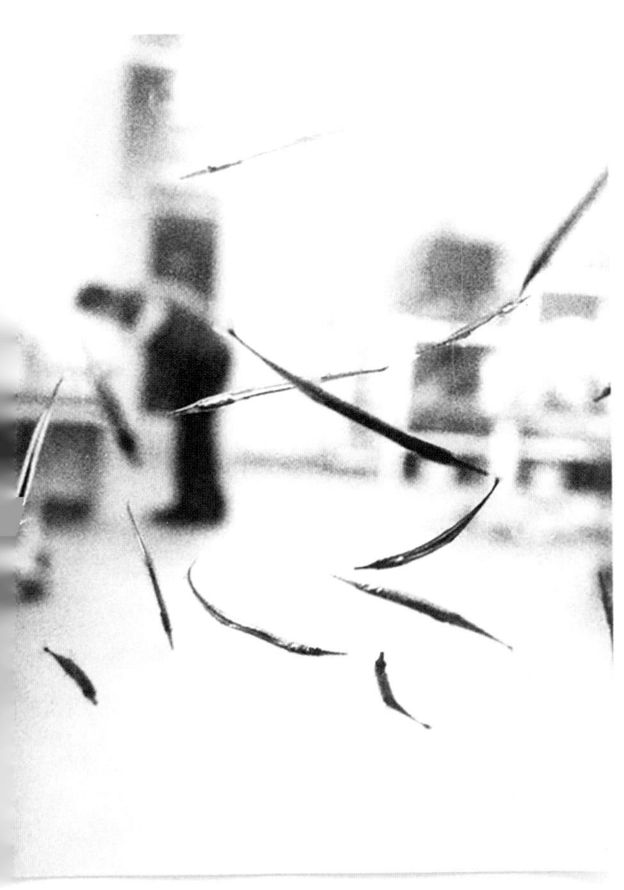

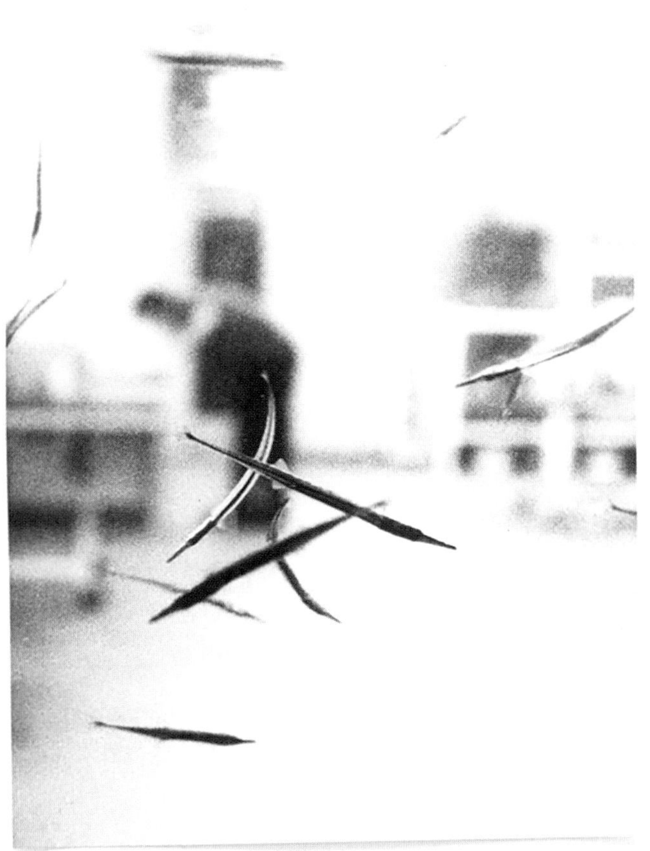

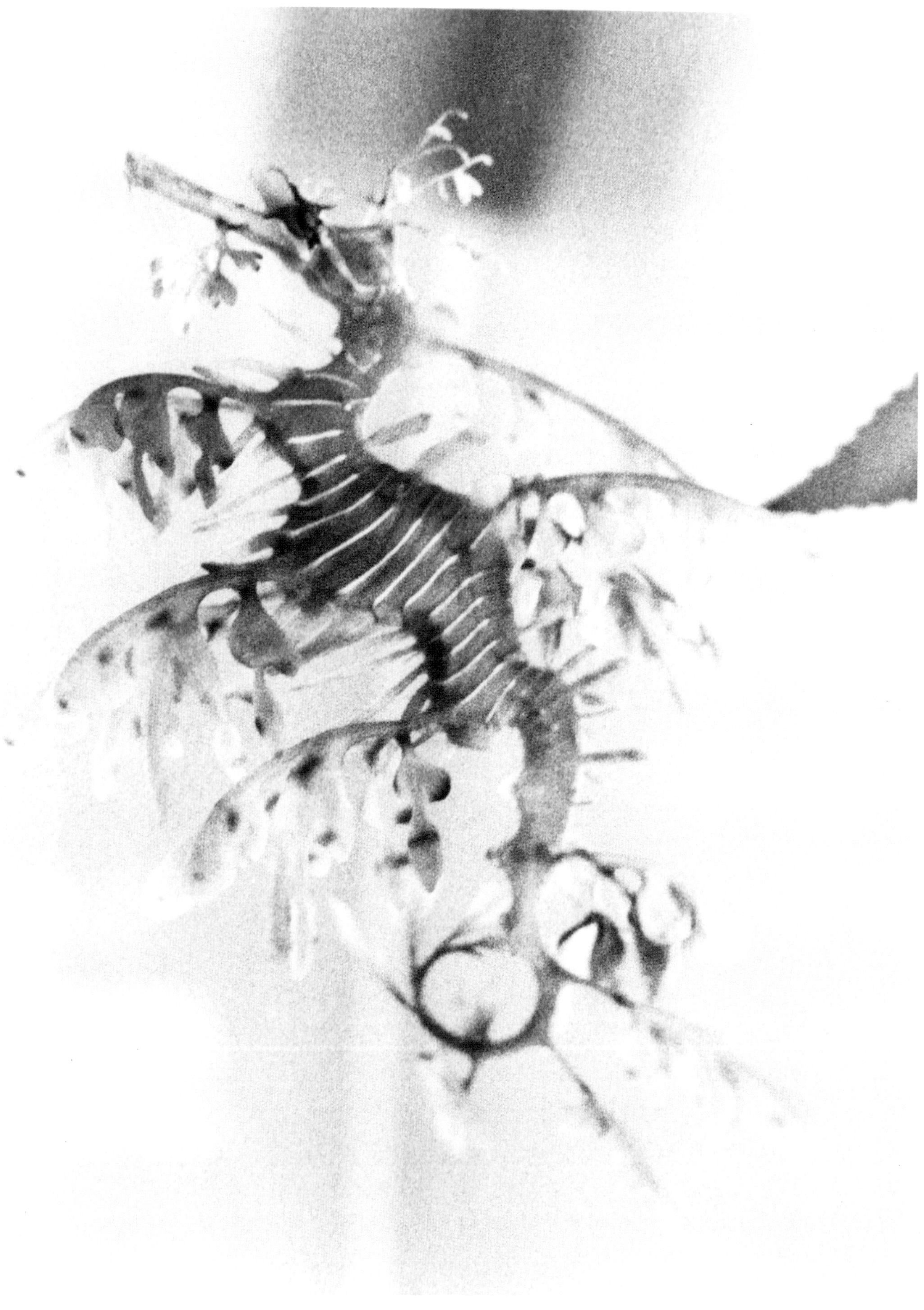

←
Untitled (Seadragon)
2016
Silver gelatin print
27 × 20 cm
11 × 8 in

→
Untitled (Automimikry)
2018
Silver gelatin print
28 × 23 cm
12 × 9 in

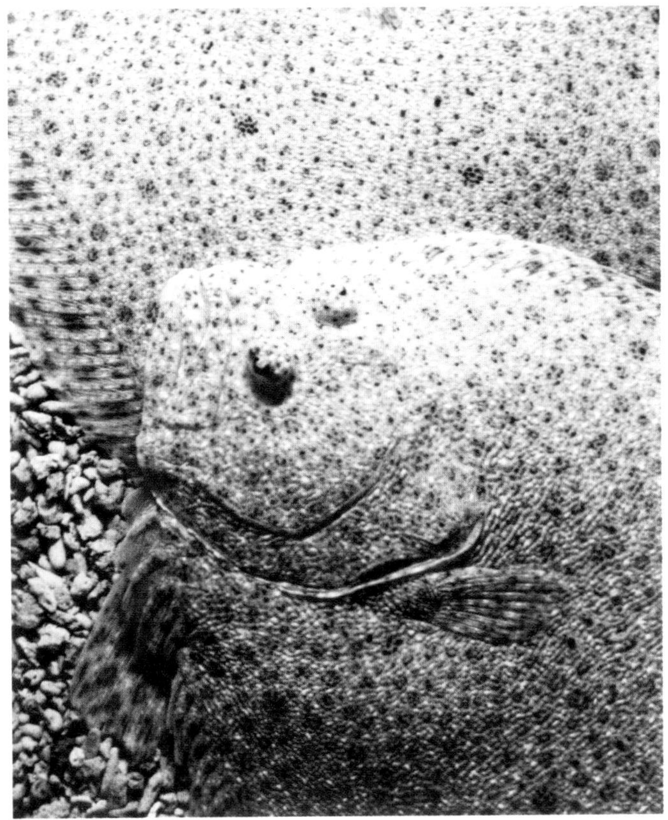

Untitled (Hand-Shell)
1934 ca
Silver gelatin print
30.5 × 23.7 cm
12 × 9 in

Dora Maar

Between running a successful commercial photography studio and various romantic and creative entanglements with the painter Pablo Picasso — including documenting the creation of *Guernica* and modeling for his iconic painting *The Weeping Woman* in 1937 — Dora Maar (1907-1997) lived through nearly the entire 20th century, pioneering the kind of radical photography practices that are now ubiquitous. Between long and intermittent returns to painting, she played with darkroom experiments like photomontage, and took her Rolleiflex camera to the streets of London, Paris, and Costa Brava, Spain, documenting workers, mothers, and everyday people. As one of the few women to ever be exhibited with the Surrealists, she moved nimbly among the worlds of art, fashion, and advertising.

Untitled (Hand-Shell) 1934, is one of Maar's earliest photomontages. A manicured hand creeps out from a shell, unclear if it is crawling out into the ominous landscape or retreating back into self-containment. With four major elements — hand, shell, sand, sky — Maar marries the chaotic visual logic of dreams with the seductive cool of a slick fashion ad. However, unlike an ad, the evocative imagery, tinged with eroticism, does not seek to direct or articulate the desires it suggests — or perhaps elicits. C.C.M.

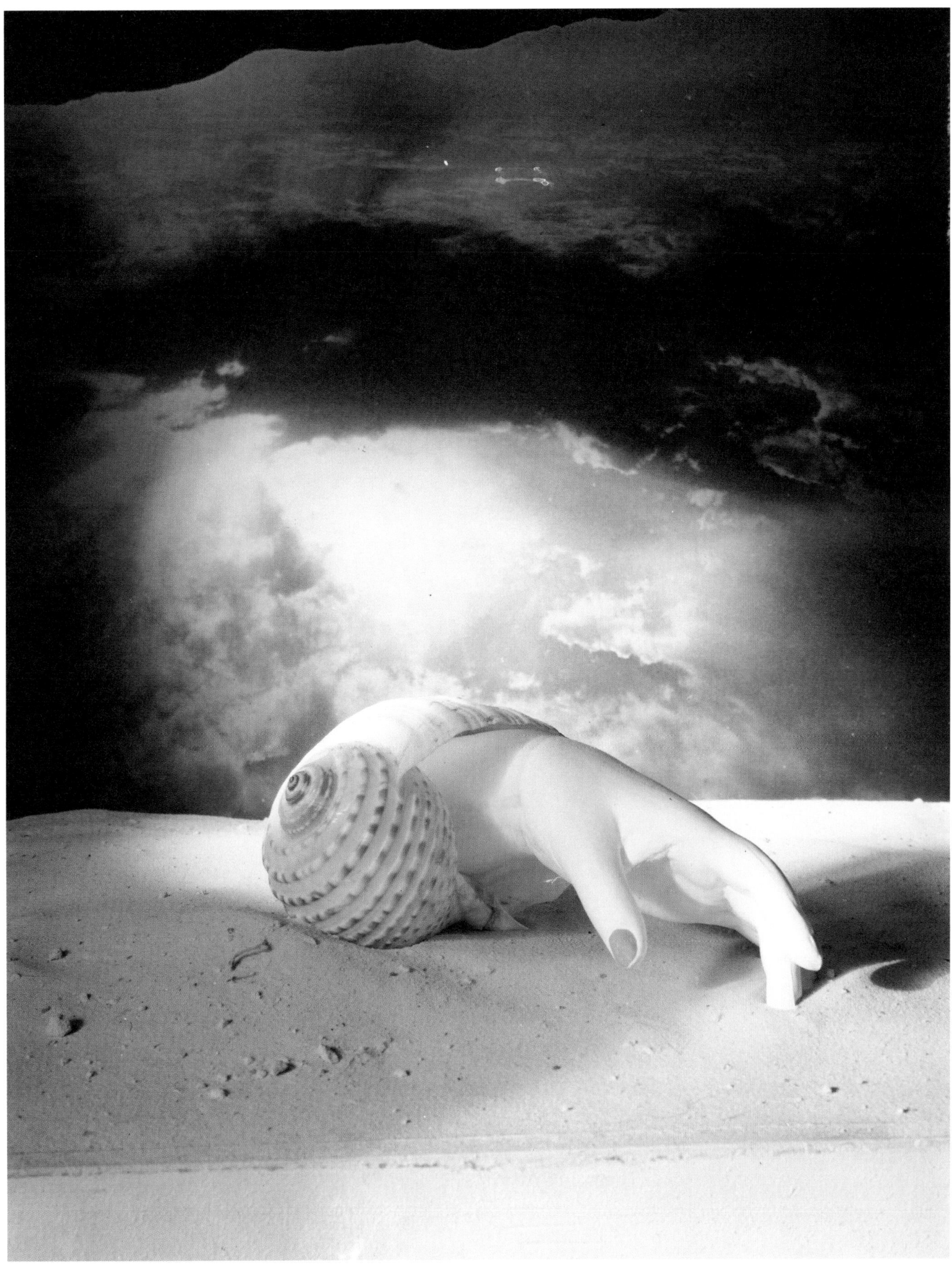

Polynésie, le ciel
1964
Low warp weaving technique,
wool and cotton
195 × 304 cm
77 × 120 in

Henri Matisse

Polynésie, le ciel is the byproduct of one of Matisse's final commissions in the last decade of his life. Approached by the state-owned tapestry factory Gobelins Manufactory (*Manufacture des Gobelins*), he designed three tapestries which Gobelins would produce including, *Polynésie, le ciel* and *Polynésie, la mer* which Matisse conceived as paper cutouts in 1946. While some of the tapestries copies were not produced until after the artist's death, they followed his specifications and were made under the direct supervision of his estate by the famous Beauvais Manufactory in Beauvais, France. Realized for an exhibition celebrating the three-hundred-year anniversary of the manufactory in 1964, this *Polynésie, le ciel* tapestry was then gifted to the city of Beauvais in memory of the tricentennial with the dates weaved on it.

The actual imagery of the tapestry was inspired both by Matisse's time in Tahiti in 1930, when he was sixty, as well as his time in Nice at different points throughout his life. The surface of the checkered light and dark blue ground is vividly animated by an apparent conflation of the sky and sea. Its perimeter is hedged in by so much algae while its interior is dominated by gamboling white seagull-like figures as well as starfish, algae, and other sea creatures. Dynamic, resplendent with light and compositionally balanced, the tapestry thrives with life. Its enchanting hard-won simplicity communicates the joy one might experience in the middle of the summer in place like Porquerolles. C.S.

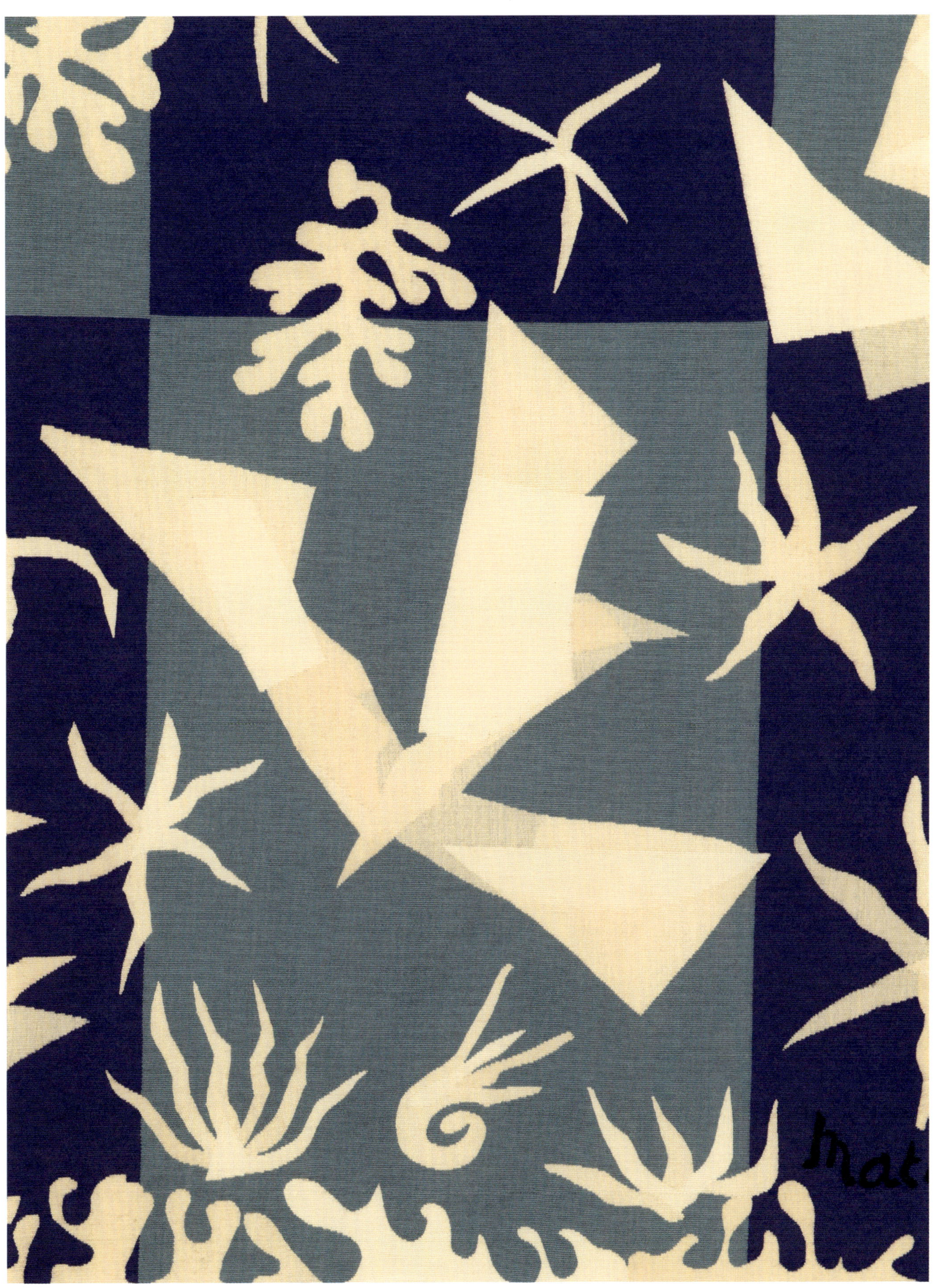

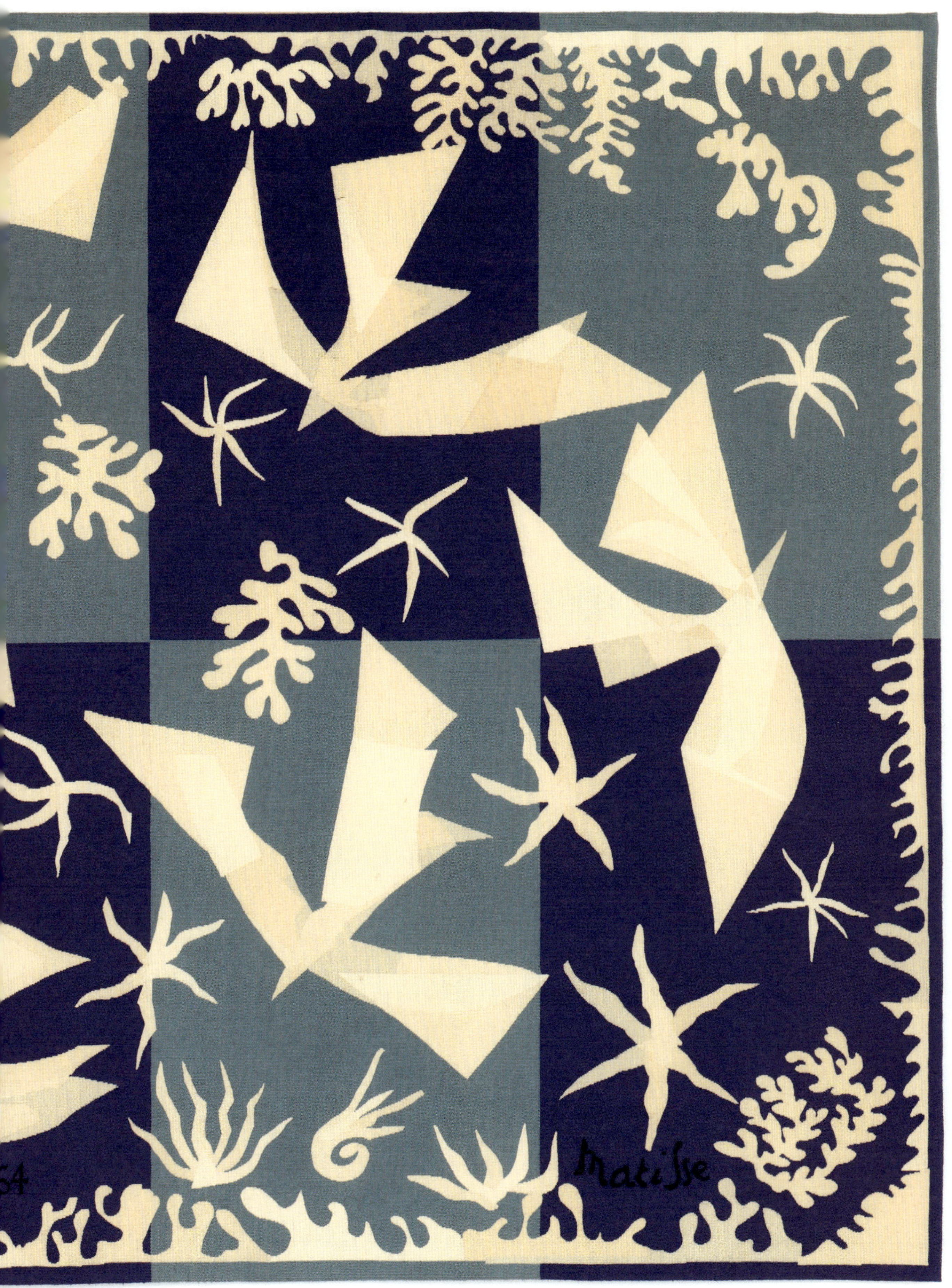
54
Matisse

Diorama (couple d'axolots)
2012
Vitrine, neon lights, dirt, aquarium, water, axolotls couple
219.5 × 180 × 330 cm
86 × 71 × 130 in

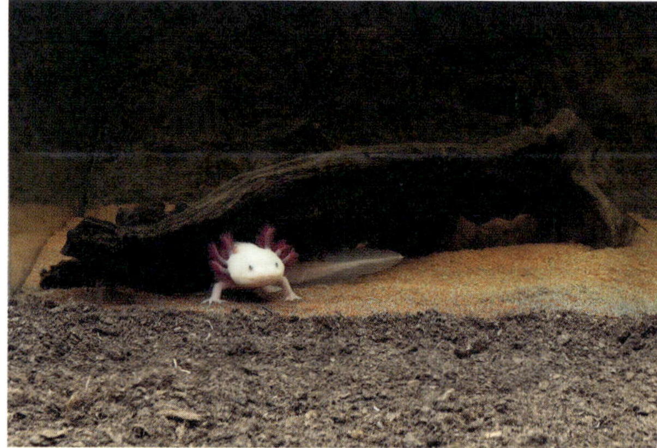

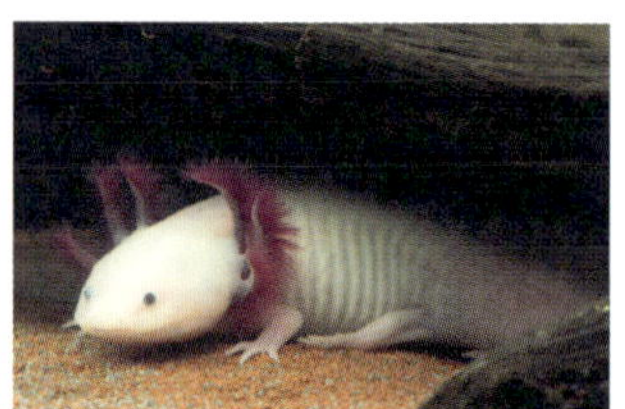

Mathieu Mercier

Mathieu Mercier (b. 1970, Conflans-Sainte-Honorine, France) is a trickster of the avant-garde tradition, taking apart its methods and signifiers, rearranging them and putting them back together in order to flip or question our systems of value. His work is a funhouse mirror of our ever-changing relationships to objects. The reduction of utopian art movements like Constructivism and De Stijl into visual styles inform much of his playful assemblages, blurring the line between functionality and aesthetic purposelessness without pitting one against the other.

Here, a pair of axolotls (clownish salamanders known as Mexican walking fish) go about their day in a small aquarium, tucked inside a larger case, redolent of a diorama. It's a matryoshka of displays, creating a mise en abyme of contexts — cage, theater, vivarium — all contained within a Donald-Judd-like minimalist cube. Much like axolotls, having developed from land dwellers into water creatures, reverse assumptions about evolution, so does the structure re-invest multiple representational narratives into the ostensibly "empty" modernist form. The context of Porquerolles extends the boundaries of the work to the viewer, a creature encircled by the island, encircled by the sea, each layer brimming with life. C.C.M.

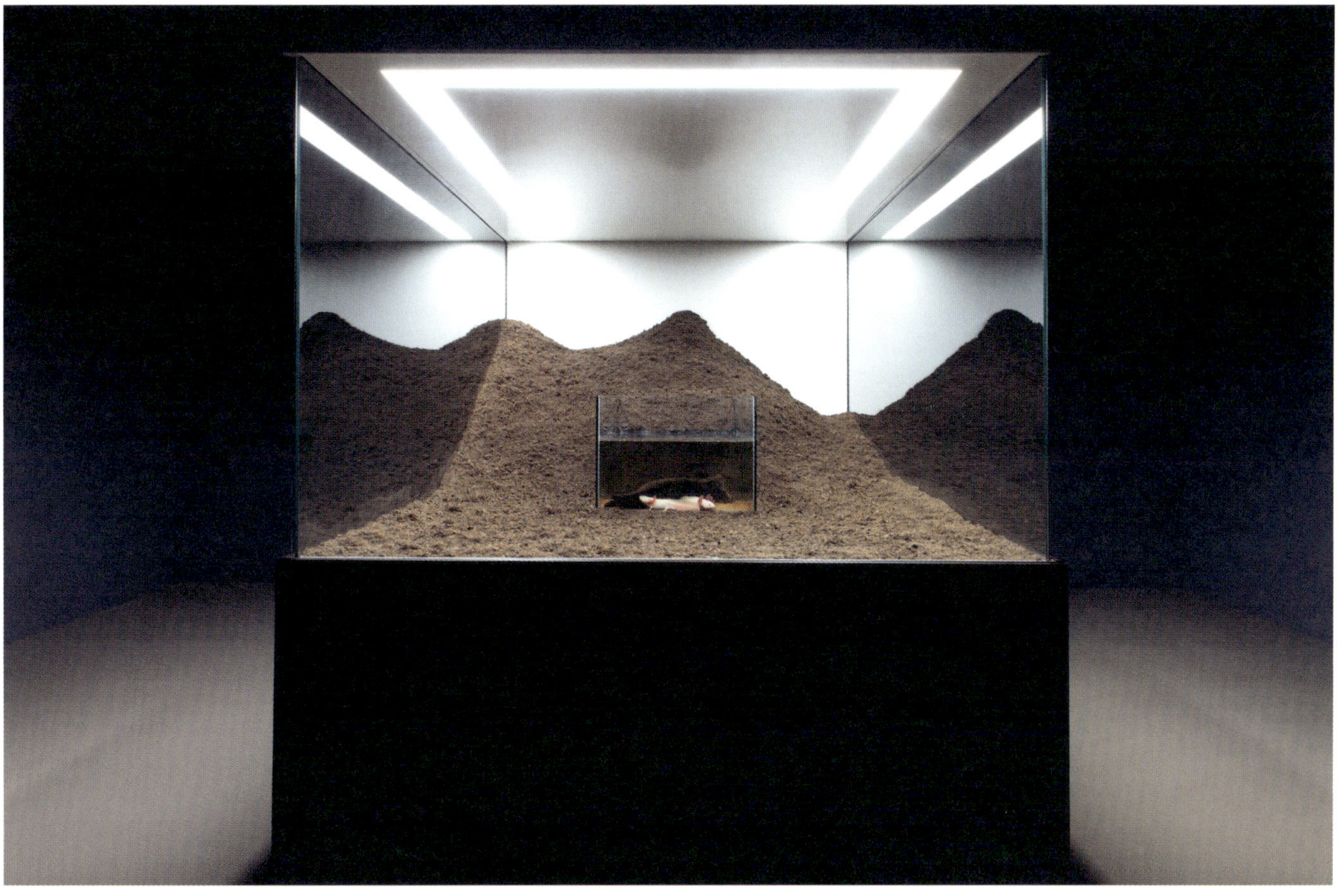

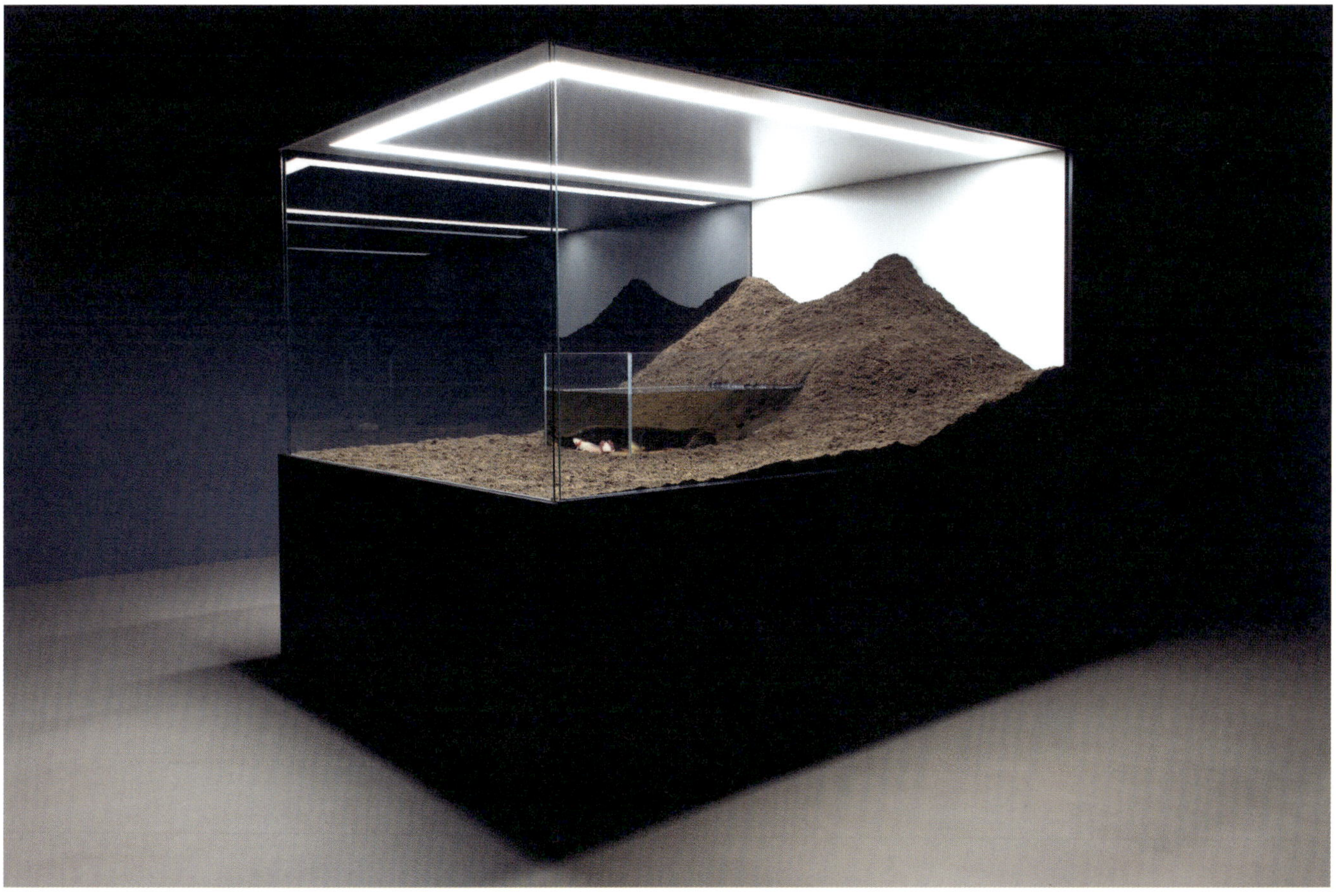

One hundred fish fountain
2005
Bronze, steel and metal
762 × 853.4 × 430 cm
300 × 336 × 169 in

Bruce Nauman

American artist Bruce Nauman's first fountain was himself, snapshotted just so in 1971. A steady stream of water spouting from his pursed lips, hands holding up the air, shirtlessly handsome as only youth can be, and dramatically lit against an inky blackness. Forty years later, Bruce Nauman continued to bend meaning to fountain just so, making life into the stuff of art with fluid flourish. Here, a hundred fish bronzed from the real swim stilly in an ocean of air, streaming water from their slim bodies into waterfalls and rain: catfish, white fish, bass, and others all caught by the artist and made to remember fishing trips from a lost childhood and a lost friend. The fanciful fantasy of fish swimming in air and breathing out water. As in many of his greatest works, Nauman flips the world upside down with deceptive ease. And here as elsewhere, the artist doesn't pretend to hide his machinations. All one hundred of these swimmers hang from wires and the tubing snakes in obvious coils feeding the water from the shallow basin, back into the school. A magician showing you exactly how the trick works without diminishing the grace of his prestidigitation. A.B.

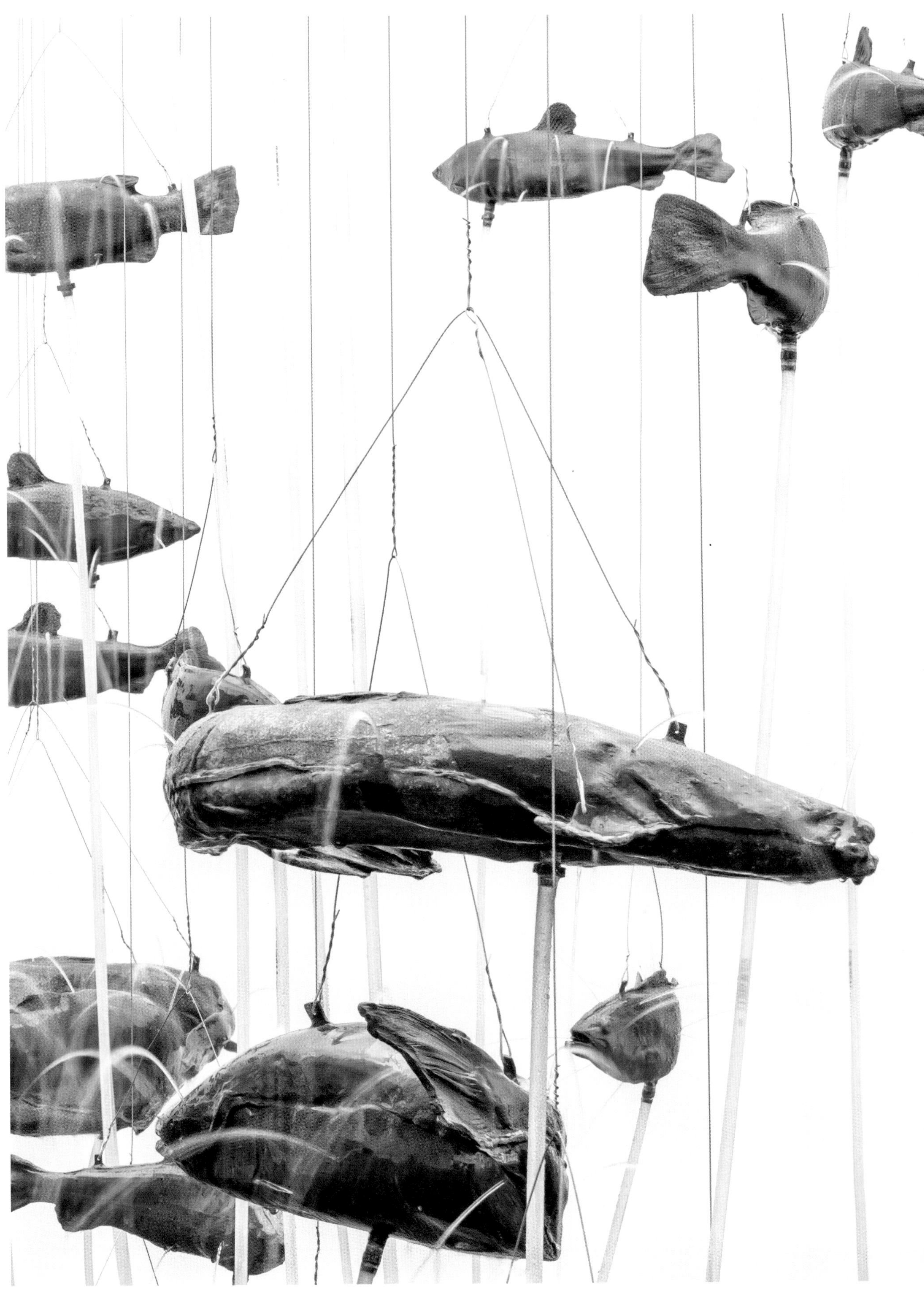

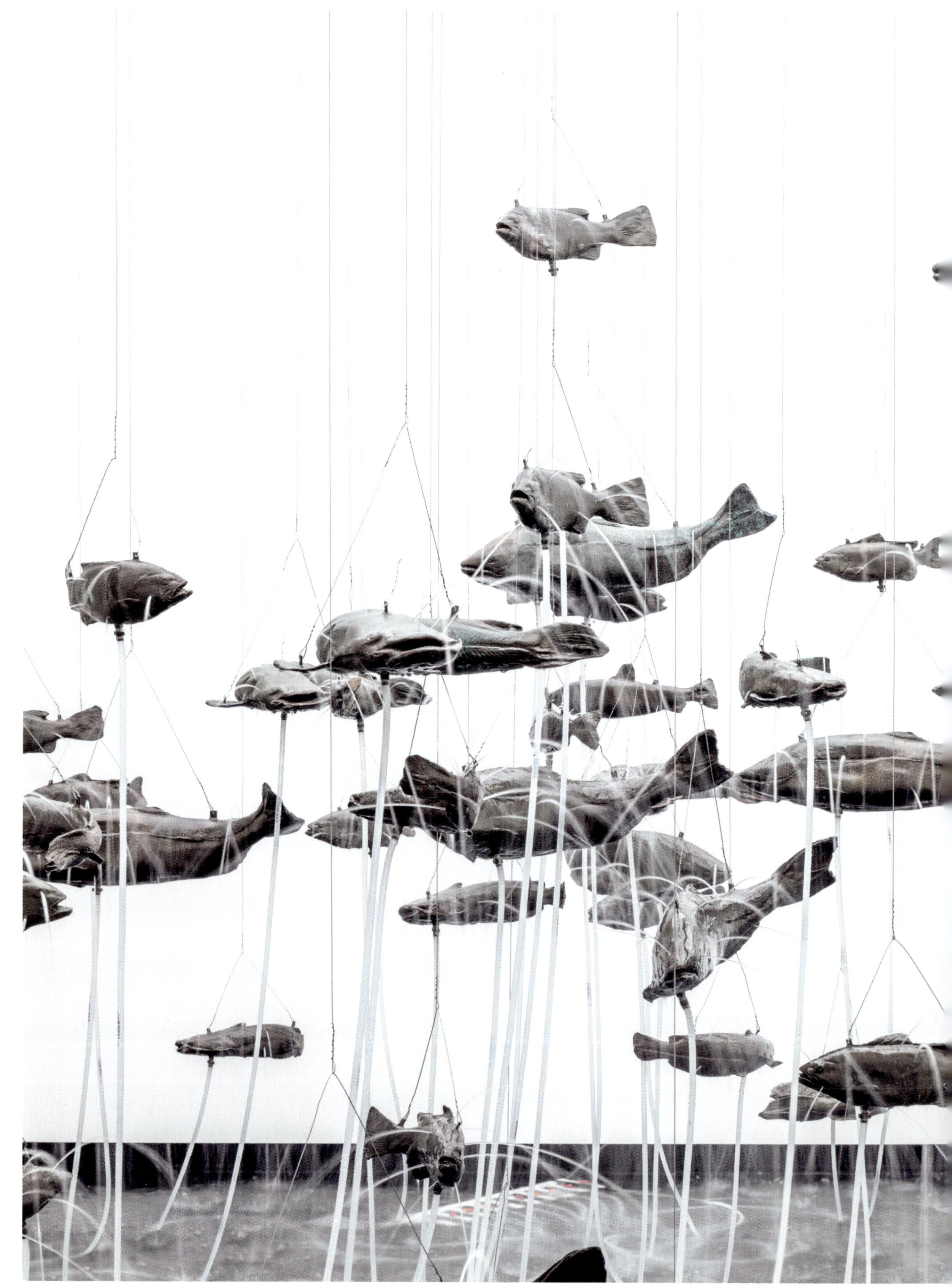

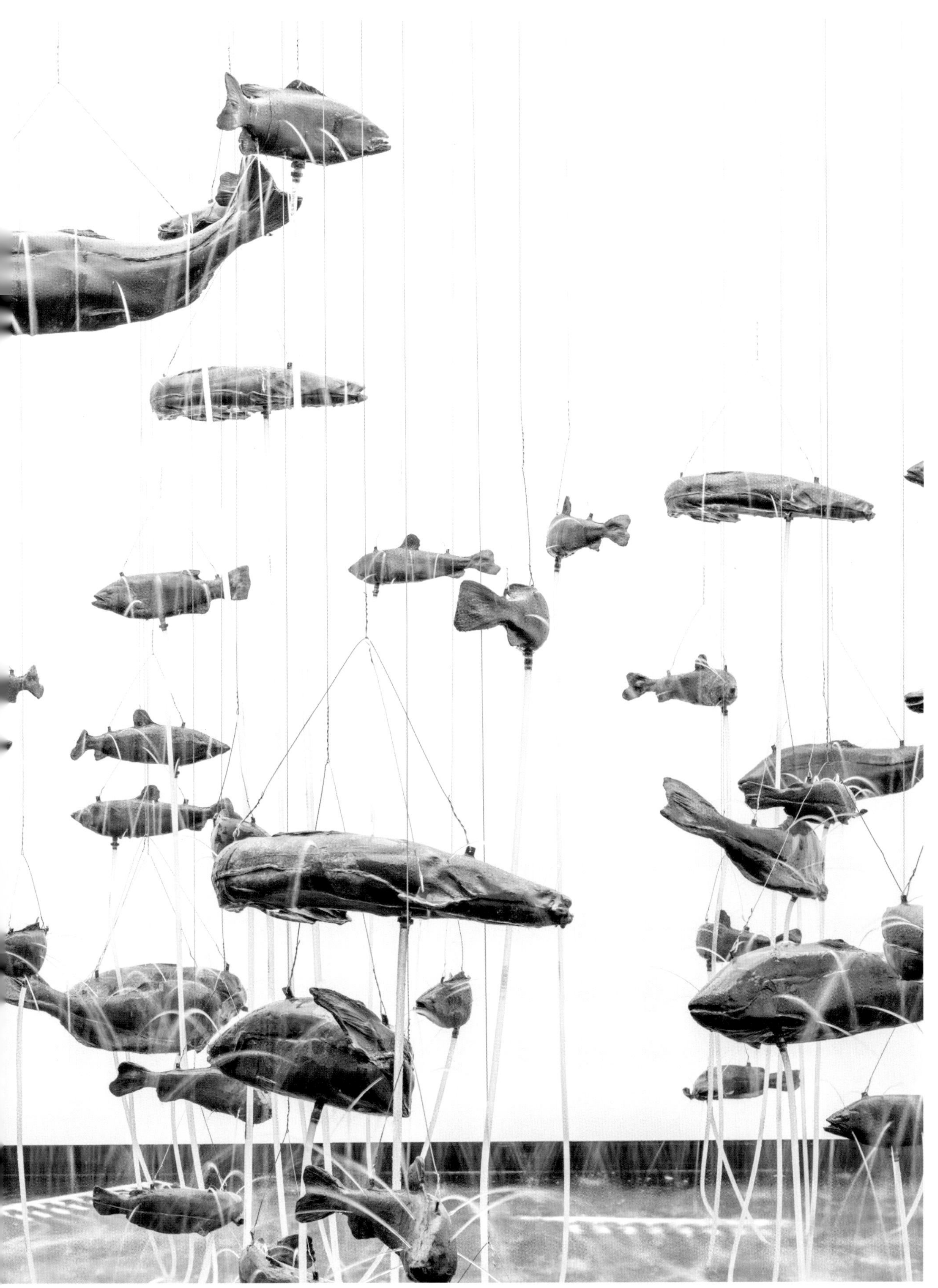

Holding onto it only makes you sick
2021
Concrete, oxide, silver, bronze, brass, ceramics, glass
Varying sizes

**the world*
2021
Stoneware, glaze, glass, wire, coated wire
Varying sizes

Kate Newby

Working with a variety of media including installation, textile, ceramics, casting and glass, Kate Newby (b. 1979, Auckland, New Zealand, based in New York) is a sculptor who is committed to exploring and putting pressure on the limits and nature of sculpture. As such, she is interested in not only space, volume, texture and materials, but where and how sculpture happens. Varying in scale, works are liable to take place ephemerally, as in the case of her ceramic skipping stones which she asks people to skip and have themselves photographed doing so, on the street in a given city, as in her concrete, poured puddles, or in the gallery proper, in subtly, but noticeably present architectural disruptions of the space itself. In every case the work bears a strong link to not just the everyday, but to the lived — it wants to experience as much as it generates experience, collecting and registering the traces of the passing world, which it incorporates and is incorporated into.

For *The Imaginary Sea*, Newby has conceived a number of interventions in the garden of the Villa Carmignac, which directly engage the immediate surrounding environment. One intervention consists of a signature puddle of colored concrete, inside of which the artist places smaller ceramic works such that the puddle resembles a patch of underwater flora. Other interventions consist of a ceramic wind chime, which sonically registers the invisible passage of one of the island's regular, immaterial visitors. C.S.

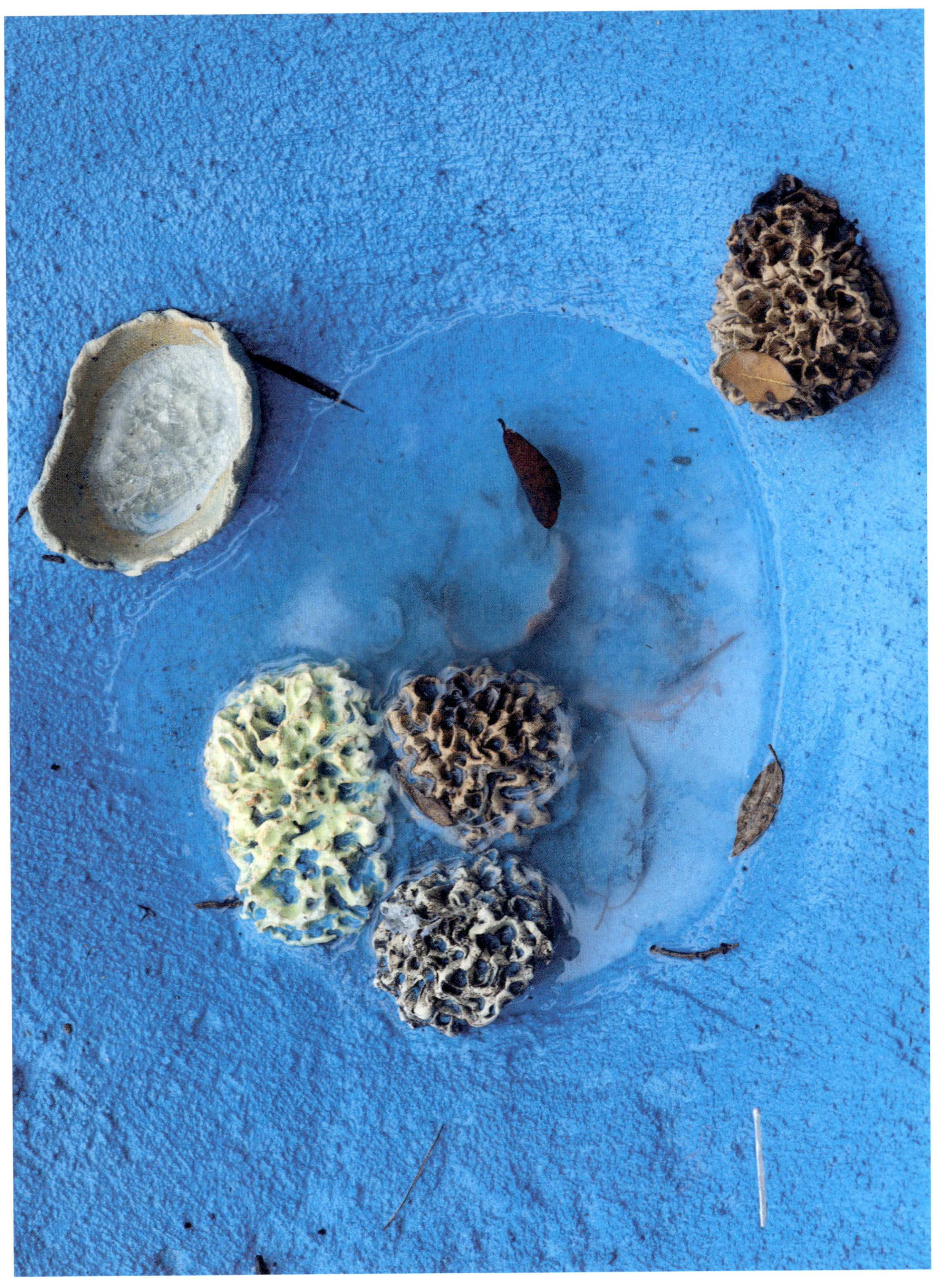

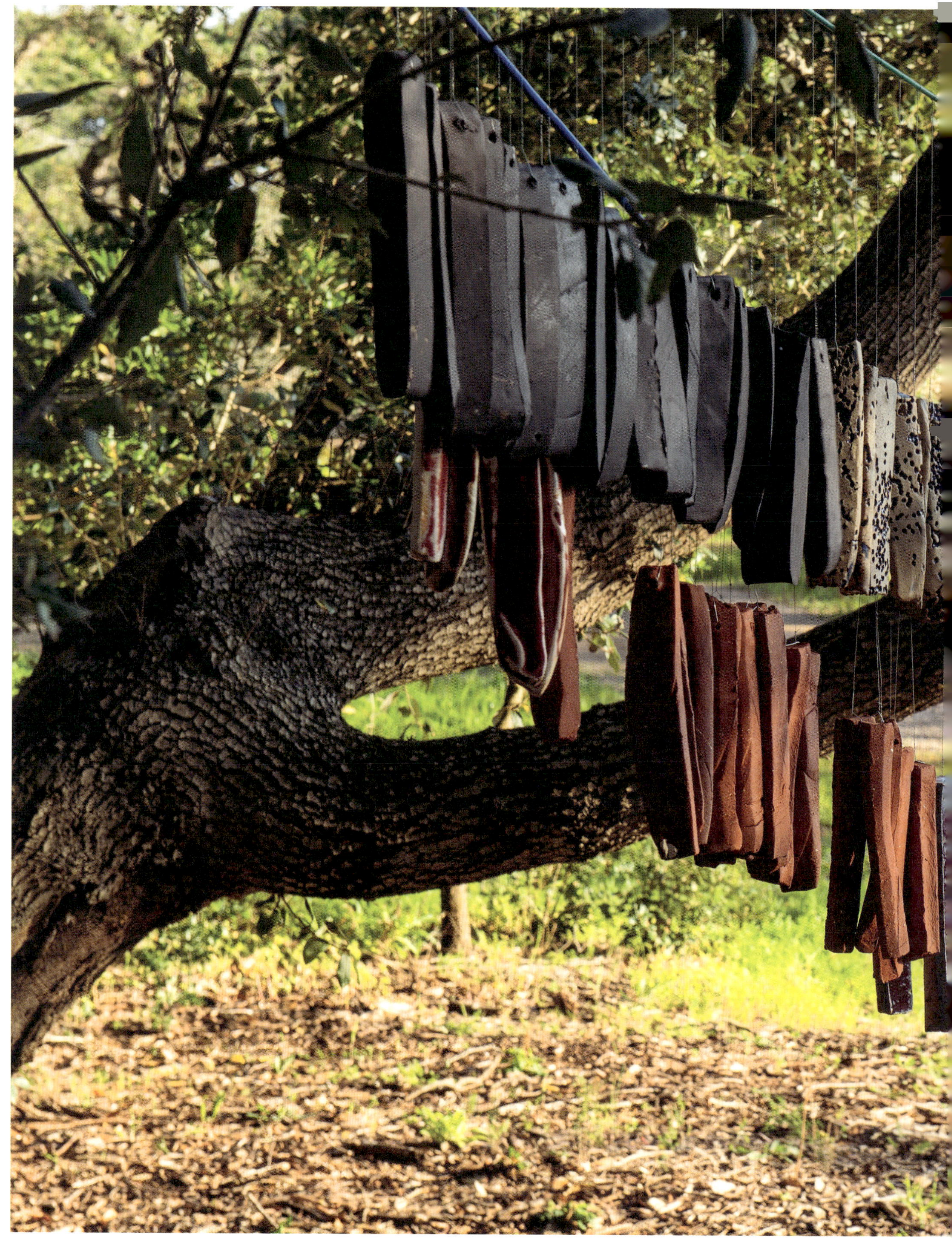

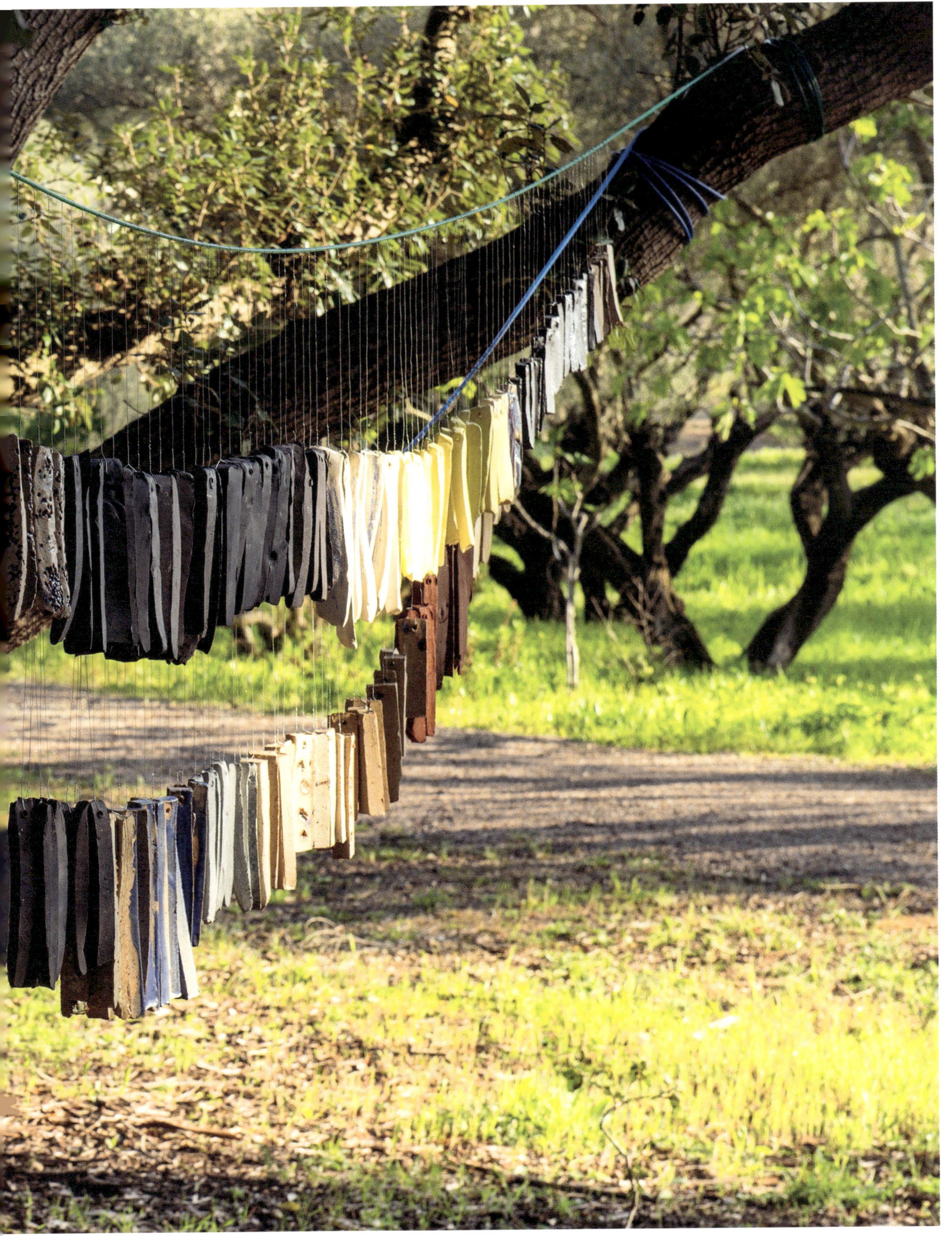

Shell
2014
Concrete sculpture
56 × 100 × 50 cm
22 × 39 × 19.5 in

Melik Ohanian

Melik Ohanian (b. 1969 Lyon, France) is a French artist of Armenian descent, and uses his background as a documentary filmmaker to explore not just his own lineage, but ideas like memory, identity, and borders writ large. He has framed mountainscapes like film stills, displayed his diary pages in lieu of an exhibition as a protest to the Iraq war, and imagined a cosmic collision between the Milky Way and Andromeda galaxies.

Shell (2014) is a sculptural work, though its themes of iteration and value are still rooted in the problems of image, and of capital. The cowrie shell is the first known object to be used as money, even before gold and silver. It was the main medium of trade in ancient China before reaching Africa via merchant ships and establishing itself as currency there. Ohanian's concrete iteration of the shell is enlarged to 100 times the scale of a cowrie. Its uncanny size bringing forth not only the tiny details and beauty of the original form, but perhaps this oversized ancient coin is poking fun at contemporary ideas of value — is bigger really better? C.C.M.

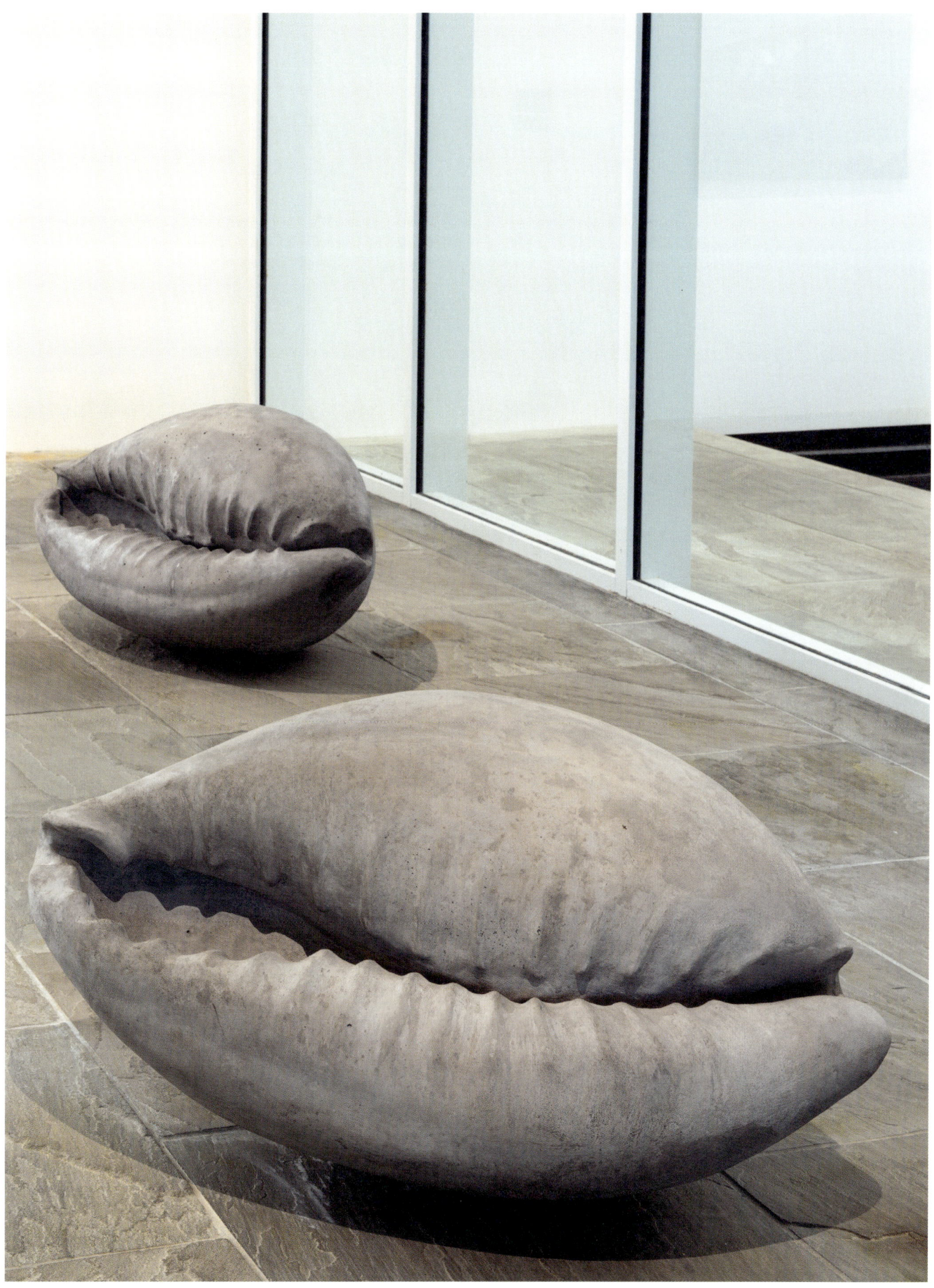

Sea Script
2020
Oil and modeling paste on canvas
180.3 × 127 cm
71 × 50 in

Ether
2017
Oil and faux pearls on canvas
180.3 × 127 cm
71 × 50 in

Alex Olson

Alex Olson (b. 1978, USA) lives and works in Los Angeles. Having studied sociology before painting, her academic background backbones her colorful optical experiments with a sense of play and undercurrents of ineffable emotion. Olson pulls from a cadre of signature techniques and formal elements, resulting in permutations that tussle with both the viewer's eye and the artists own historical references, which range from Surrealism and Op Art, to idiosyncratic signposts from the artist's hometown of Manchester-by-the-Sea in Massachusetts, USA.

In Ether (2017), bristly curls of paint in dark jewel tones dance up and across the face of the canvas. The swath of crescents is buttressed on both sides by straighter strokes that sprout up from, and zig zag across the inky black background. The tessellation of strokes evokes a swatch of midcentury wallpaper and an undersea landscape. A delicate scattering of faux pearls further attests to the picture's aquatic affinities while adding yet another layer of depth for the eye to juggle. *Sea Script* (2020) contains many of Olson's signature marks — often inspired by textiles and graphic design, always self-evident records of their own construction. The result is a riotous euphony of movement and color, much like the sea itself. C.C.M.

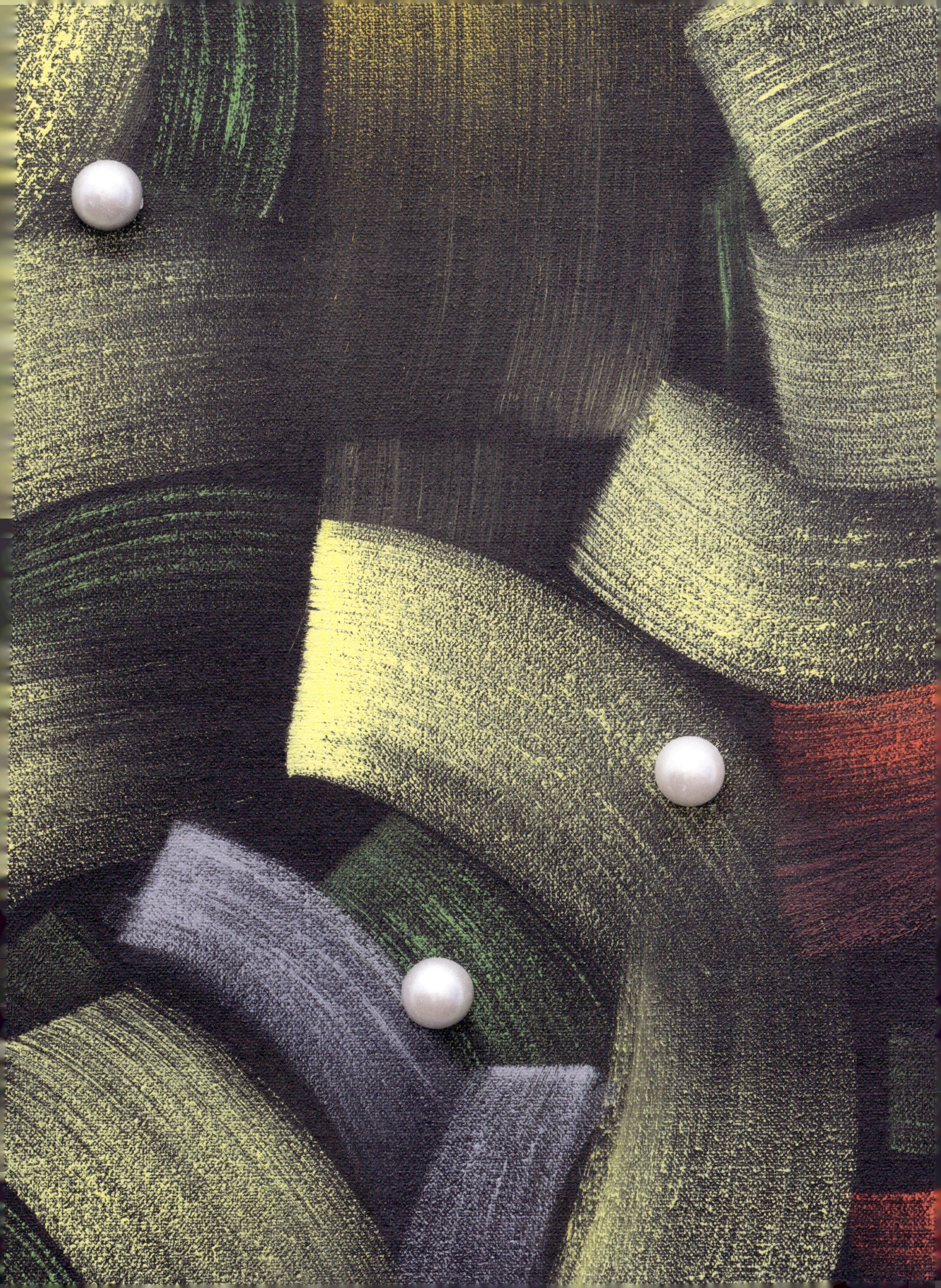

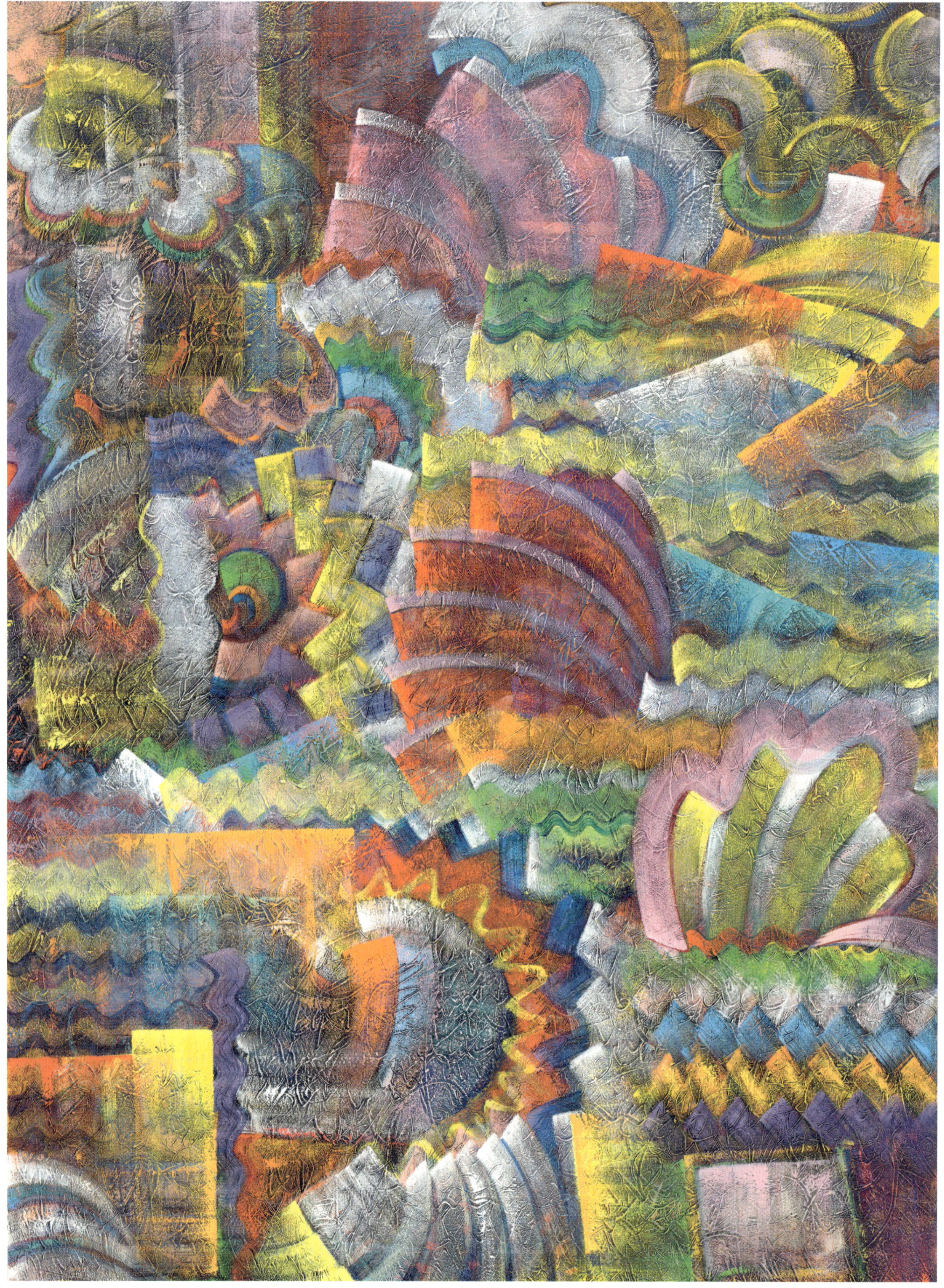

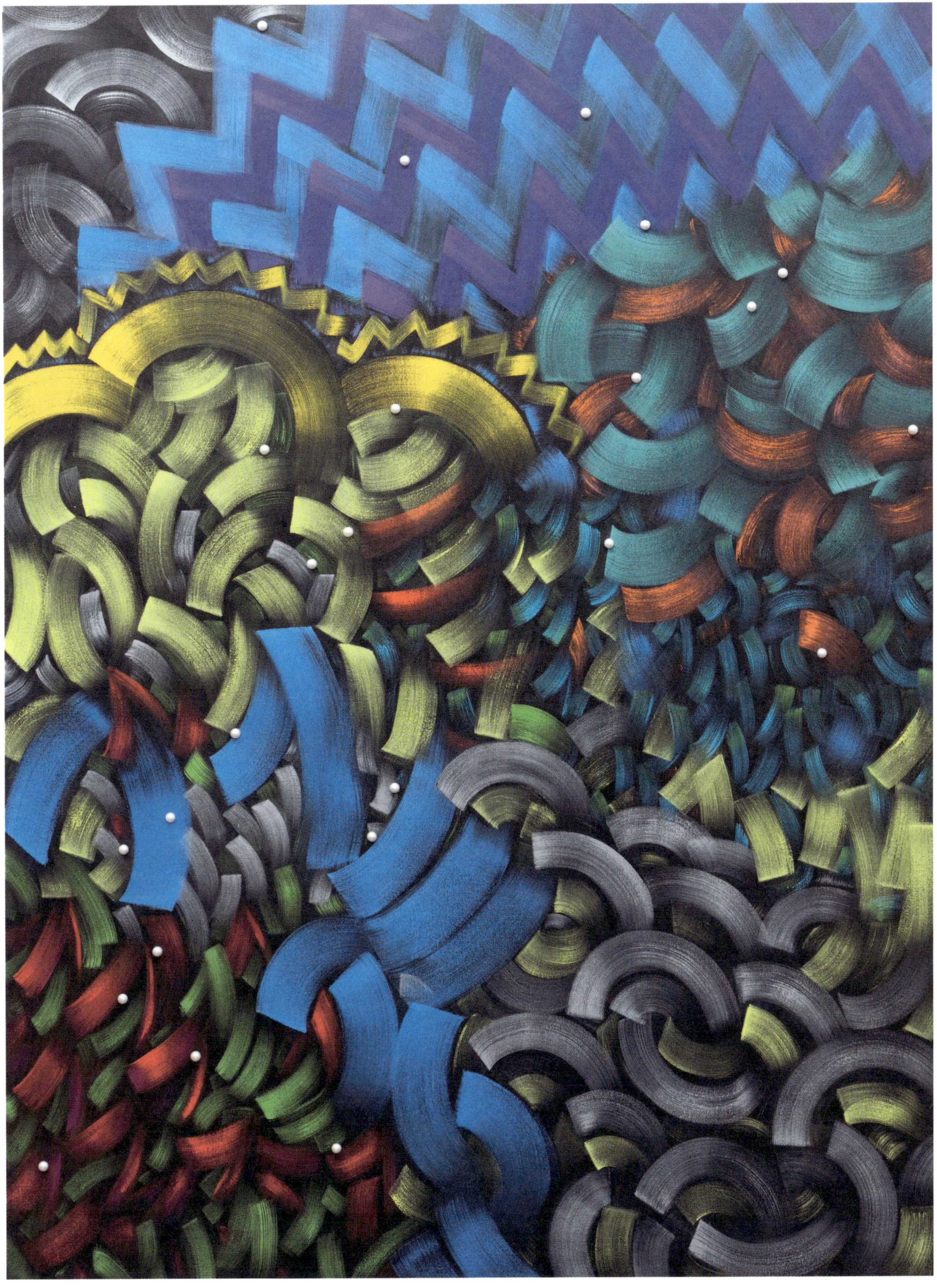

Spume 5
2003
Polyurethane foam
57.15 × 104.14 × 154.94 cm
22.5 × 41 × 61 in

Spume 6
2003
Polyurethane foam
109.22 × 162.56 × 101.6 cm
43 × 64 × 40 in

Gabriel Orozco

A poet of the political everyday, geometrist of the organic, and peripatetic philosophical gamester, artist Gabriel Orozco found himself in Brooklyn with polyurethane molds, not intending to make a sculpture of any particular shape. When he stuck these together just so, they came together in ways that were both organic and inorganic. Whether prehistoric creatures or post-modern robots, they look ready to swim. A *spume* is the froth or foam found on waves, often in the wake of a whale, a creature that's found form in other works by the artist, particularly *Mobile Matrix* (2006), an assembly of a gray whale skeleton held together with a metal armature and patterned with a graphic drawing to hang in the vast atrium of José Vasconcelos Library in Mexico City. In the *Spume* series, the inorganic finds organic form; while in *Mobile Matrix*, the inorganic pattern renews and elevates this creature's bones into something new and powerful, all and both majestic creatures swimming the imaginary sea. A.B.

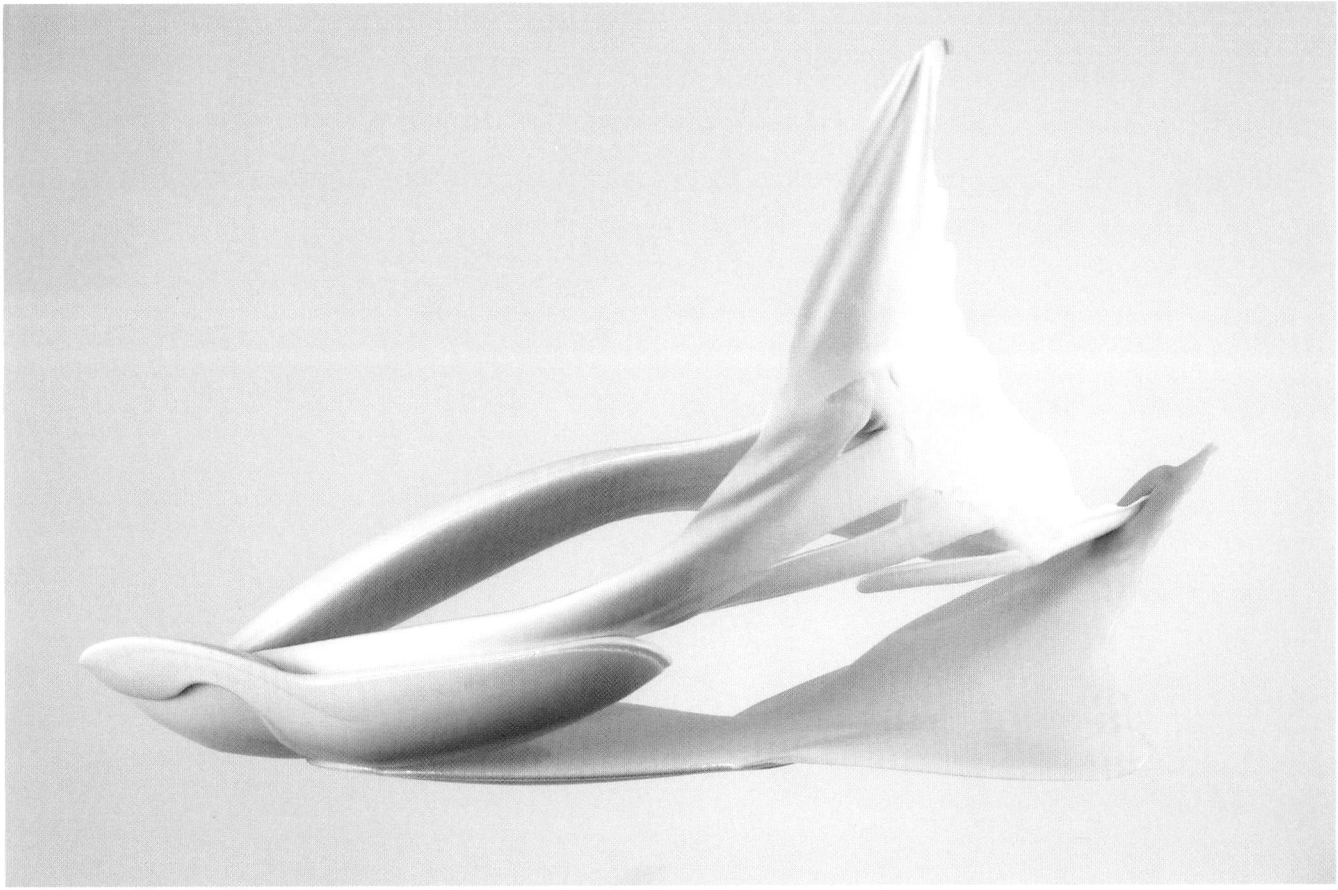

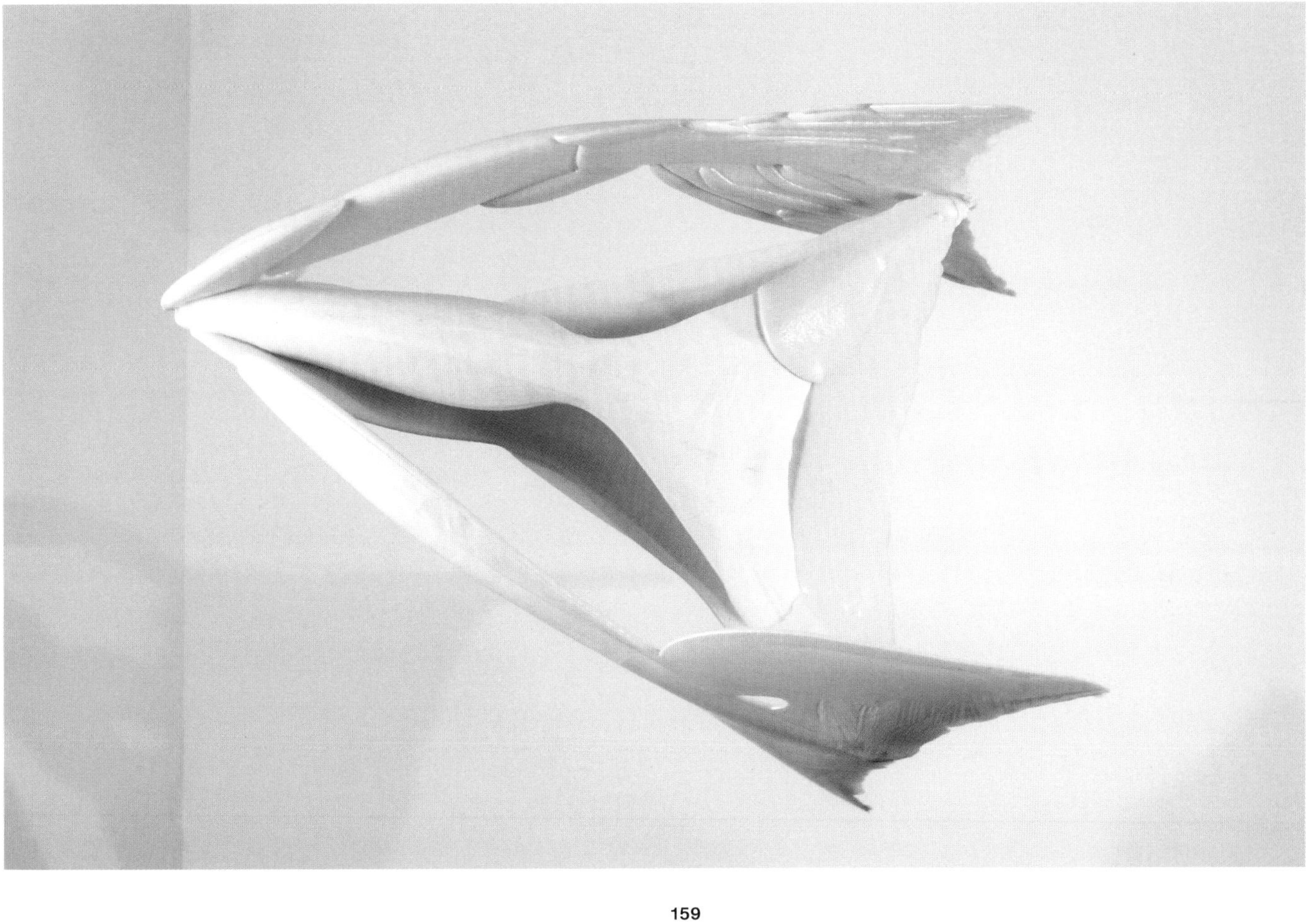

Buste de l'Hippocampe
1931
Unique vintage print
141 × 98 cm
56 × 39 in

Jean Painlevé

Jean Painlevé (20 November 1902 – 2 July 1989) occupies a very special position in this exhibition. As a pioneer of underwater filmmaking and photography, not to mention as an amateur scientist who made over 200 notoriously unclassifiable films in his lifetime, Painlevé exists at the crossroads of the poetic and scientific in his will to portray and understand marine life. Initially esteemed by his scientific peers as an unmethodical crank, he has come to be regarded as an important filmmaker in his own right over the years. His depiction of sea creatures, ranging from everything from the sea horse to the sea urchin to the love life of the octopus, is, at times, characterized by a tendency to anthropomorphize, and at others, to scientifically apprehend, and finally, at others, by an impenetrable sense of mystery. As such, his idiosyncratic spirit suffuses virtually every aspect of *The Imaginary Sea*, energetically inhabiting its many double entendres.

The Imaginary Sea features Painlevé's first publicly screened film, *La pieuvre* (The Octopus), 1928, as well as a selection of photographs. Allegedly the origin of his interest in studying zoology, the octopus, first encountered by Painlevé in Brittany at the age of nine, is here depicted in all fascinating strangeness as escapee of dreams and narrow places as well as something quite close to us, which courts, feeds, fights, mates, and dies. Meanwhile, the selection of photos consists largely of details of sea life, oneiric in their capacity to evoke and obscure the entirety of whatever is portrayed, such as a crab's pincer, the penumbral tentacles of an octopus, or an extreme close up of a seahorse's head. C.S.

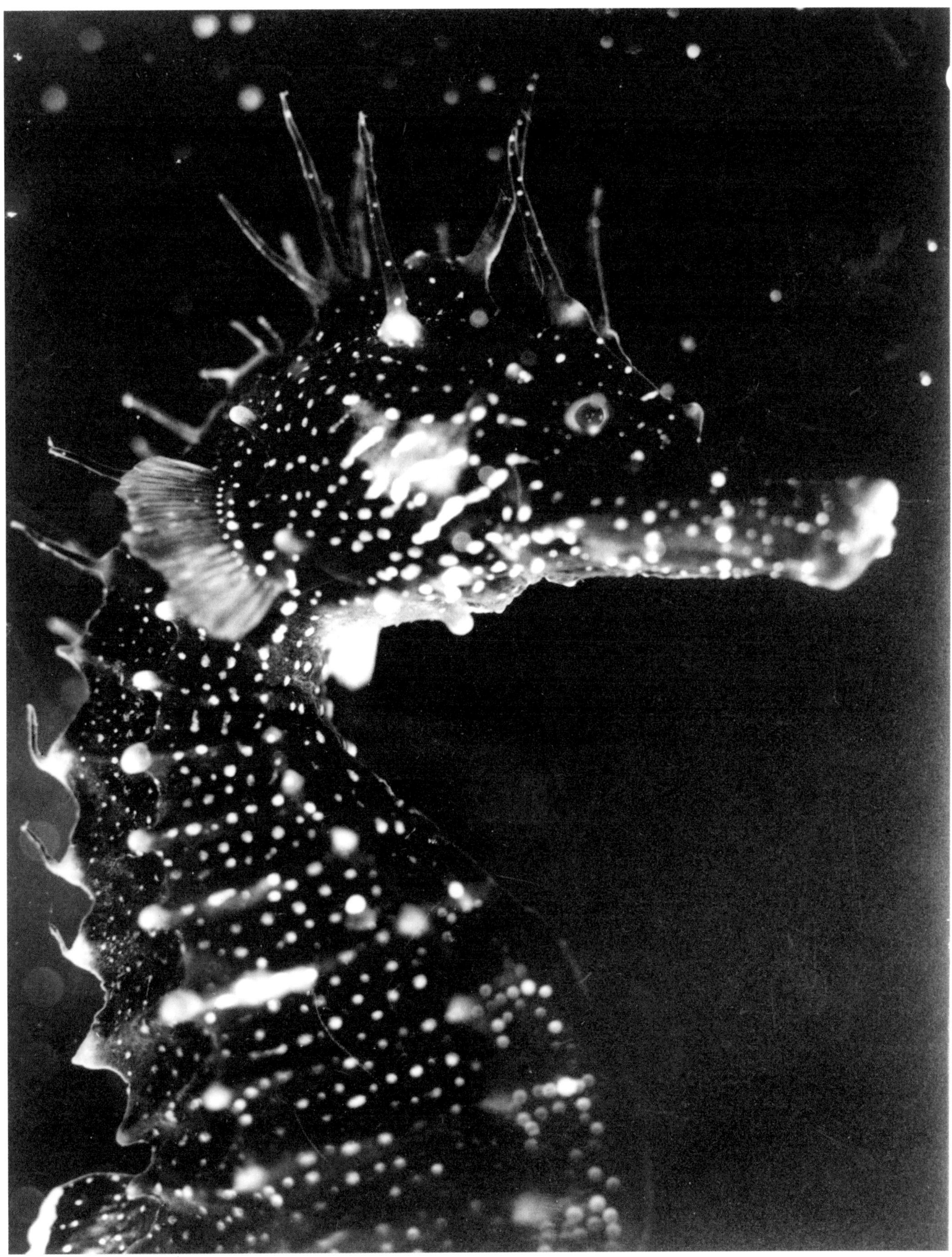

La Pieuvre
1928
Video
35 mm, stained black and white/silent, 12 '

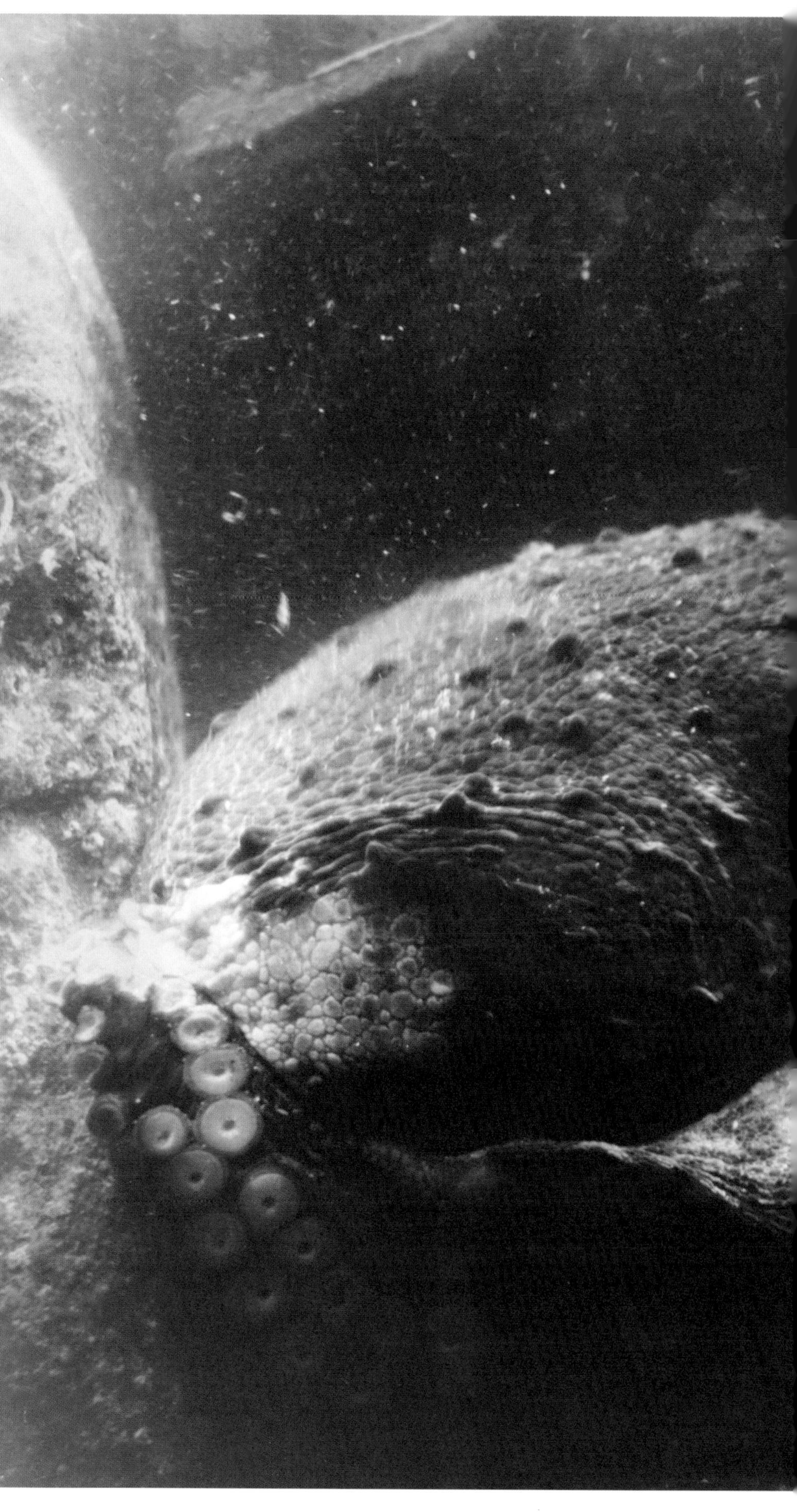

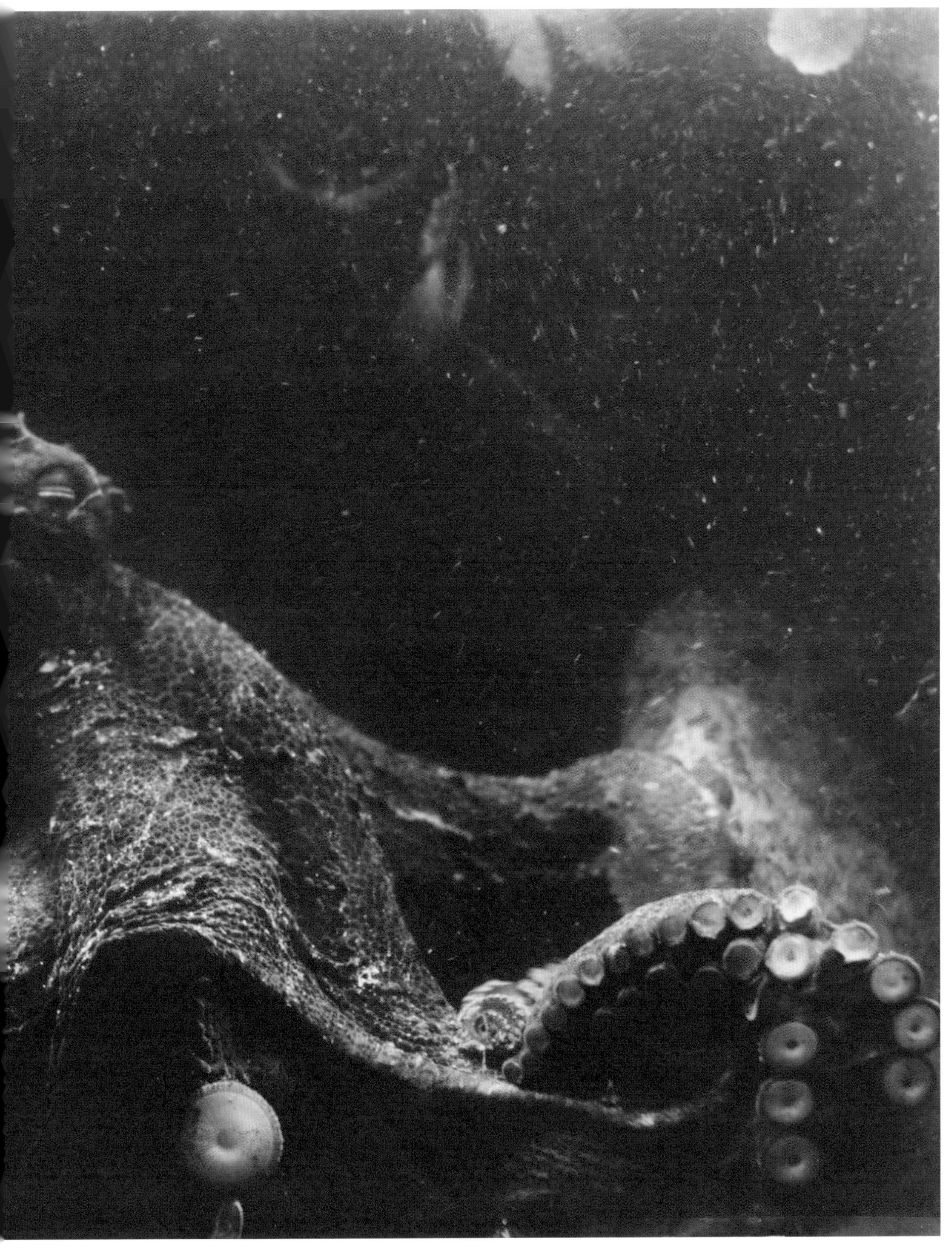

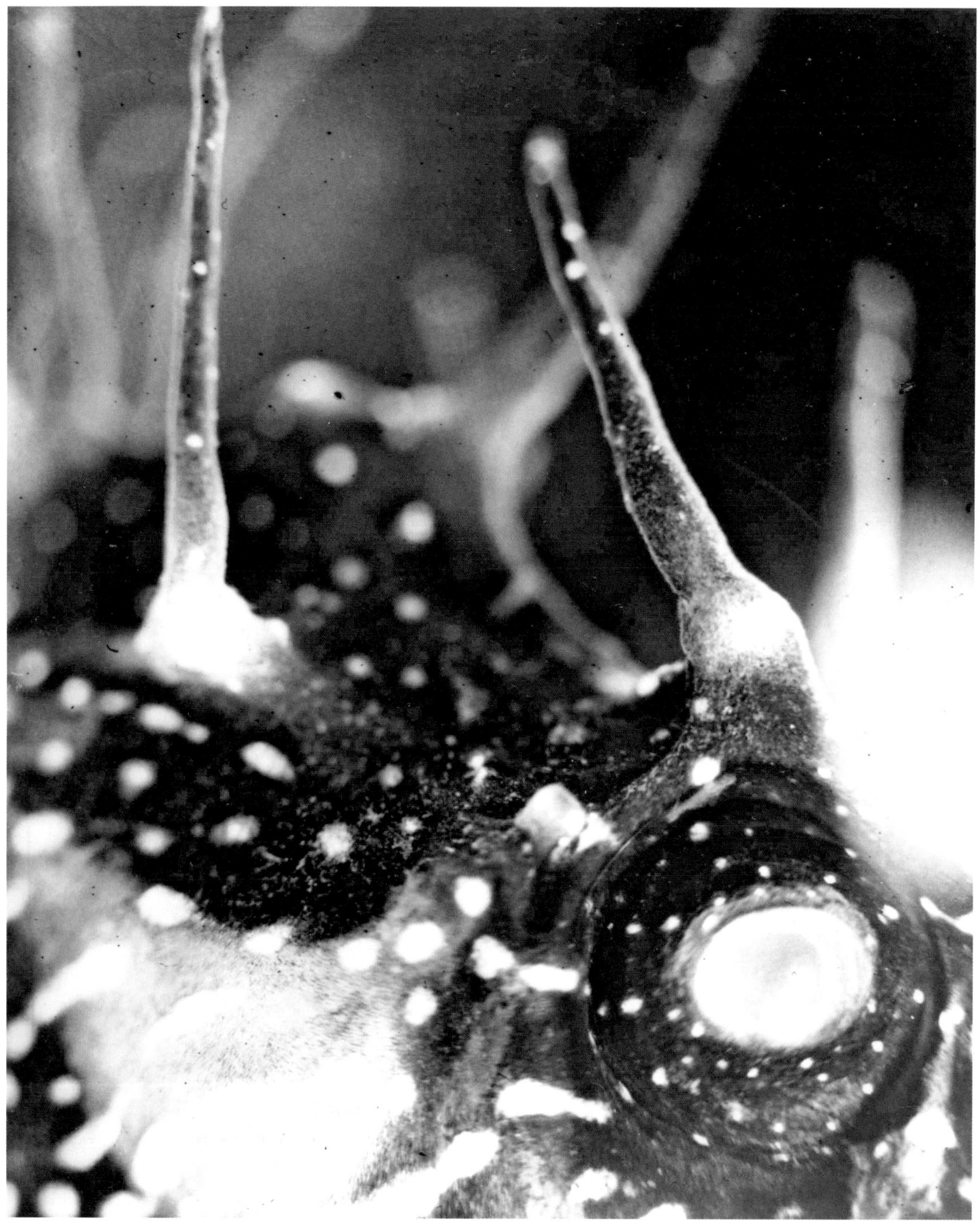

→
Tentacules de la Pieuvre
1927
Printed on Hahnemühle glossy fine art
59 × 77 cm
23 × 30 in

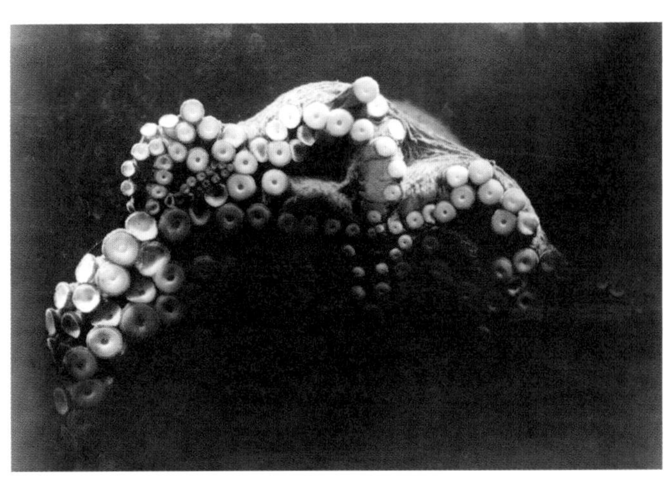

←
Tête d'Hippocampe d'Arcachon
1931
Printed on Hahnemühle glossy fine art
77 × 64.5 cm
30 × 25 in

↓
Pince de homard
1929
Printed on Hahnemühle glossy fine art
77 × 60 cm
30 × 24 in

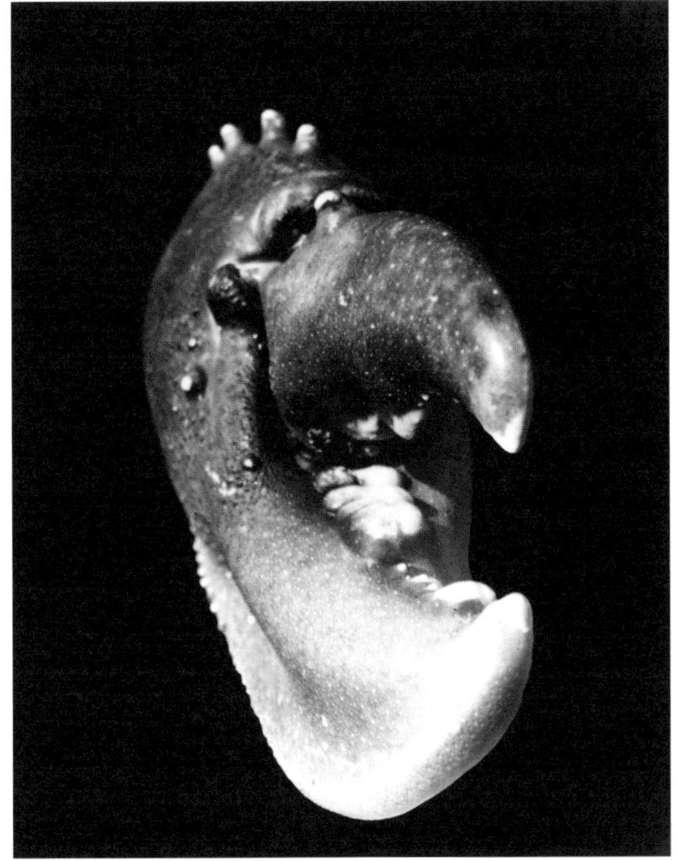

Sans titre
2000-2001
Silicone, silk, pearls and lace
59 × 90 × 40 cm
23 × 35 × 16 in

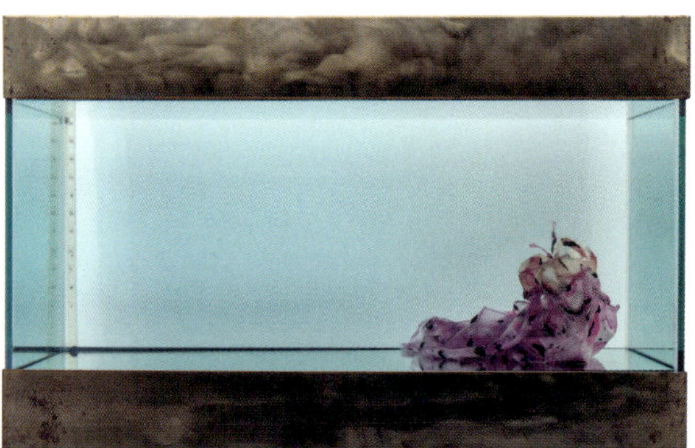

Bruno Pelassy

Bruno Pelassy (1966, Vientiane, Laos – 2002, Nice, France) made a singular, if difficult-to-classify contribution to the history of French art at the end of the 20th century. Diagnosed with HIV at the age of twenty-one in 1987, Pelassy's entire subsequent career and artistic production was marked by the impact of AIDS on his life. His domestic-sized baroque production, which was largely sculptural, took its cues as much from the legacy of kitsch and camp as the films of Kenneth Anger. Objects, such as those in the series *Bestioles*, are fabricated from wigs, feathers, textiles and repurposed mechanical toys, while others are fashioned out of jewelry, glass pearls and velvet, look like fetish objects, or ultimately, religious reliquaries. A sense of inevitable evanescence is built into a good part of what he produced, such as his video, *Sans titre, Sang titre, Cent titres* (1995), understood as his aesthetic and political manifesto, which was recorded on VHS, and therefore meant to gradually degrade and erase after each viewing. Another series, *Créatures* (2000-2001) — an example of which is featured in the *The Imaginary Sea* — made at the very end of his life, was particularly fragile and vulnerable to dissolution. These consist of delicate fusions of silicon, silk, lace, pearls and crystals, which are placed in water-filled, mirrored aquariums, and which float, bend and twist with the slow, muted lyricism of a semi-transparent underwater organism. C.S.

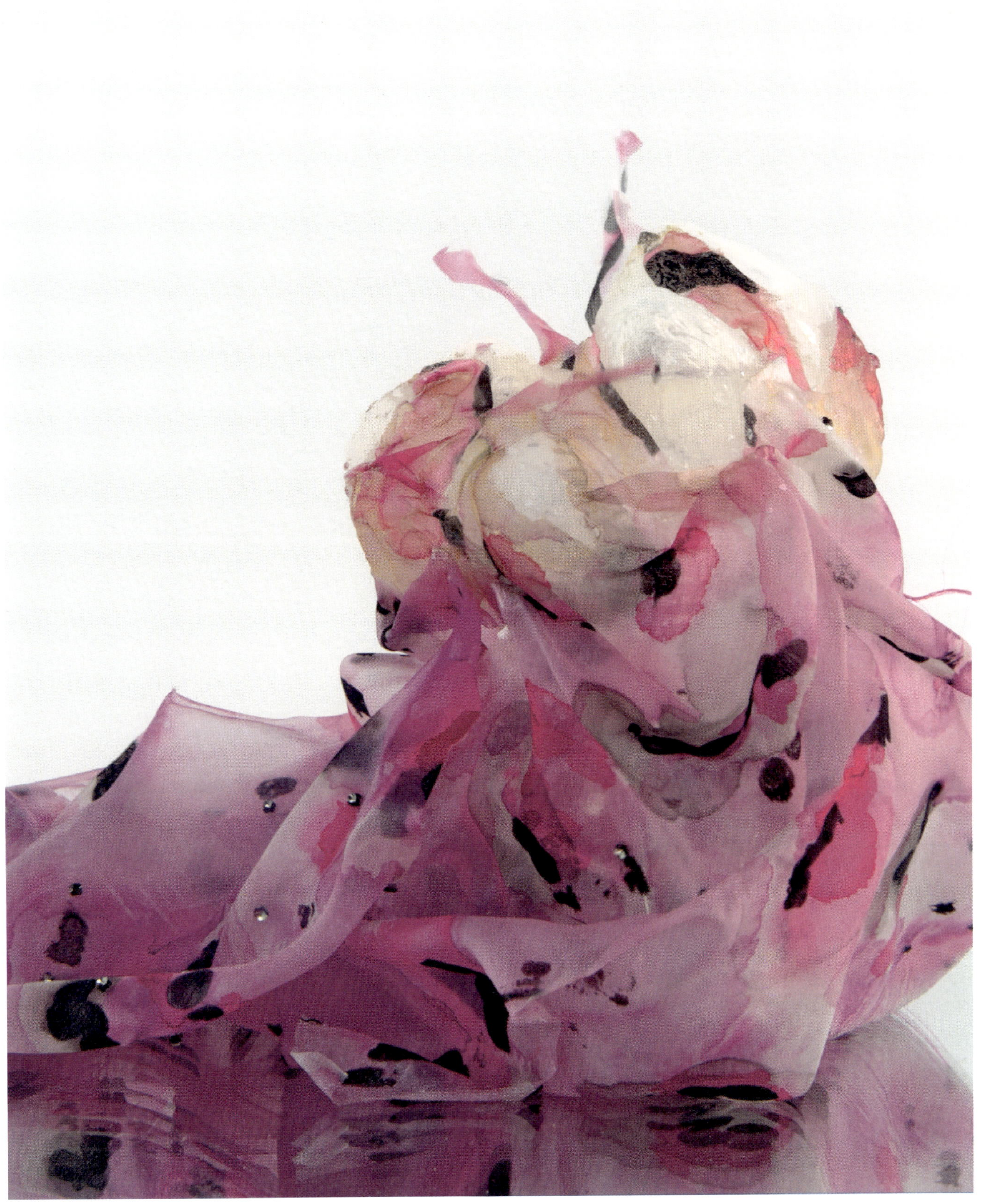

Teneen Albaher/
Sea Dragon Relief
2020
Styrofoam, steel, acrylic paint, wood
173 × 268 × 51.5 cm
68 × 105 × 20 in

Lin May Saeed

Lin May Saeed (b. 1973, Würzburg, Germany; lives and works in Berlin) makes sculptures, sculptural reliefs, drawings, works on paper, and video. Known to use non-traditional materials, such as and especially styrofoam, Saeed's work is directly linked to and thematically informed by her interest in animals and her commitment to animal activism. Her work deals with the exploitation of animals, their depiction, liberation, and potentially harmonious relationship with human beings, and the self-seeking meanness of the latter. Saeed's iconographic frame of reference is rich and varied. It includes Egyptian statuary, Greco-Roman sculpture, and scientific and natural history museum displays, among others. Generally eschewing noble materials, such as marble and wood, she is drawn to styrofoam precisely because it is a fundamentally ugly and difficult material, which she seeks to aesthetically redeem, despite and because of its essentially ruinous use of and impact upon nature. Hers is a sculpture in which there is virtually no gap between her political convictions and the formal and conceptual considerations of her medium.

In a new, large-scale relief in styrofoam, plaster and pigment, Saeed brings to *The Imaginary Sea* a submerged urban environment. The work imagines a post-current sea level civilization in which sea life is free to exuberantly and abundantly exist, with a surface brightly populated by a menagerie of seahorses. C.S.

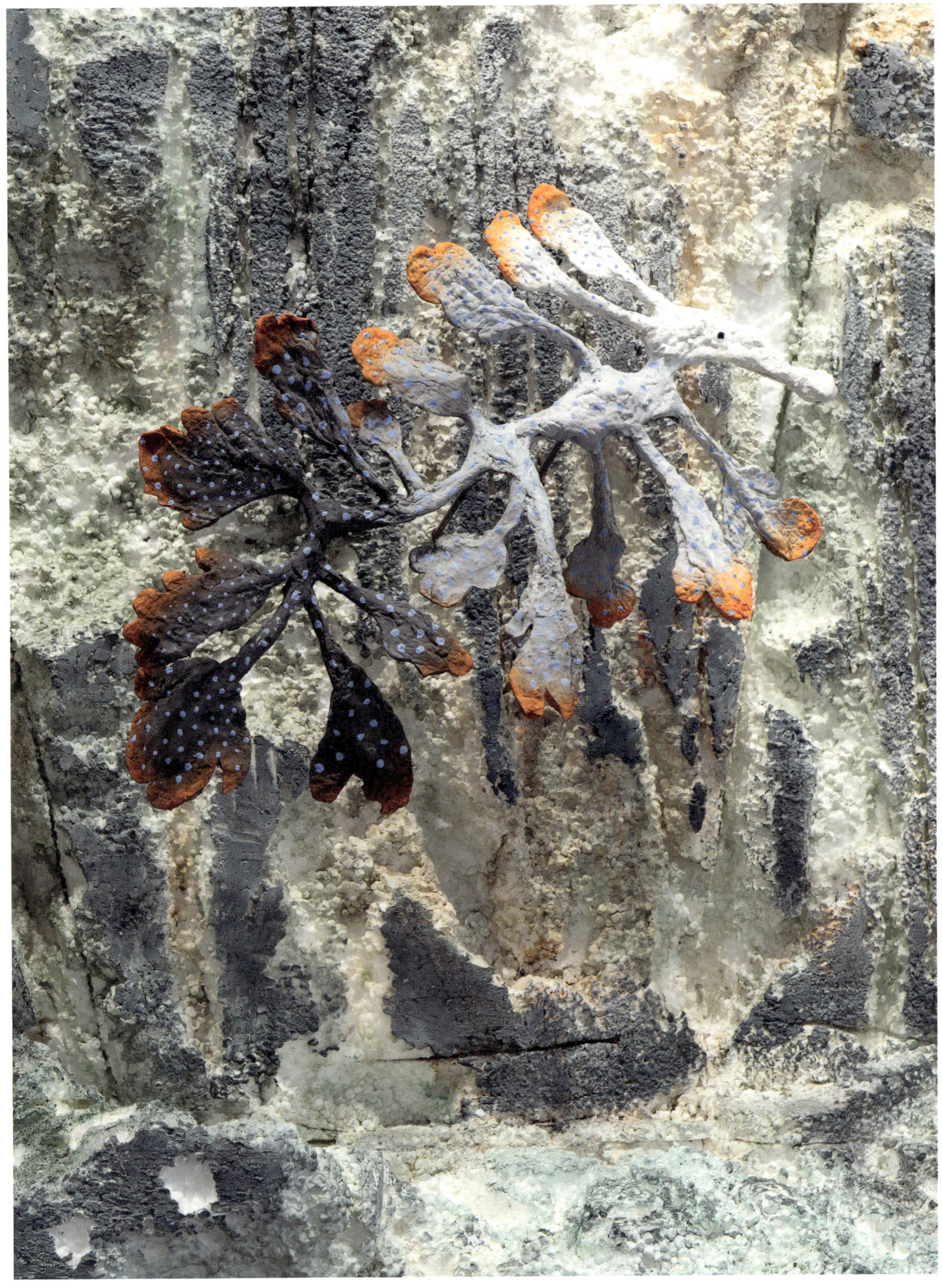

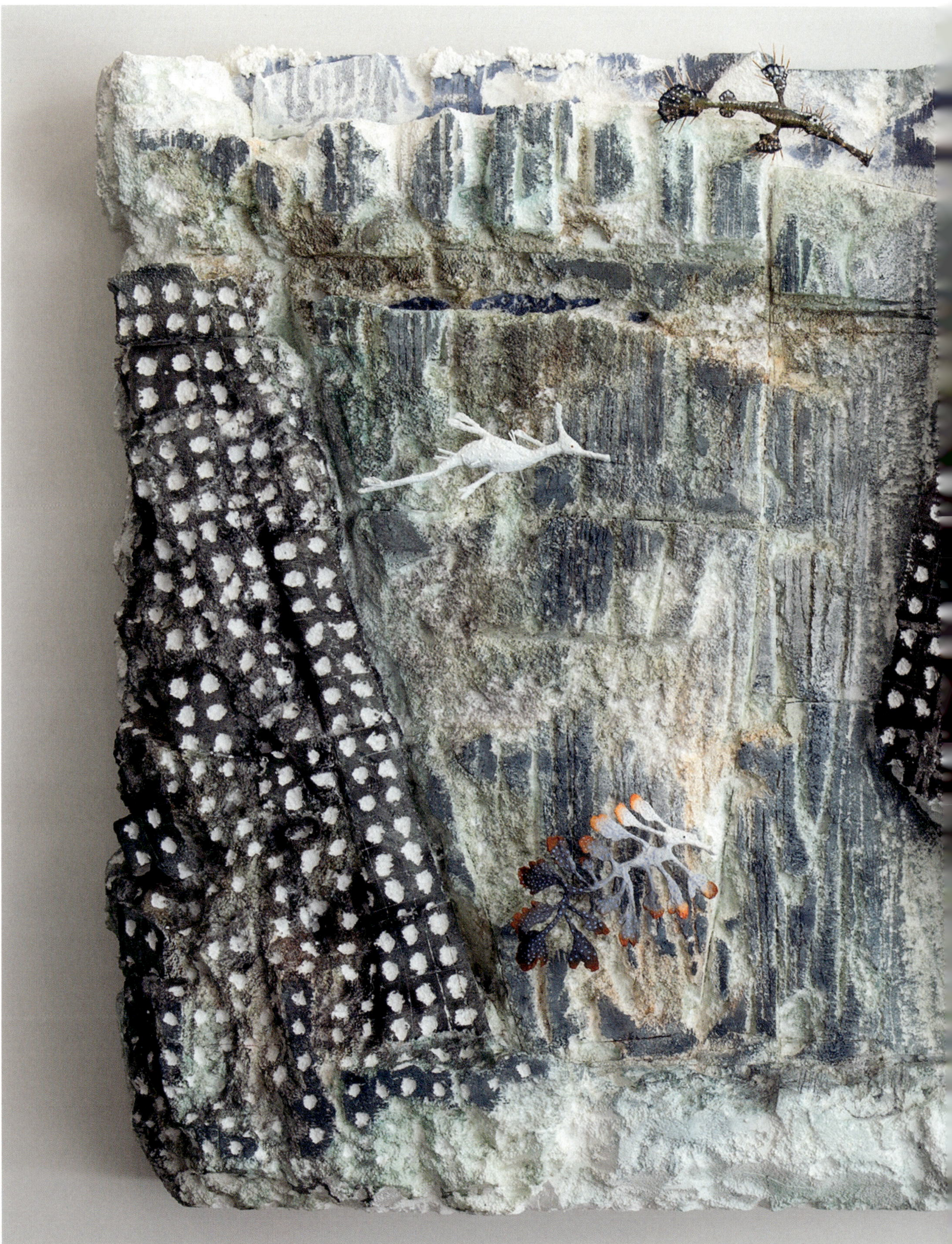

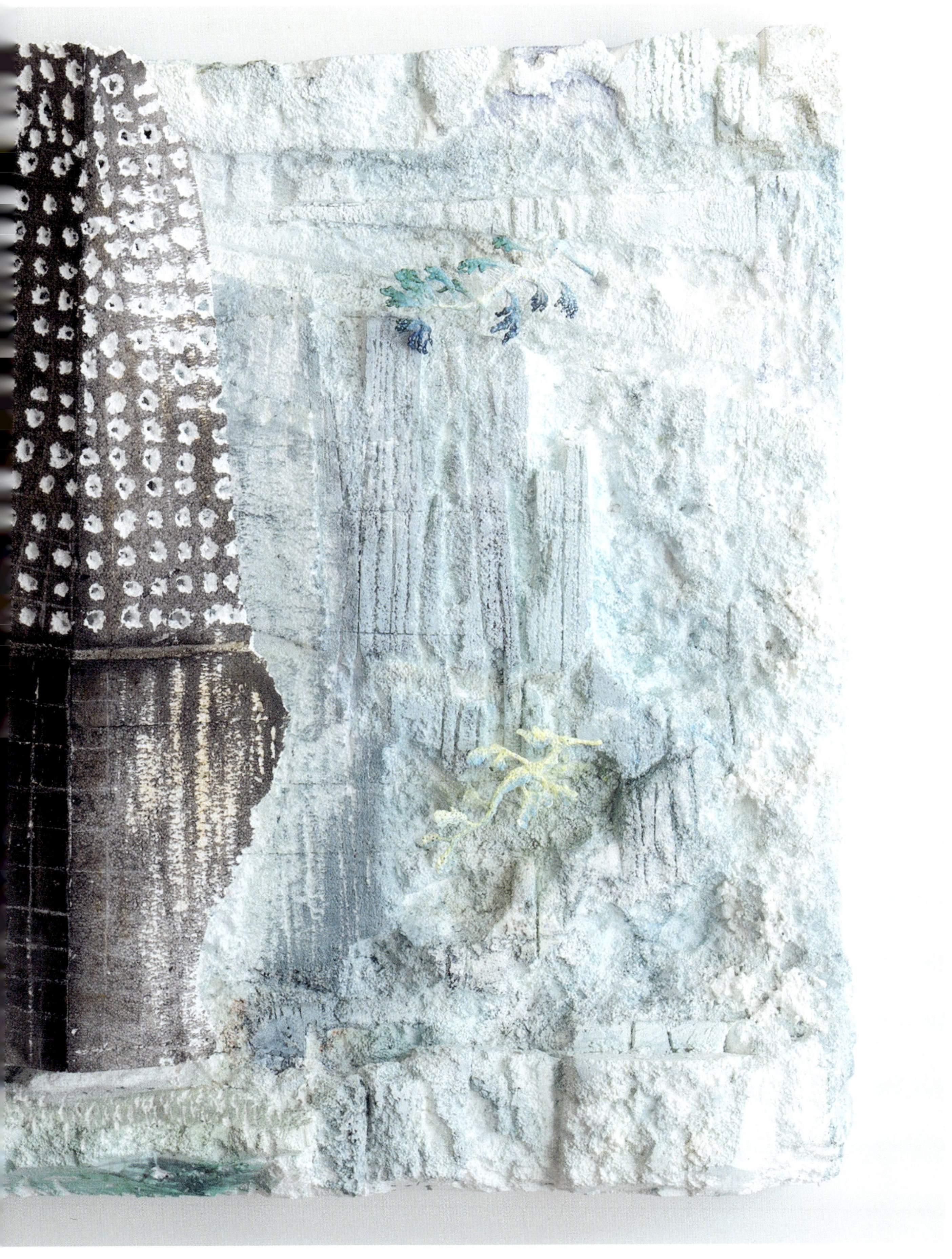

Leaves swim
2011
Mini DV transfered
on DVD, colors, silent
2 min. 30 sec., loop

Shimabuku

Shimabuku (b. 1969, Kobe, Japan) is a tour guide of the everyday, showing us the uncanny and poetic potentials tucked into the nooks and crannies of peripheral experience. He has sharpened a laptop computer into a functioning axe, photographed deceptively similar fruits, and brought bags of ice to Japanese snow monkeys raised in Texas, wondering if their play might reveal some secreted recollection of their ancestors' home climate. His work contains profound epistemological inquiries, often wrapped in a playful shrug: *what do we know?*

Leaves Swim (2011) is video footage of a *phycodurus eques*, also known as a leafy seadragon, engaged in a louche, balletic dance with the invisible currents of the water. The directness of Shimabuku's gaze bubbles up all kinds of questions about how and why we classify living things the way we do. The movement of the dragon is doing its own ontological dance with the title of the video itself — which might be understood as an assertion of the quiet magic that can exist in the twinship of flora and fauna. C.C.M.

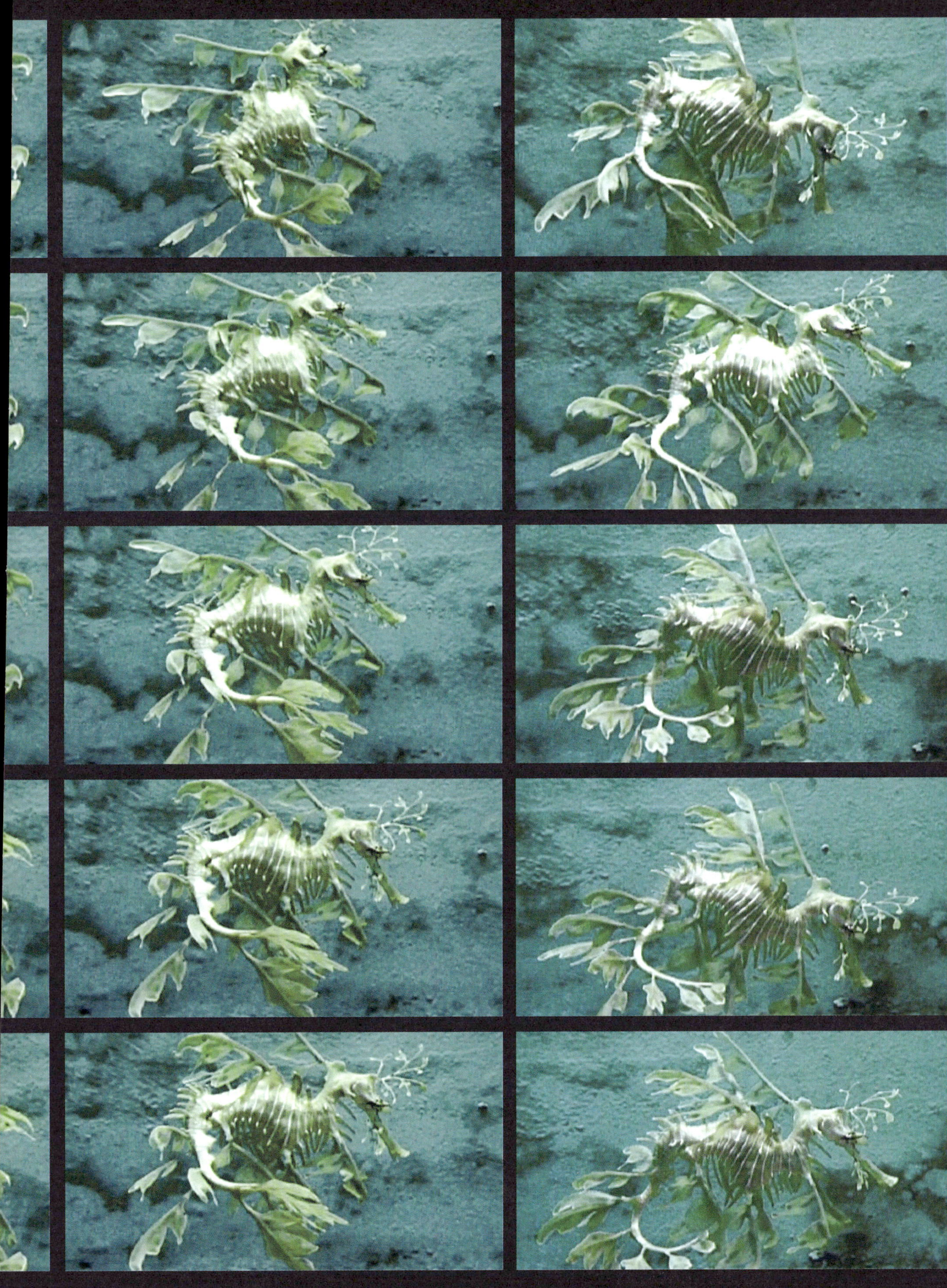

Untitled
2017
Fish, metal, plastic
163 × 30 × 23 cm
64 × 12 × 9 in

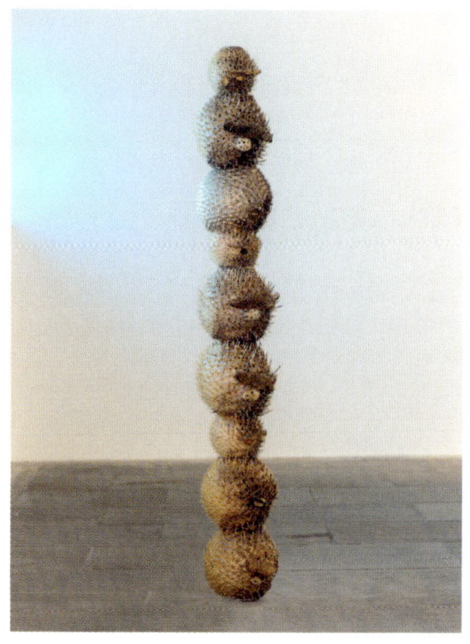

Michael E. Smith

Michael E. Smith (b. 1977, Detroit; based in Providence, Rhode Island, USA) has earned a well-deserved reputation as one of the most radical sculptors of his generation for his dark, aesthetic prognostications. An evoker of aftermath, human fragmentation, and urban desolation, he has a strong penchant for unusual materials ranging from plastics, protective gear, automotive components, foams, animal parts, to industrially produced comestibles, human bone, and textiles. When not re-contextualizing a given object or quite simply disfiguring it, his sculptures are often the byproduct of strange and improbable conjunctions (to wit: a piece of human skull inserted into a fragment of a laptop computer; weed whacker engines dipped in oatmeal; clarinets stuffed into PCV piping). His work brings to mind the absorbed and idiosyncratic industry of the garage-bound tinkerer, yet contrary to the harmless stereotype, his variety of tinkering borders on the psychopathic.

Smith presents a variety of works here which deal with the animal kingdom and the sea. A small, seemingly quaint photo depicts a group of oddly colored goldfish which, it just so happens, is an appropriated image of the first genetically modified, commercially available animals on the market roughly a decade ago. Meanwhile, a couple of starfish have been dismembered and reconfigured to resemble a geometric cube, while a group of blowfish have been totemically stacked upon one another, as if to ironically collapse the nature/culture divide. C.S.

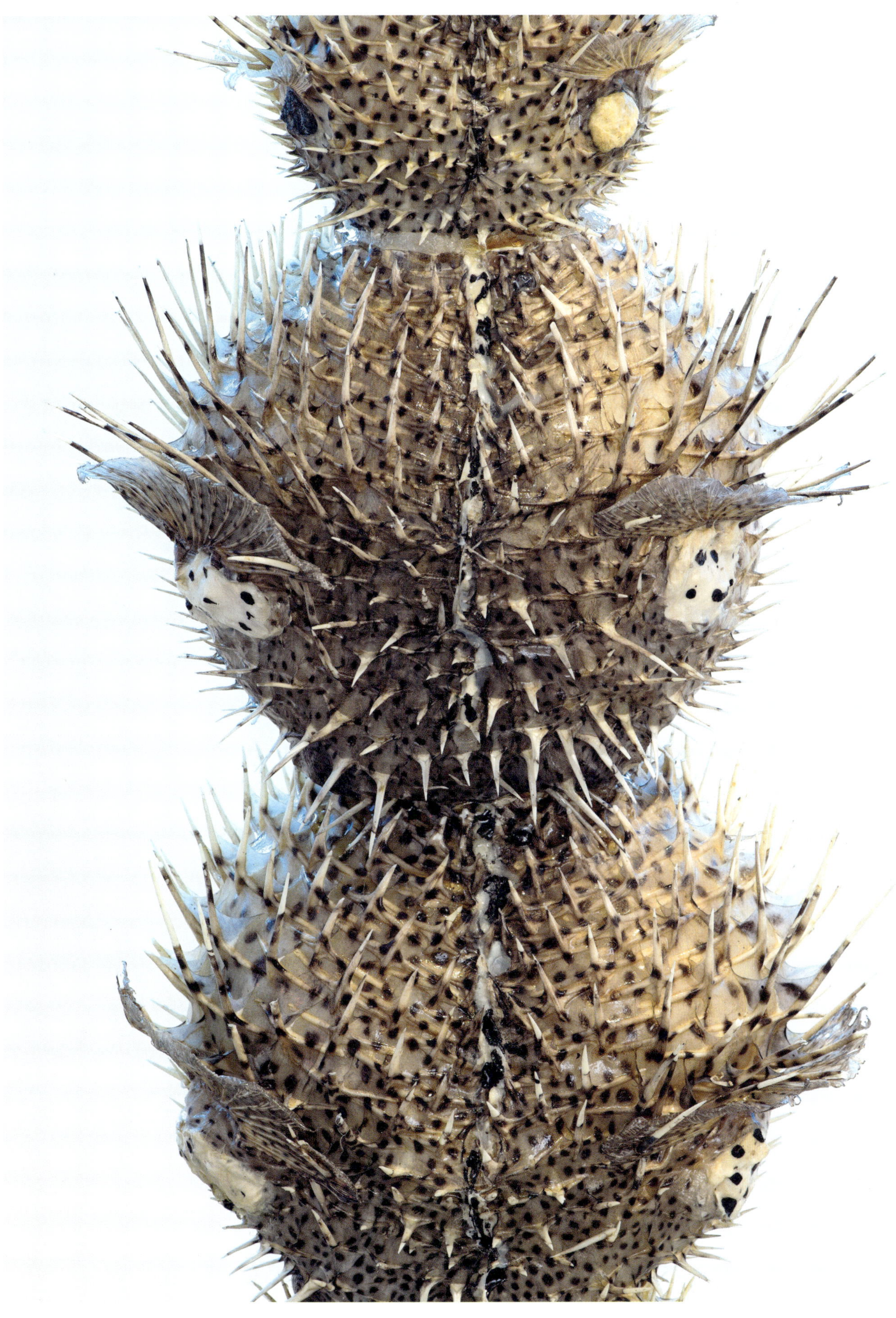

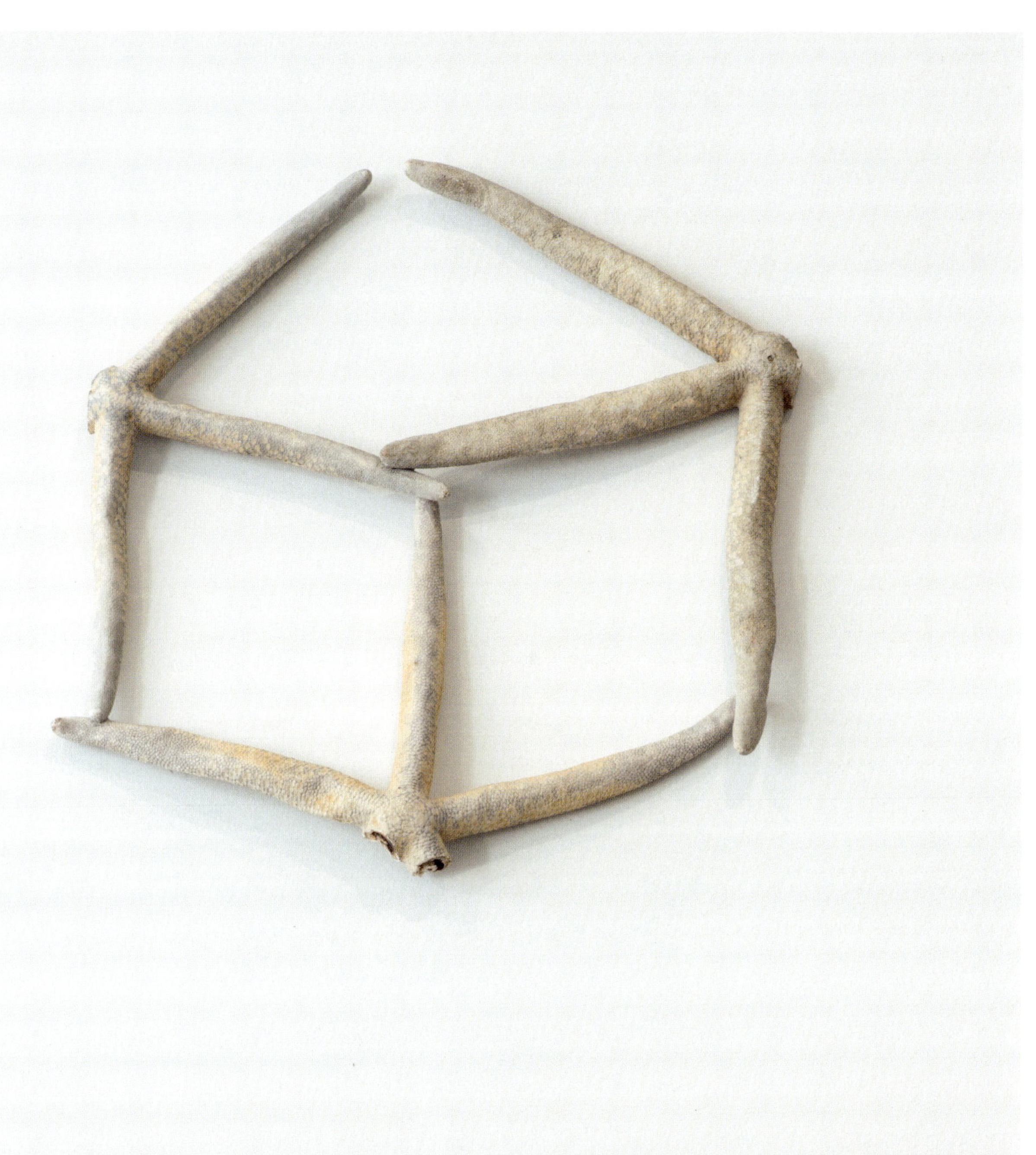

←
Untitled
2018
Starfish
50 × 50 cm
20 × 20 in

↓
Untitled
2011
Archival pigment print
18.41 × 22.23 cm
7 × 9 in

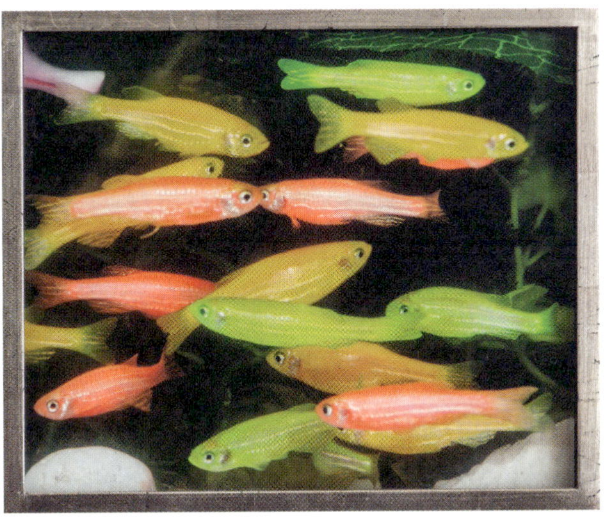

La Lune virevoltante
2021
On-site project

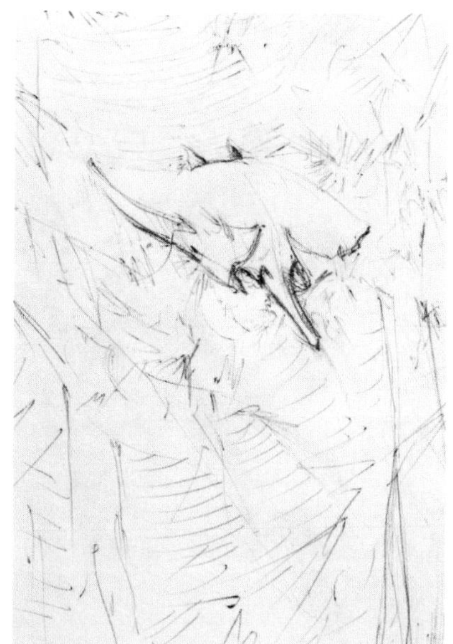

Martin Soto Climent

Martin Soto Climent (b. 1977 Mexico City; based in Tepoztlan, Mexico) has gift for foregrounding the sensuality of materials. In what he makes, anything is liable to assume a sensual, fetish quality. Departing from an ethical principle of low impact consumption, Soto Climent's production is often characterized by the temporary modification of readymade materials, which range from women's clothing, to window blinds, to old black-and-white photography magazines, among others. Although used for photographic reproduction, a sculpture, or an installation, they are often capable of being restored to their original function. No matter how artificial his materials and forms may seem, nature, as a generative principle, is never far from what he makes.

The relationship to nature and the cycles of the Moon and its influence on the ocean are crucial to his presentation in *The Imaginary Sea*. Entitled *La Lune virevolante* (2021), his outdoor intervention project consists of a group of floating creatures, strung between trees, like so many indescribable beings. Their forms are inspired by the evolving reflection of the full moon on water, and the way in which it is formed and unformed, ultimately flickering away into its shimmering surface. Arrested in mid-flicker, Soto Climent's folded, curvilinear sculptures seem to contain this inward and outward motion at one and the same time, while bringing to mind the existence of some kind of flying sea creature. C.S.

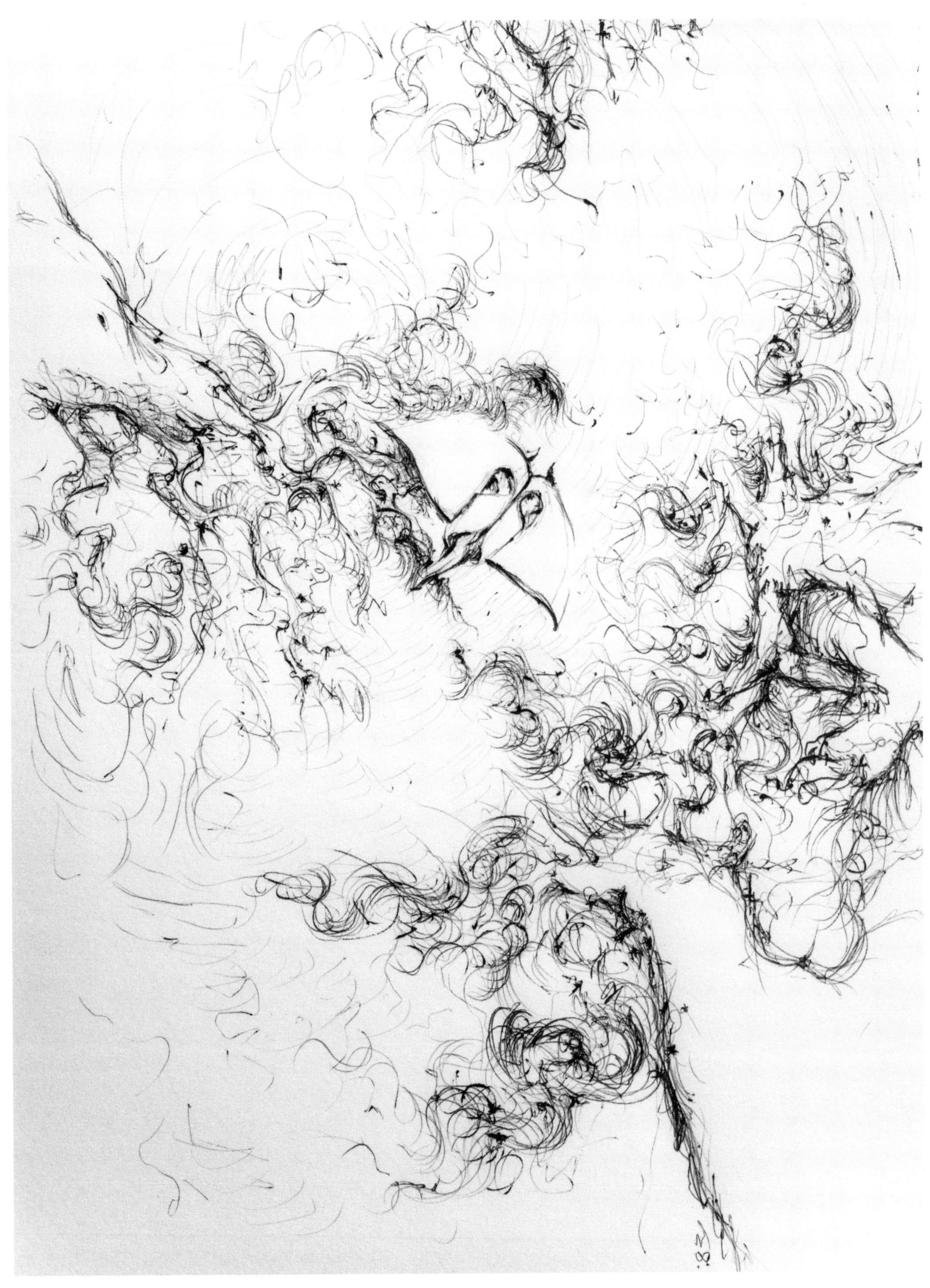

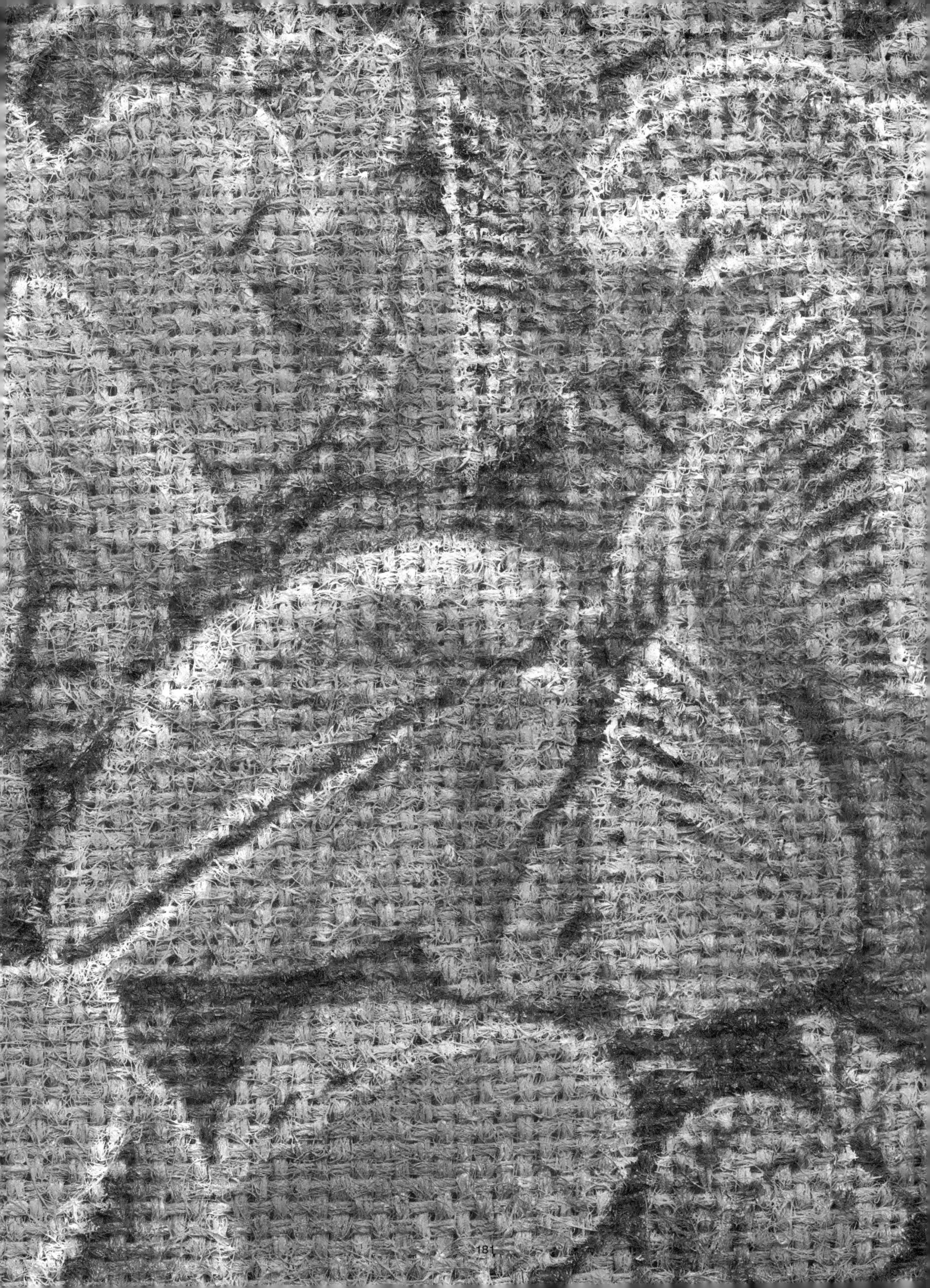

Biographies — **Authors**

Andrew Berardini

Andrew Berardini is a writer, editor, and curator from California. He has curated exhibitions at venues including MOCA (Los Angeles), Palais de Tokyo (Paris), Castello di Rivoli (Rivoli), and the Pavilion of Estonia at the 2019 Venice Biennale. Best known for his poestic and corporeal writing, Berardini has been a longtime contributor to *Artforum*. Since 2008, he has been faculty at the artist-run free school the Mountain School of Arts (Los Angeles) and has occasionally run a residency for art writers at the Banff Centre (Banff, Canada). A contributing editor at Momus and Mousse, he is the author of the book Danh Vo: Relics (Mousse, 2016).

Christina Catherine Martinez

Christina Catherine Martinez is an interdisciplinary artist, writer, and actress based in Los Angeles. She writes for numerous publications, monographs, and museum catalogs, as well as television. Her live act is a blend of performance art, stand up comedy, and clowning. She is a recipient of the Creative Capital / Andy Warhol Foundation Arts Writers Grant (Short Form Writing, 2018), and the author of the essay collection *Aesthetical Relations* (Hesse Press, 2019).

Vincent Normand

Vincent Normand is an art historian. He is a contractual PhD student at the Centre de Recherches sur les Arts et le Langage at the Ecole des Hautes Études en Sciences Sociales (Paris), teaches at the ECAL/Ecole Cantonale d'Art (Lausanne), and has recently published with Tristan Garcia the collective work *Theater, Garden, Bestiary: A Materialist History of Exhibitions* (Sternberg Press & ECAL, 2019). He has curated exhibitions at the Centre Pompidou (Paris), LABOR (Mexico), David Roberts Art Foundation (London), Kadist Foundation (Paris), Fondazione Nomas (Rome), and Forde (Geneva). He is a founding member and co-editor of *Glass Bead*, a bilingual journal devoted to the relationship between art, science and philosophy. His texts have been published in various exhibition catalogues, collective works and reviews.

Filipa Ramos

Filipa Ramos is a writer and curator based in London. Her research focuses on how art and culture address ecology, in particular the modes in which contemporary art fosters interspecies relationships across humans, animals, and machines. Ramos is co-curator of *Bodies of Water*, the 13th Shanghai Biennale (Shanghai, 2021). She is a curator for Art Basel Film and a founding curator of Vdrome, a programme of screenings of films by visual artists and filmmakers. She is a lecturer at the Master Programme of the Arts Institute of the Fachhochschule Nordwestschweiz (Basel). In the past, she was Associate Editor of *Manifesta Journal*, Editor-in-Chief of *Art-agenda/e-flux* and contributed for *Documenta 13* (Kassel, 2012) and 14 (Kassel, 2017). She authored *Lost and Found* (Silvana Editoriale, 2009) and edited *Animals* (Whitechapel Gallery/MIT Press, 2016).

Chris Sharp

Chris Sharp is an independent writer and curator who co-founded the independent art space Lulu (Mexico City), presented at the Palais de Tokyo in the exhibition *Prince.sse.s* des villes (Paris, 2019). He co-curated the New Zealand pavilion at the 2019 Venice Biennale for artist Dane Mitchell and has organized major exhibitions around the world (Australia, USA, Canada, Mexico, Austria, Hungary, Italy, Switzerland...). In France, he has curated several exhibitions, including *Tom Wesselmann* at the Nouveau Musée National de Monaco (Monaco, 2018); *Martin Soto Climent: Travaux et Jours*, at Atlantis (Marseille, 2017) and also at Parc Saint-Léger (Pougues-les-Eaux, 2014) and at CREDAC (Ivry-sur-Seine, 2014).

Credits

Yuji Agematsu
Courtesy the artist
and Miguel Abreu Gallery,
New York

Gilles Aillaud
Private collection
ADAGP, Paris, 2021

Jean-Marie Appriou
Courtesy the artist
and Jan Kaps, Cologne
Photography: Marc Domage

Miquel Barceló
Fondation Carmignac
ADAGP, Paris, 2021

Bianca Bondi
Co-production Fondation
Carmignac, Bianca Bondi
and Mor Charpentier, Paris
ADAGP, Paris, 2021
Photography: Marc Domage

Cosima von Bonin
Collection Syz, Geneva
Courtesy the artist
and Petzel, New York
Photography: Jason Mandella

Leidy Churchman
Courtesy the artist
Collection of Laura Belgray
& Steven Eckler
Collection Milovan Farronato
Photography: Lewis Ronald

Julien Discrit
Fondation Carmignac
Courtesy the artist and
Galerie Anne-Sarah Benichou
ADAGP, Paris, 2021
Photography: Julien Discrit

Hubert Duprat
Co-production Fondation
Carmignac, Hubert Duprat
and Galerie Art Concept, Paris
ADAGP, Paris, 2021
Photography: Marc Domage

Nicolas Floc'h
ADAGP, Paris, 2021
Photography: Marc Domage

Camille Henrot
Fondation Carmignac
Courtesy the artist and
kamel mennour, Paris/London
ADAGP, Paris, 2021

Adam Higgins
Courtesy the artist and
HunterShaw Fine Art,
Los Angeles
Photography: Ruben Diaz

Allison Katz
Courtesy the artist
Collection Allison Katz

Paul Klee
Courtesy Projet Pangée
Photography: Marc Domage

Yves Klein
Private collection
Succession Yves Klein
c/o ADAGP, Paris, 2021
Photography: Marc Domage

Jeff Koons
Fondation Carmignac
Courstesy the artist

Micha Laury
Courtesy the artist
ADAGP, Paris, 2021
Photography: Marc Domage

Jennifer J. Lee
Courtesy the artist and
Klaus von Nichtssagend
Gallery
Photography: Marc Domage

Jochen Lempert
Courtesy BQ, Berlin
and ProjecteSD, Barcelona
ADAGP, Paris, 2021

Dora Maar
Courtesy Centre Pompidou,
MNAM-CCI, Dist.
RMN-Grand Palais / image
Centre Pompidou, MNAM-CCI
ADAGP, Paris, 2021

Henri Matisse
© Succession H. Matisse
Ville de Beauvais
Photography: Marc Domage

Mathieu Mercier
Co-production Mathieu
Mercier and le Crédac, Ivry
Courtesy the artist
ADAGP, Paris, 2021
Photography: Marc Domage

Bruce Nauman
Fondation Carmignac
Courtesy the artist
ADAGP, Paris, 2021

Kate Newby
Co-production Fondation
Carmignac and Kate Newby
Courtesy the artist
and The Sunday Painter Gallery
Photography: Marc Domage

Melik Ohanian
Courtesy the artist and
Galerie Chantal Crousel, Paris
ADAGP, Paris, 2021
Photography: Marc Domage

Alex Olson
Courtesy the artist and
Altman Siegel, San Francisco
Photography: Jeff McLane
and Phil Bond

Gabriel Orozco
Courtesy the artist and
Marian Goodman Gallery
New York/London/Paris
Photography: Catherine Belloy

Jean Painlevé
Les Documents
Cinématographiques, Paris

Bruno Pelassy
Collection MAMCO,
Donated by the Pelassy family
Courtesy Famille Pelassy
and Galerie Air de Paris
Photography: Marc Domage

Lin May Saeed
Courtesy Jacky Strenz
Frankfurt/Main and the artist
Co-production Fondation
Carmignac et Lin May Saeed
Photography: Marc Domage

Shimabuku
Courtesy the artist
and Galerie Air de Paris

Michael E. Smith
Courtesy the artist
and KOW, Berlin.
Collection De
Vleeschouwer – Pieters
Collection Sébastien Peyret
Collection Laura Bartlett, London
Photography: Marc Domage

Martin Soto Climent
Courtesy the artist

The Imaginary Sea
From May 20th to October 17th 2021
Guest Curator
Chris Sharp

Fondation and Villa Carmignac would like to thank the artists, art lenders and institutions who contributed to this exhibition. Special thanks go to Anaël Pigeat for her intuition and Marie-Claude Beaud, patron of this exhibition.

Fondation & Villa Carmignac

President
Édouard Carmignac
General Director
Charles Carmignac
Director of the Villa Carmignac
Anne Racine
Collection and Art Project Director
Amélie Blanchy
Art Project and Publishing Manager
Kévin Le Squer
Registrar-Archivist
Alexandre Bagnod
External Relations Director
Valentine Dolla
Digital Communication Manager
Adrien Briand
Communication Manager
Camille Protat
Executive Assistant
Frédérique Yourath
Carmignac Photojournalism Award Director
Émeric Glayse
Carmignac Photojournalism Award Project Manager
Margaux Granjou
Technical and Security Manager
Jean-Marie Toche
Venue and Public Relations Manager
Béatrice Gallyot
Administrative Manager
Thibault Garnier
Intendant
Emmanuel Hoyez
Gardeners
Nicolas Nast et Olivier Haberey
Shop Manager
Florian Bruno

Exhibition

Set Design
Jean-Julien Simonot
Lighting
Abraxas
Graphic Design
Savannah Lemonnier
Art Transportation
Chenue, Fræme, FredExpress, Léon Aget, MMCI, Aldéric Trével, Nicolas Giraud
Printing and Framing
Dupon
Conservation
La Réserve
Insurance
Morel & Cie
Skeleton fabrication
Dasplet Monsters
Mathieu Mercier's work's veterinarian
Mathilde Prevot - Univet
International Press Relation
Sarah Greenberg - Evergreen Arts
Exhibition poster Design
Jésus & Gabriel
Mediation
Fraeme, Keren Danan, Flora Kuentz, Olivier Millagou, Victor Remere
Reception and Shop
Marianne International
Herbal tea infusion Design
Gauthier Dupont

Partners

Culture
Réseau Plein Sud
Artistic project
Parc national de Port-Cros, Villa Noailles, École des Arts Décoratifs - Paris
Media
Arte
Mediation
Espace Mer, Iléo Porquerolles, Porquerolles Plongée

Catalog

Publishing
David Desrimais and
Mathieu Cénac, JBE Books
Kévin Le Squer, Fondation Carmignac

Editing
Samantha Calteau

Graphic Design
we-we.fr

Exhibition views
Marc Domage

Translations
Cassandra Katsiaficas (English)
Hélène Planquelle (French)

Proofreading
Monique Gross (English)
Sylvie Philippon (French)

Thanks
Aure Bergeret
Olivia de Smedt

Distribution
D.A.P. Artbook
(North America, Latin America, Asia)
Antenne Books (United Kingdom)
Interart (France)
Vice Versa Distribution (Germany)

I would like to acknowledge my debt of gratitude to Giovanni Carmine, with whom a curatorial forebear to The Imaginary Sea *was conceived in Sao Paulo a number of years ago, but never realized. I owe a huge thanks to the inspired vision, douce folie and incisive feedback of Charles Carmignac who sought me out in Venice in 2018 to invite me to visit Porquerolles. I am equally indebted to the entire team of the Fondation, Amélie, Kévin, Anne, Alexandre, Valentine and Frédérique; without their commitment, rigor and support, none of this would have been possible. I would like to thank David Desrimais and his team for their excellent work on this publication. A special thanks to Filipa Ramos and Vincent Normand for the thoughtful contributions to the catalog, as well as Andrew Berardini and Christina Catherine Martinez for theirs. Last but definitely not least, a humble thank you to Édouard Carmignac for creating such a unique and beautiful institution and allowing it to be filled with these treasures of the sea and the imagination.* **Chris Sharp**

Jean Boîte Éditions
51 rue Claude Decaen,
F-75012 Paris
jbe-books.com

Legal deposit: May 2021
First edition

Printed in Lithuania